A Mother's Story

Mercury HeartLink
www.heartlink.com

A MOTHER'S STORY

Angie Doesn't Live Here Anymore

a memoir of recovery by

Maggie C. Romero

Contents

THREE

for my children, grandchildren—

and their children

ACKNOWLEDGMENTS

This writing journey began several years ago as a story about my daughter and her drug addiction. I was well into the body of it when my coach, Merimee, pointed out what should have been obvious to me: that I needed to dig much deeper into my life in order to get to the real story. "Keep excavating!" she pushed. "Then you'll find your story." My deepest appreciation goes to her for her endless encouragement and belief in this project. She waded through several drafts helping me distill many words into a simple story about love and resilience.

I also want to thank my fellow writers Georgia, Cindy, Blake, Sandra and especially Jenn for creating the writing seminar where I learned so much about the craft of writing. Their feedback is invaluable. Thanks, also, to my editor Jeanne for her sharp eye and professional expertise. And heartfelt thanks to fellow travelers Allison and Laura for helping me keep my eye on the ball.

My sister, Lucy, understands the healing power of writing and has supported my efforts all along. Gene put up with sharing me with my computer for the better part of two years, and for that he deserves a medal. Thank you, love of my life. Finally, my son, Carlos, his wife Carrie, and my daughter Caroline, have welcomed my need to write this memoir, of which they are an integral part. They are my heart. And Angie is my soul. It is for them, their children, and all who come after me, that I've written this story.

Prologue

"Angie doesn't live here anymore because she's gone." That's what I used to say to all the creditors who called about those endless bills that came. "Angie doesn't live here anymore. Don't know where she went. No phone number. Sorry, I can't help you, so please stop calling here." Pleading under my breath, *Please leave me alone! Don't remind me of what she's done and what might have been if she hadn't been stricken with this horrific illness, if she hadn't plummeted into the relief of drug abuse and lost all hope for recovery, if she hadn't let herself succumb to addiction, pushed onto the darker side of that relief, into a living death.*

Where might my daughter be now if fate, or genes, had been kinder to her? Now, several years into her illness, I am coming to terms with the terrible legacy that began generations ago in my own family and which I have unwittingly passed on to my daughter. All these years I've diligently searched for answers, clarity, and solace in the face of terrible pain. Like a gift from the universe, it has come to me slowly, and it is with me now. But it's been a hard won victory.

In the summer of 2001 Angie turned twenty-two. At first I was blindsided by her drug addiction; I didn't see it coming. I didn't know how to deal with the bizarre behavior—all the lying, the stealing, and the terrible language. When I wasn't in denial I lived in fear. At times I reacted appropriately, but more often I did not. I distracted myself with work and, like a child wishing on a star, hoped it might go away like a bad dream.

Looking back, it's hard to believe Angie ever could have been such a joyful child. True, her start in life was, between the colic, screaming, and subsequent hernia operation at a mere three months, not a smooth one. But she bounced forward into childhood so that I never imagined what would be down the road many years later. There were signs, yes, but I never saw the enormity of full-blown drug addiction coming. In any case there's nothing I could have done to prevent the dreadful onslaught that would engulf my family.

I liken the effect addiction has on families to a bomb exploding in the living room with everyone nearby. The shrapnel hits us all in different places; none of us is left untouched, though some may be wounded more than others. Some even ignore the explosion or block it out as the insidious effects of addiction take root in these bewildered individuals.

What happens when a bomb drops anywhere? Doesn't everybody run for cover? That's what happened in my family. Angie's brother and sister got out of the way as much as possible—a healthy response, I suppose—shrapnel wounds can be pretty dreadful. It broke my heart to see them pull away from their sister. But now Angie was so isolated in her family. And so began the long journey, Angie's father's and mine, of carrying her, much of the time, on our backs.

When I decided to have children, I didn't spend my time dreading the future. Christ, kids were my future. I said I wanted to have kids because I wanted to enjoy raising them. But there are hidden truths behind all that. Some of us want to do a better job than our parents did. I certainly did, as ill equipped as I was. Some of us feel the need to pass on a legacy, or something that remains after us. Call it ego, whatever.

Well, if ego entered into my reason for having children, then mine has been shattered ten-fold. And that's a good thing. We all need to be reminded of our place in the universe, which is essentially nothing in the scheme of things. But tell that to a mother who feels her baby grow inside of her, sacrificing her teeth and her hair so that this baby could be born strong and healthy, nursing her through soreness and mastitis so that she would be immune to many diseases. Tell that to a mother who nurtured and loved this child until she left home at age twenty-one. Tell that to any mother who had hopes and dreams for her child. And many will tell you that "No, we are all-important, the center of our children's world!" But I will tell you that "No, once disease strikes, whether it's cancer or HIV, a mother's love can become frustratingly ineffective." And facing the powerlessness of that, and releasing our children to the universe, is one of the hardest tasks any parent can face.

I have — and this is my story of learning to let go.

So he planned by day
and he
dreamed by night
Of how he could reach
The Great
Shining Light . . .

INTRODUCTION

"Look back without staring…"

(*Courage* 216)

Mirror/Mirror

Fall, 1967

When I drove off in my little VW last month, I absorbed the look of disappointment on her face. Mom and her sister were knockouts when they were young. My father had been completely besotted with my mother when they got married, and she was still a very attractive woman. It must have killed her to have a nineteen-year-old daughter so fat and out of control. What an awful reflection on her. What would she tell her friends? That my metabolism over the summer had suddenly shut down, like a broken furnace? I guess she was out of explanations, so she decided to drive down to school on the pretense of visiting a friend who lived nearby. Like a stalker, my mother drove all the way to college to confront me. It was only forty miles, but she rarely made the drive down.

It was a crisp fall day. There wasn't a cloud in the sky, and there was just enough of a breeze to kick the fallen leaves up into the air. I could smell the apple orchard across the street. She was on time. My classes were over for the day, and I spent too much time primping for her visit. I couldn't fit into pants anymore so I wore one of my long, flowing dresses that concealed my body nicely. I had raced over to the hairdresser for a quick blow dry before my ten o'clock seminar that morning and my hair looked good. But I think I had too much makeup on. Dang — an old habit from high school. I just wanted so much to look pretty for her. She really needed me to be pretty.

I stood in the parking lot as she pulled in, motioning where she could park. Turning off the ignition she looked at me through her window. Still there that look of bitter disappointment. She hadn't seen me in a while so I hoped she might have missed me. Screaming inside my lonesome heart I searched her eyes for some unconditional love, begging, *Mom, I know I'm fat, but please love me anyway.* Instead, I tried kissing up to her.

"Mom, you almost never drive down here. I know it only takes an hour, but you hate the drive. I could have come home this weekend."

"Oh, I wanted to go see Martha anyway. She hasn't been feeling well. And since I was so close I thought I'd stop by and see you."

*Uh-oh. I know that tone. I was in for another lecture about my weight. Doesn't she understand that all this pressure just makes me want to keep eating? I can't stand her relentless criticism; it's as though everything I am is a reflection on **her**, as though my whole purpose for living is to realize **her** unfulfilled dreams. Why won't she just let me be? Goddamn bitch. I'll show her!*

I was nervous and scared, but I'd always been terrified of my mother and the control she had over me. I just didn't have the will or integrity to stand up to her and assert myself. Maybe letting myself go like this was one way to get back at her.

I went to hug her when she got out of the car, silently pleading for some kindness and understanding. But she didn't return my hug, seemed very distracted and brittle. After the "How are you doings?" and other pleasantries were dispensed with, she got right to the real purpose of her mission while we walked around the pond.

"Maggie, you've got to get a hold of yourself. Have you looked in the mirror lately? Judy's wedding is next June. What if the bridesmaid's dresses are sleeveless? Won't you feel self-conscious?" she said, barely concealing her anger, smiling and gritting her teeth at the same time. She had a dazzling smile; it was easy to be drawn into her web.

"Mom, please, I promise I'll go on a diet." I whined, feeling angry too but at the same time utterly defeated. This was one of the many times that I had wanted to strangle my mother. But instead I would continue to abuse myself for years.

"Yes, good. But I think it should be under a doctor's supervision. I made an appointment for the day after Thanksgiving when you'll be home from school."

She'd said what she came to say. I got the message, for the umpteenth time. I felt overwhelmed by her, completely lost in her presence. How could she be so ruthless, cold and unfeeling? I'm sure she felt that she was trying to help me. But she was seeing only the outward symptom of my aching, lonely soul. How could an intelligent woman be so disinterested in answering my clear cry for help?

"Can you stay and have dinner with me in the cafeteria? The food's really good."

Not addressing my invitation, she barked, "Maybe if you try to get your eating under control, it won't be so embarrassing when you see the doctor. Now I've got to run and get your father's dinner at home."

Daddy was an alcoholic, and she'd tried every trick in the book, from crying to shaming him for thirty-two years, unsuccessfully, to change him. So she turned her attention to me—fixing me became her project—and she took no prisoners. I know now that she was consumed with her own aching, lonely soul, and wasn't willing or able to deal with me effectively. Just as many years later I would be an ineffective parent to Angie, lost in my own self-absorption, guilt and shame. Though unaware of it at the time, Mother and I were very much alike. She was my role model, a sad, driven woman with an alcoholic husband and now with a daughter visibly out of control like him. As she grew more desperate to control her surroundings, she could be very cruel.

Racing to get into the car, she ignored my hand on her shoulder and drove off.

"Bye, Mom," as I fantasized about the fried chicken, spaghetti and chocolate cake that were waiting for me in the dining room. Sweet oblivion.

These days they have a term for this kind of behavior: emotional abuse. My mother hurriedly married my father before she knew that he was the latest in at least two generations of alcoholics. Back in 1935 when she eloped with him, what did anyone know about the disease of alcoholism or the effect it would have on the people who lived with it? My hapless mother was trapped before she knew it with three children and a husband who enraged and disappointed her. But she couldn't control him or the disease that was progressively claiming him.

So, with my older brother away at boarding school and my sister wrapped up in ballet and my father's affections, she turned her efforts to control to me from a young age. I was lonely and vulnerable, had no one in the family in my corner, and so I allowed myself to be swallowed up by this woman and her ambitions. I was a compulsive overeater before I was five. I ate out of fear and loneliness, and also to numb my pain, but turning myself into an obese teenager was also a giant F-You to my mother. It hurt us both: it hurt my health and it embarrassed her terribly, so terribly that she would drag me to a diet doctor and expose me to the fangs of a rattlesnake hidden under a rock: drugs.

The Day After Thanksgiving

"Come on, Maggie. Let's not be late," she said, nervously looking at the kitchen clock.

"Do I really need to see a doctor to lose weight? I can do this on my own, Mom. I'll just stop eating desserts. That'll do it. I'll just eat three meals a day and nothing in between."

"The wedding is in June, Maggie. You need a lot of help to get your eating under control. It'll take time to lose all this extra weight," she said grasping my broad hips from behind as if to remind me of the work ahead. I could feel her fingernails.

I can still see how determined she was, the set of her jaw, as she drove me to the doctor's office. I remember feeling like a wooden doll, devoid of any feelings. Every time I tried to express them to my mother she deflected them or brushed them off. **My** feelings! Her message was clear: feelings are a nuisance; they are not important. No wonder I kept stuffing them down my throat with food — no one would listen to me in my family. So I just learned to shut down my feelings.

The appointment was embarrassing and shocking. Approaching the scale seemed like a death march. I weighed nearly 200 pounds. Well, it **was** the day after Thanksgiving! *No excuses, Porky,* my inner voice of self-loathing reminded me. I was mortified, disgusted, a total disappointment to my mother. I wanted to get out of there. But the doctor assured me that the weight would come off quickly.

"Just take one of these orange pills an hour before mealtime as well as this capsule at 4:00 p.m.," he said, writing out the two prescriptions. "You'll see the weight come right off."

A lifeline to my mother's approval, I grabbed them. Mom and I rose to leave:

"Thank you, Dr. Smith," my mother enthused. "You're a lifesaver!"

Appetite suppressants — diet pills — Dexedrine — the granddaddy of today's methamphetamines. The weight did come off, mostly because I was being chemically programmed to lose interest in food. But because of her ambition and perfectionism, she led me to a very dangerous place. By taking me to a diet doctor I would discover a whole new avenue for dealing with my depression. She didn't know what an "addictive personality" was at that point, but I was about to embark on several years of drug abuse.

"Mom, Dr. Smith only gave me a three-month supply of pills. What should I do when they run out? Can I go see him and get more?"

"You'll be back to yourself again, Maggie. You won't need any pills."

Back to myself again? That's a scary thought! I won't need any pills?

Appetite: Webster calls it an inherent craving. Craving for what? Food? Love? Acceptance? Being a happy child?

Up until our mother's death in 2009, when my sister revealed to me that she'd gone to live with our aunt before I was born, I'd been haunted by a mystery: why did my sister, it appeared to me then, resent me so much? I look in old family albums, searching for clues, grainy black and white snapshots of the two of us together — Christmas mornings, outside in the snow with our dog, Corky. I'm always smiling like a Cheshire cat and there she is, often stone-faced next to me. Maybe if I'd never been born she'd have smiled more in pictures.

By the time I came along in 1948, my mother was thirty-eight, approaching middle age. We were still living in New

Jersey that year. Depressed a lot of the time, with a husband who disappointed her, she found it daunting to be having a third child, so my sister, Lucy, who was five years older, was sent to live with my mother's sister for about a year. Somehow my mother felt less overwhelmed by her life with one less child in the house. My brother, the oldest, was ten and very busy with soccer and, I guess, not in need of much supervision.

But the dynamics of our family had profoundly changed, and we all, in varying degrees, carried the weight of that decision for the rest of our lives. Lucy did return to our family and we all moved up to Massachusetts from New Jersey. But the damage had already been done. If I'd been my sister, I wonder how I'd have felt toward that new baby.

We moved to a small town on a lake the year I was born, and our new house was a remodeled schoolhouse set back from the street. Lucy was awarded the big, beautiful room with a walk-in closet and a nice view of this lake. I was given the tiny room, not much bigger than a walk-in closet. There was just enough room for a single bed and a dresser. My father built shelves along the wall as you walked in so I would have some space for books and knickknacks. He also put a piece of wood on legs underneath these shelves to act as a desk. Daddy was very good with his hands.

In the spring of 1954 I was six years old. I had always felt eclipsed by Lucy in our family. I resented all the attention our father gave her. It's hard to know why a parent bonds more easily with one child than another. Maybe it's just chemistry and nothing deliberate. Or maybe he was trying to compensate for sending her away before I was born. But I was nevertheless jealous of my lovely and talented older sister — so totally unaware of the pain she must have felt to be sent away, like an extra, unwanted child, at the tender age of five. My six-year-old eyes saw only that Daddy loved her best and seemed to love me very little. I was a very angry child and craved the companionship of my big sister, but it wasn't forthcoming. So I retaliated by sneaking into her closet, taking her shoes and wearing them around the house.

One day, I knew she wouldn't be home till later. Our brother was away at boarding school so, for a couple of hours, I felt like the house princess instead of Lucy. I had the run of the house because Daddy was in the basement and asked me not to come down. Mom was taking a nap and had asked me not to disturb her. So I could do anything!

Lucy had a growing collection of shoes that she was very proud of, and I liked them too, so for a while I would pretend they were mine. Her door was closed but not locked. I'm sure she would have liked to lock me out but there was no lock in the doorknob. I was relentless; I kept coming back no matter how much my sister protested. I listened to make sure our mother was still sleeping and went into Lucy's room — such a beautiful room with opposing windows that let in light and a nice view of the lake. I'd wished it had been my room. While she was out, I was pretending it was.

I looked at all her ballet costumes hanging in the closet. The pink tutus were so pretty. She was a dancing student and was very graceful, everything I was not. She was such a star, but I wanted attention, too. I looked at her dressing table, smelled the toilet water, the talcum she used on her feet. I looked at myself in the mirror — *just for a little while*, I told myself. Her shoes were all carefully lined up. I just wanted to wear them in the house a little. Maybe then some of her power would rub off on me. So I shuffled around a bit, swimming in them and struggling to keep them on my feet. My princess time was running out; Lucy would be home soon. I didn't feel any different, but for an hour I felt like I had supplanted her a little, and taken her place in our family. For a little while I felt as loved as she was. But I guess I wasn't careful to put them back as she had left them.

As soon as she came home, Lucy went to check in her closet to see if her things were as she had left them. How did she know they might not be? Why did I allow my trespassing to be so easily discovered? Exploding out of her room she confronted, not me, but our mother, who had awoken by now, about my latest theft from her closet. Tears streaming down her face, she implored:

"Mother, Maggie has been in my closet again. She took my favorite shoes. You always let her get away with this. Please **do** something this time!"

"Lucy, you're the older of the two of you. **You** do something."

Listening to all this, crouching in my little room, I felt neither triumphant nor scared. I don't remember feeling anything. This was the corner I'd boxed myself into over and over as a child. Intervention was needed; I should have been disciplined, but I was not. I don't remember ever being punished when I behaved outrageously. This was such a miscarriage of justice for my sister—and for me. The mismanagement of matters between us destroyed what was from the beginning a very tenuous relationship. All three of us, my brother included, grew up essentially like only children, without a sense of unity and loyalty. There was too much unaddressed dysfunction—too much unfinished business — for any of us to come out of our family unscathed.

Our mother, when she wasn't preserving jelly from our Concord grapes, cooking, gardening, or washing, was silently sobbing on her bed. She was bitterly disappointed in her husband, and in her life in this little lakeside town far from the ocean she had loved as a girl. She was inaccessible more often than not and Lucy, in her rage and frustration, simply shut down toward me. Who could blame her? There was no justice to be found in our house.

So a few years later I went into the woods across the street from my house — on the other side of the brook — and made my own little house/courthouse. I cleared away bushes and created separate little rooms: four bedrooms and the central area with a big granite rock sticking out of the ground was the room where we gathered as a family. On this rock I often lowered one of my father's big hammers and pronounced the verdict:

"Maggie, I find you guilty of jealousy and theft. You are sentenced to eternal alienation from your sister."

"But I just wanted to get her attention," protesting loudly through my tears. "I'll do anything to get her attention! Please try to understand. I'm not a bad person. It's just sometimes I do bad things. I'm so lonely in that house. My brother's gone now. And I need my sister."

"You're a worthless little thief and you must pay for what you did to her. Guilty!" as the hammer came down on the rock. For most of my life I would be riddled with guilt for violating my sister's space as I had done over and over again, without any punishment. I longed for a closer relationship with Lucy but she couldn't trust me. In subsequent years I sometimes felt her anger simmering just below the surface, and I was often terrified of her.

What lessons were taught to the people who lived in that schoolhouse? What did I learn about family, about right and wrong, about how to work difficulties out within the safety of the family unit? As a child there was no healthy resolution — only intense judgment both self-inflicted and otherwise — that would serve to punish me when my parents didn't.

I found a lot of refuge in nature. I've always loved hurricanes. Carol swept through southeastern Massachusetts in August of 1954 and did a lot of damage. I remember going out in the street with trees downed from one side to the other so there was no traffic. I was safe from any cars and it felt like my playground. Jumping up in the air I grabbed the leaves that were prematurely separating from the trees. I twirled around and around in the wind, wishing it would carry me away and put me down, like Dorothy, far away from Kansas.

There was so much dysfunction inside that schoolhouse. I was happiest outdoors away from all that stress. I wanted to attach myself to the natural world, like lichen on a rock. But eventually I had to detach from my woodland and go back inside. Outdoors I could create my own world, a natural world full of power and beauty and though trampled on too much by humans, it had great resiliency.

I learned about survival studying nature—dead tree trunks, hosts, all over the forest floor, covered with plants, or epiphytes, growing on them. I climbed Mt. St Helens a few years ago, and at the top I surveyed the damage from the lava flow on the back of the volcano. Back down on the road I saw the regenerated forest that had been destroyed by the fire decades earlier. Nature is powerful and resilient. Much later on, I would discover my own resilience.

My father was a handsome man when he was young, and he had an electrifying sense of humor. He really swept my mother off her feet with his charm and good looks when they were twenty-five, and after a brief, three-month courtship they eloped to New Hampshire. He was of medium height, about five feet ten, with green eyes and thin brown hair fast receding into a memory. He had terribly bowed legs that would become very painful to walk on in later years. Arthritic knees, too, prevented him from getting much exercise, so later on he spread out quite a lot around the middle, though as a child I remember a trim figure. Later on my teenage eyes would watch him morph into a bloated, overweight man. Like a balloon that kept inflating and deflating, my father's body changed with the gin and beer it consumed.

Daddy worked for himself. Radios and televisions were starting to get popular in the 1950's, and my father had his own business selling and renting this equipment to the local hospitals. He did very well for a number of years. He loved us all very much and worked hard to provide for us. Working for himself gave him a lot of freedom to pick his own hours, be home a lot, and work on his ham radio hobby he had pursued during World War II. A fun advantage to having a father in the TV business was that we had TV's all over the place, nearly in every room several years later. To this day, I love to watch TV; I think it's a way to stay connected to my father.

As a child he had been hit with a baseball bat and had terrible vision in one eye, and so he wasn't allowed to serve in the war. Patriotism was in the air and Daddy felt terrible that he couldn't serve. So he stayed behind but served very well, I think, by using his ham radio to keep families in touch with each other during the war. Still, he felt inadequate, and he had his own demons to battle from his childhood with an abusive father. Daddy had always been a big drinker in college. And in our house, I imagine he drank in the basement, though I never saw him drinking when I was a young child. But he had graduated from college twenty years before, and he was hardly a teetotaler. He was often irritable with me and when I asked to come down to the basement he loudly told me not to. He was usually such a loving man. I don't know how else to interpret his neglect of me during those years.

I had been there a number of times but mostly I just sat at the top of the stairs wishing he would let me come down and be with him. It was an underground basement and not finished like many are today. I can still smell the mustiness from humidity seeping through parts of the walls that were still exposed rock and dirt. Some of the floor was dirt too, but Daddy had done a great job of covering it, putting up shelves, and creating space to store all the televisions and radios.

He had a long bench to work on his radios, and I'll never forget the soldering line on his thumb from all the work he did with his hands. That must have hurt so much when it happened.

I remember coming home from school one day in 1957 and calling to my father, "Daddy, are you down there? Can I come down?"

"Not now, Maggie, I'm busy. Go check on your mother upstairs."

Climbing the stairs to her bedroom, I heard my mother sobbing on her bed— choking, protracted sobbing. I couldn't bear to face her, so I just stood outside her door listening. I felt so helpless, and so incredibly angry with her. She was not available to me, she cared nothing about my needs in that moment, so consumed she was with her own misery. My sister was long gone by now, immersed in her own interests, and I wasn't one of them.

My mother was a beautiful woman when she was young. I have her hazel eyes, her high cheekbones, and her oval face. She had a long Roman nose like her father's, but none of us got it. We're the same height, five feet three, but she had attractive thin legs. My father always liked her to wear dresses or skirts so she could show them off. My legs are short and stubby, and no matter how thin I've gotten over the years they were never as lovely as my mother's.

She ate with an indifference that always infuriated me— the way she could leave half a meal on her plate if she didn't have much appetite. She picked at a meal I could have inhaled in five minutes. She never abused food and had no trouble with her weight. Even so, she always had a thick waist. As early as I can remember I think she wore a size ten dress, which is big by today's standards. By the time she would age into a woman in her nineties, she was wearing a fourteen just to get the waist to close.

As lovely as my mother was, her beauty was cut in half by the melancholy she carried within her. And it wasn't just around my father and his alcoholism. It goes way back to her childhood growing up in New Jersey with her parents and sister, Lila. Her mother and father enjoyed a very happy marriage and were devoted to each other. But Grammy was very critical of my mother and less so with Lila, who my mother told me was the favorite. There was quite a lot of triangulation going on with the three women in that family. Mother recounted an incident once when my aunt and grandmother were happily involved in some activity that my mother had been left out of. So she went to her room and cried.

"Oh, Peggy's gone to sulk again," my mother overheard her mother say.

Later on there would be a lot of triangulation between my mother, my sister and me as well. Mother would play us off against each other, set up competition and not play fair. My sister and I were puppets of her manipulation for years. She often dangled her possessions, from oriental rugs to her valuable diamond ring, in front of us to watch us jump. Well into our adulthood, I'm embarrassed to say, we were still vying for some of our mother's material possessions — until I finally lost interest in the game.

I was quite a rebel, and my sister played better by Mother's rules. More than once she yelled at me in frustration, "Why can't you be more like your sister?" As a teenager, I felt terribly ganged up on when the two of them would confront me about something outlandish I had just done. Whenever they faced me with all their rage and indignation, all I could think was:

I am alone in this family, totally alone. There's no one in my corner to defend me. I feel invisible to these people, and what they do see is either an embarrassment or a reason for shame. I never should have been born.

This is shame at a molecular level. And for much of my early life I indulged in self-annihilation and self-abuse, just as my daughter Angie does now. This pattern of illness has been passed down from my father and mother, to me, to my daughter — three generations of men and women experiencing addiction in its many forms — and reeling from living either with it or around it.

My sister was never an ally for me the way many siblings band together in dysfunctional families. My mother's behavior had always driven a wedge between us. I've often felt that perpetuating this triangle, with Mother in power this time, was her way of working through her anger at her own mother, which was considerable.

I've learned in recent years how tremendously freeing it is to let go of the resistance we encounter — like a brick wall — when we try to change things we can't. If Mother had stopped trying to change the man she married, she would have been much happier. She used to tell me that she thought all men were like her father. He was a kind, loving man who would never let drinking interfere with his marriage. Having very little experience with men when my handsome father swept her off her feet, she entered into this union pretty naïve. Their marriage lasted for forty-nine and a half years, until my father died of a massive coronary at the age of seventy-four. But she had packed her bag a few times during those years. Still, I believe she did the best she could for her family, given who she was.

But a nine-year-old child didn't have the wisdom of years to know that. So I turned around and walked back down to the kitchen.

The kitchen — the hearthstone — the center of activity in so many homes. Well, it's where the food was anyway. For as long as I can remember, food has comforted me when I felt lonely or anxious or, come to think of it, felt anything at all. Feelings, good or bad, were uncomfortable to me. Food served to numb them. I used to salivate on my way home from school thinking about the apple pie Mom had made the night before. I didn't start smoking till later, and I was never even curious about climbing into my father's gin bottle, though that would have been one way to get closer to him. Food was my drug ever since I was first a fat baby, then a fat child growing up in the Fifties when that seemed healthy.

But I always felt sad in that schoolhouse. When I was born in New Jersey and my sister was sent away, my big brother Bill doted on me. I felt his affection and enjoyed his attention, but not for long. When I was five, he was sent away to boarding school and that was that. I felt terribly abandoned by him. He was fifteen then with interests of his own. My father didn't pay much attention to me. I had started acting out against my sister by now, and when Bill came home he heard all the bad reports. I remember hearing him complain to my parents about what a spoiled brat I was. I was devastated to hear that. I wondered, then, how much he ever could have loved me.

I have some good memories of my brother, though. He was an expert sailor and he taught me how to sail on the lake, quite a challenge because of the shifting winds. I enjoyed sailing for many years, both in summer camps and on the lake, and I thank my brother for that. But largely I think because of our ten-year age difference we haven't enjoyed much of a relationship since I was a very young child. He got married right out of college and had a family of his own very soon. I just wasn't on his radar, and what he did hear about me wasn't very good. So, he concentrated on his own busy life. I don't blame him for that. But it would have been nice to have at least one advocate in my family.

I felt very isolated much of the time. And one day, I think I was eleven, I sat on the family room step facing the driveway, took a piece of glass I'd found, and cut my wrist. I still have the scar. But either I wasn't seriously suicidal or I was pretty dumb about anatomy because the cut was on the far side of my wrist, as far away from the vein as you can get.

Mother was alarmed at the sight of my bleeding wrist and asked me how it happened. *Well, that's one way to get you out of your bedroom*, I thought to myself. I lied to my mother and told her I fell on a piece of glass in the driveway. She believed me and the incident was forgotten. In fairness to my family members, my parents in particular, I had become very adept at covering up my pain. They were distracted with plenty of their own, so I just went underground with it. Was this a cry for help? Of course! It was one of several in the next few years that would be ignored or loudly sighed about. My cries provoked much anger and frustration. I was definitely "the problem child" in my family, which kept everyone from confronting, a few years later, the alcoholic right under their nose.

It's funny the things you remember. I was twelve years old in seventh grade, and it was weigh-in time in gym class. I think I weighed 120 pounds: I was very chubby. I can picture my gym teacher right now: dirty blonde ponytail, maybe thirty-five, and well over 250 pounds. She was a very large woman. While I was on the scale, I heard some of the girls giggling as she called out my weight to the person writing down the weights next to our names. I was mortified and embarrassed; I just wanted to disappear. My teacher saw how badly I felt and joked:

"Hey, don't be upset. I weighed that when I was born!"

I think she was trying to make me feel better. But I just became more and more self-conscious about my weight. My whole adolescence would be one diet after another, up and down on the scale, bouncing from slim, to chubby, to chubbier, to obese. My weight became such a huge, overriding issue that food became much more than the body sustenance it was intended to be. My food addiction masked far more basic hungers in me, feelings it would take years for me to sort out and face in therapy.

When I was thirteen, in 1961, we moved away. My mother hated that house and that town. She wanted to be closer to the salt water, having summered growing up on Long Island and swimming in the Atlantic Ocean with her sister late at night. She was a very good swimmer. My father wanted to please my mother and, as soon as he could afford it, he found a way to get her near the ocean. In July of 1961, he bought a beautiful house on a hill located on the South Shore of Massachusetts, and that was my home until I moved out ten years later. Mother called our new home "Terraces."

My depression worsened in this new house. For one thing I was a teenager, and that's no fun. Daddy often drank during the day, and I was too embarrassed about him to bring any friends home. So I wasn't popular, and I always felt like an outsider. But I had become a food addict from a very young age and this addiction would soon, at age nineteen, turn into a full-blown eating disorder. I remember all the time I spent in the kitchen negotiating with my mother over what I could eat for dinner. I had gotten used to skim milk, but it still tastes like water to me.

"No more salt, Maggie. You'll bloat up like a balloon. Use the Lawry's. You'll get used to it."

I kept wishing she'd leave the kitchen so I could eat some cookies and ice cream. I did plenty of that anyway, after my parents had gone to bed.

Daddy's alcoholism got worse and became more apparent as he got older. The elephant was in the living room, clear as a strident cowbell. But there was no serious intervention. This was the early Sixties, when alcoholism wasn't so openly talked about, at least not in our family. So everyone turned their attention to the baby of the family. I had acted out, first as a child against my sister and then in other ways as I got older. I would rebel a lot in subsequent years and give my family plenty to focus on. I felt like the family scapegoat. And the weight of it, through most of my childhood and young adulthood, was very hard to carry.

My father usually stayed in a back room off the garage where he could tinker around with his radios, smoke and drink gin. Daddy was a very loving man, but when he was sauced he could be really ugly. I have a deformed toe on my right foot, and when, all red-faced and bloated, he saw me walking around barefoot one day, he growled,

"Maggie, put some shoes on. You've got the ugliest feet I've ever seen. I don't want to look at them."

Had I been healthier emotionally maybe I could have brushed that off. But for a long time I hated to wear sandals with open toes. Not anymore.

Yet, on another day, when I failed to become an American Field Service Finalist at my high school, I went into his back room after school looking for consolation, and I got it. He hugged me for a long time and assured me that he was proud of me, win or lose. I melted within the warmth of his arms. I knew then and I know now that my father has always loved me. He was a very good and loving man. But he was sick; gin and cigarettes killed him way too soon. I've tried not to judge him, any more than I would judge Angie. I know too much about addiction and how it robs us of those we love.

My mother, on the other hand, had a different sort of malady. She wasn't driven by addiction of any kind, unless you could call ceaseless and unrelenting ambition a form of addiction. If she could have confined her need for elevated social standing to herself it would have been one thing. But she used me to fulfill dreams that were too late for her. To use one's child to live out one's own ambitions is, I think, incredibly selfish. I was well into my thirties before I seriously thought about breaking free of the mold my mother had poured me into. But it's amazing how many people feel utterly justified masking these passed on dreams as expressions of love.

Dreams like being a debutante. I didn't give a hoot about my mother's social pretensions. I just wanted to be loved and accepted for who I was, not as an extension of her. But I went along with her, got the long satin gown and squeezed into it, embarrassed about displaying my flabby upper arms as I took a bow with my father. I don't think my dear Dad cared much for all this play-acting either. I felt like such a puppet, and I was angry.

This anger toward my parents played itself out a lot while I was a teenager. Mother tried to choose my friends, but I rebelled plenty by choosing my own. I had a friend named Peggy my mother did not approve of because she was from a working-class family. We used to go to bars in Boston with her older sister, even though I hated to drink. We were just sixteen.

One Friday, we skipped school, got a ride to the interstate highway and started hitchhiking, just to see what it felt like. What lunacy! Boy, were we lucky. Our ride dropped us off somewhere in Connecticut. When we got nervous and decided to turn around Peggy and I put out our thumbs and got lucky again. We got a ride close to our town in Massachusetts, where her sister came to get us. I have often felt in my life that I had an angel on my shoulder, saving me from certain disaster.

Mom and Dad were beside themselves with worry. It was eight o'clock at night when I slowly snuck in the back door. I went upstairs to apologize, but I could see how disappointed in me my mother was. I didn't blame her. I lied about what we had done that day. I didn't dare tell my parents the truth. I couldn't be sure what they would do. I told her my friend and I had skipped school and just hung out with a friend of hers in a nearby town all day.

"Maggie, get in the car. We're going over to talk to Peggy's father," my father ordered, nervously shimmying into a pair of pants and an old polo shirt.

I could smell the gin on his breath, but I think this sobered him up pretty quickly. Dad drove me over to Peggy's house to talk about this incident with my friend's father, who had been equally upset by our disappearance. The four of us sat on opposite sides of the living room glumly staring at each other. My father spoke first:

"So, Jack, what are we going to do with our wild little girls?"

"They're not little girls anymore. That's the trouble. Who knows where they were or what they were up to? How do we know they were really at Judy's house?"

Then he turned to his daughter. "Peggy, what on earth got into you, skipping school like that and coming home so late? Didn't you think we'd notice?"

Peggy just sank deeper and deeper into the sofa cushions, trying to hide from her father's angry glare. I wondered where her mother was. I knew where mine was, too mortified to be here. Peggy had nothing to say, and I took my lead from her.

"I've grounded Peggy for the rest of the school year. That's what **I've** done."

My father, chastened by this man's seriousness and realizing this was not the time for any levity, agreed.

"I think that's a very good idea. Maggie, that goes for you too. You come right home from school and no more going out till school's out."

Peggy and I just looked at each other, pretty pissed off to be having this confrontation with our dads, but secretly glad that it was May, not October, and summer would begin soon.

Dad shook hands with Peggy's father as we left. It was all very civilized; there was no name-calling or blaming one of us over the other. I think both of our fathers suspected that this conversation wasn't going to cure the wild streak in their daughters. The best they could hope for was to put a finger in the leak for a little while. And they were right. I would rebel again in a big way while I was in college.

I was glad that my father had intervened to discipline me like this. On this occasion I felt protected by him, and loved. This wasn't the first time he would show how much he cared about me and it wouldn't be the last. Despite being an alcoholic, he was devoted to all of his children. His progressive illness may have interfered at times with how he expressed his devotion; the gin may have clouded his judgment at times. But I'm grateful to have had this man for my father.

I'm not sure what makes kids rebellious. But I felt my mother had stepped into my shoes from an early age, and I needed an identity of my own. And like many rebels, I went pretty far in the opposite direction.

For two summers while I was in college, I was a volunteer English teacher on a mission in Puerto Rico. I loved living among these simple people, learning their culture, eating their food and getting to know the young men who were fascinated by this *gringa* with *mucha carne*. I was nineteen, weighing nearly 200 pounds, and this was very attractive to many Hispanic men. So I fell in love with one of them, a young man who picked sugar cane in the fields, and I wrote a letter home about it. I was really seduced by the simple life I had discovered there. It was the exact opposite of everything I'd known. I talked about leaving college to stay there.

You might well imagine how my parents reacted when they got my letter. They were terrified of losing me, and they were on the next plane. I met them at the airport, we rented a car, and I began to proudly show them around the island. I'm a nightmare behind the wheel and they were pretty nervous driving with me around the hills, honking around every bend to let cars know I was coming. In the dark you have headlights. But this was the Puerto Rican daytime defense from crashing along unprotected mountain roads, decorated with crosses and flowers every few miles as a reminder to keep honking.

At the mission, I introduced them to my boyfriend and they politely shook hands. That's all they saw of him. He was in a hurry to catch the truck to work in the fields. I can only imagine what they were thinking: *What the hell has gotten into you? Are you seriously considering giving up the life you know to live in a shack, eat bacalao and platanos, and have children with this sugar cane cutter?* I tell you, I was rebellious — and romantic. I believe I was testing them, and myself, to see if I was capable of taking such a strong stand — and to see if they would let me. Once again I capitulated to my parents' wishes. I broke up with the sugar-cane cutter, much to their relief, soon after they left, and I returned on schedule to finish college.

In my 1966 high school yearbook, I quoted the first two lines of a Louisa May Alcott poem under my picture, "I slept, and dreamed that life was beauty; I woke, and found that life was duty." I'm not sure if I gave in to my parents out of a sense of duty or out of fear. In any case, I had miles to go and years of my life would tumble away before I could become my own person and assert my independence with confidence instead of anger.

Still, I was left with a new and better understanding of my parents. They were a product of their own culture: white, Anglo-Saxon, Protestant, and from New England. And of course I was their daughter. But though they quite understandably clung to the culture that they knew and valued, they were starting to accept that their youngest child had a mind of her own and an independent streak that would take her far from her family. My sister and brother both married people from the same cultural background as our family. But I did not. My experience in Puerto Rico opened my eyes to a whole new culture.

But back in the United States, I wasn't a sought-after *gringa* with *mucha carne* anymore. In the culture of New England I was just plain fat and I wasn't attractive to the college kids I knew. I was back near my family, unable to escape the depression that I had sought relief from by getting away and doing something different.

When my doctor-prescribed diet pills ran out, I panicked and felt sure that if I let myself experience the sadness that was just a pill away I would need to drown in food to numb myself. So I schlepped from diet doctor to diet doctor waiting in lines around the block, to keep getting more—and more— and more. Food and weight was a secondary issue because while I was in college I had discovered from other girls how to throw up to avoid weight gain from excess food. Depression was the primary issue, and amphetamines took away my sadness. I was self-medicating, and thirty-five years later I would watch my daughter do the same thing.

I was feeling such overwhelming sadness much of the time, especially when I was with my family. My brother and sister had families of their own by now and they weren't interested in my emotional baggage. I didn't even try to hide my sadness. I was in my twenties, but not really focused on anything in particular. When I came home on weekends sometimes, and binged and threw up in the downstairs bathroom, my mother never said anything, even though the next morning I could still smell the vomit that I hadn't bothered to clean up.

In retrospect, I'm sure that she knew what I was doing in the bathroom. But I think she never said anything because she knew that vomiting would keep me thin. What could be worse, to her, than being fat and out of control? How many young and not so young women in our society today have felt subjected to the same pressures? To my mother appearances were everything, and so I rebelled against her perfectionism during my college years by letting myself get fat. Then the pendulum would swing back with my efforts to get thin. Eating disorders, anorexia and bulimia, are all about one's need to establish a sense of control in one's life. *At least I can control what I put in my mouth*, I thought to myself. But I was still very young and full of longing and self-doubt. My mother was still firmly in charge. I wanted to be free, but I didn't know how to be. Our love-hate battle would continue for many years.

I had graduated from college in 1970 and after living at home briefly following graduation, I moved into Boston with a friend who needed a roommate. I was a secretary at Harvard University where I dated a number of graduate students there, every one of them foreign. There was a Portuguese guy who drew my portrait. There was Juan from Puerto Rico. There was a Frenchman who took me up in his glider and nearly killed us both when the wind currents shifted. There was a Czech architect — Kazimir Janovsky — who dumped me for his former girlfriend whom he loved more. I loved the romantic sound of his name. That's when I got into Smetana and listening to *The Moldau* all the time — until he dumped me, that is. And then, there was Xavier.

Xavier Romero was a Cuban teaching fellow at Harvard University, my father's alma mater. All five feet six inches of him swooped into the office where I had been working for a year and swept me off my feet. He fell instantly in love with me, and I wasn't far behind. He wasn't a big man, but he had a big heart, and he literally charmed the pants off of me after a couple of dates. We saw each other steadily for three years. But we were separated for one of them when he went to Colombia to finish his Ph.D. thesis.

During that period I quit my job at Harvard and decided to go to art school. This was way out of left field; I had never even drawn pictures or been interested in art. I enrolled in a two-year interior design program in Boston and determined to complete it in one year. I was on a fast track and put myself under incredible pressure to complete all my class work with excellence. I was a terrible perfectionist. Somehow I thought that squeezing two years of work into one would be a source of pride. "Do the difficult," I heard my mother's voice hounding me. Well, I certainly did, but the cost was great.

Since I was twenty I had been actively bulimic. Purging was a habit I picked up in college from some other girls in my dorm. At the time, I thought I had discovered a way to continue my food addiction without getting fat. I was delighted. This secret pattern of self-abuse played itself out during my early twenties, while I was dating and working at Harvard. But in the spring of 1973, after I had left Harvard and before I began design school in June, I became anorexic. Anorexia can be characterized, not by the excesses, but the opposite: bare, subsistence level calorie intake. This is how a typical day went:

I got up at 6 a.m. sharp and made myself a cup of black coffee. For breakfast I had exactly one half cup of Wheatena, eaten very slowly while I watched the early news. Lunch was exactly two of the rectangular Venus wheat crackers I don't see in the store anymore. I can still taste them after all these years. With the crackers I had exactly one cup of (diluted) Campbell's tomato soup. Then dinner was the same as lunch at 6 p.m. sharp. When my classes started in June and I wasn't home for lunch, I ate a cup of plain yogurt instead of soup and crackers. Needless to say I had to isolate myself and avoided all of my friends most of the time. I could never let myself go out to eat and enjoy myself. This rigid ritual lasted for six months. Rigidity is a key concept in anorexia. Any flexibility around food might allow one's natural instinct for survival to take over, and normal eating might return. But like many compulsions, my anorexia was a matter of degree and was short-lived. I just couldn't stand the hunger.

I was also popping amphetamines every day, so some purists might say this wasn't anorexia because I didn't feel intensely hungry. That might have been true at first. But after a few months on that subsistence level diet, I was always hungry. The amphetamines enabled me to stay "up" and awake until 2:00 in the morning so I could do all my drawings. I spent hours on my drafting board and routinely got four hours of sleep at night. But body wisdom is very smart: I was starving and it knew it. I thought about food all the time and how strong I was to resist it. Before this, when I was in the midst of a food binge, I felt just the opposite: weak and incredibly self-indulgent. I hated myself then. When I restricted food intake, I admired myself. My whole life before recovery would be a wrestling match—a love-hate battle with my self-esteem—using food as the arbiter.

This was a deadly combination—hard drugs and little food or sleep—and after six months I began to crack under the pressure. I started to hallucinate and suffer from paranoia. It was November, and I remember going to see my college advisor to tell him what I was experiencing. Maybe he had seen this before in the high-pressure atmosphere of design schools. He told me to go home and take a longer holiday break. It was good advice because as soon as the pressure to perform was off my sanity returned, along with my ability to nourish myself. I rested through the holidays, started eating again, and my weight returned to normal. I went back to school in January and graduated with honors the following June. But the effects of my drug abuse had scared me, and I weaned myself off of the amphetamines over the next two years. I never abused hard drugs again.

I think of all the addictions, food is one of the hardest to conquer, simply because we can't give it up entirely, like booze, or drugs, or gambling. We have to eat to survive. But I would gradually learn to put food in its proper perspective, as a means to nourish my body instead of a weapon to punish or reward myself.

I think my parents honestly didn't know how to deal with me from a very young age. And I think they were really starting to wonder if I was ever going to be OK. So to their credit they made sure I started seeing a psychiatrist twice a week for a couple of years.

The intensive therapy did show some results. By the time I was twenty-six, I was at a normal weight, though I went underground with my food addiction. I had some serious issues to deal with, and I realize that they were never completely resolved. But at the time my depression seemed to lift like a coastal fog, burning off in the morning sun, and freed of the paralyzing sadness that had been holding me hostage, I was able to move forward with my life. When Xavier came back from South America we decided to move in together to see if it would work.

It did. His parents came to Cambridge to see us. His father and I together refinished a sideboard that I still have in my dining room. I've always been very fond of my in-laws, and was saddened when Xavier's father passed away a few years ago. There's quite a story behind Xavier's coming to America, and though my life was no fairy tale, neither was his.

He and his family flew to Miami in 1960, a year or so after Batista had lost power in Cuba, so Xavier was twelve when he emigrated here. As an ESL teacher, I know that that is the age when we cling to our first language, and acquiring a second one is less easy. To this day Xavier has a Cuban accent you can cut with a knife, proudly holding onto his heritage. I've always loved that about him.

But he and his family endured significant trauma when they first arrived in Miami. Xavier's mother went from being a privileged housewife to a garment worker in a factory almost overnight. The family of four slept on sofas of friends in the newly arrived Cuban community. A proud, hard-working family, they must have suffered terribly from the harsh adjustment to American culture. But just as Miami has flourished from the first wave of Cubans who have turned it into the vibrant city it is, so too Xavier's family survived and did very well. Xavier's sister finished college and graduate school. And Xavier graduated from Harvard University, was a Knox Fellow at Oxford University in England, and later received his doctorate from Harvard.

When Xavier and I began to live together, he was still a teaching fellow at Harvard and I was a secretary down the road at MIT. My year in art school had certainly been volatile, and I learned much about myself from the experience. But the time apart had tested us, and we missed each other. I think we'd both grown some and were ready to settle down. I was pleasing my parents by considering marriage, which was definitely what I was expected to do. Be a debutante: check;

graduate from college: check; marry: check; a Harvard man: double check.

During Christmas of 1974 Xavier came out to Terraces, sat on the sofa with my father, just the two of them, and asked for my hand in marriage. Mother and I were sneaking looks around the corner from the dining room, delighted that Daddy had welcomed Xavier into the family as his son-in-law.

This was no small thing. This was my mother and father being open-minded enough to accept my marrying out of my culture. These were my parents flying to Puerto Rico to rescue me and being rescued themselves from their own cultural prejudices.

I was now twenty-seven, pushing spinsterhood in their eyes, and I think they were glad to be marrying me off. I didn't care. At the time I felt delighted to be running off to Washington, D.C. with this exciting man. I think I was delighted to be running away from the town I'd grown up in, full of many sad memories. Hell, I know I was delighted to be running off — period.

On September 6, 1975 we were married in my hometown. It was a lovely, sunny day. The reception was at Terraces. We hired a guitarist to play beautiful Spanish music during the reception. All of Xavier's family came from Miami. It was a joyous occasion, and we both raised a glass to toast our parents for all they had done for us. My therapist, Dr. K, to my great surprise and joy, even came out to see us get married.

Recently, a friend of mine, who has accompanied me on this painful journey with my daughter, marveled at "my strength." I was quick to give credit to the sound principles of living that I've learned along the way. But as I look back, some of the good doctors I've seen over the years also deserve credit for helping me to deal with my depression. Xavier and

I had every reason to believe that we would have a good life together. And in so many ways we did. My recovery from addiction and the effects of addiction have kept me in tune with all of my good fortune. In spite of everything, I have lived a very blessed life.

My Favorite Person

My favorite person is my mom. It's not that, I don't love my dad. I do. It's just because he's gone most of the day, so I end up seeing more of my mom than him. Suppose my brother started bothering me, who would I go to, but my mom. I also always help her cook, clean, etc. Unlike my lazy brother and sister. Not just because I have to, I like to help her. I also spend alot of time showing her my drawings and asking her opinion. My brother and sister could care less. I guess theres a special bond between us.

My Daughter/Myself

May 1984

"Be careful, Angie, you'll fall on your head!" I shrieked, my heart in my throat. I often took the kids to this park after their morning in preschool. We didn't have any equipment or swings in our yard, and I wanted them to work off steam as much as possible. But Angie was like a monkey the way she swung around, turning so effortlessly. Such agility, I was dizzy just watching her, grateful that she never lost her grip.

"Mama, please come push me. I want to go high!" shouted Caroline, her little sister, as I ran to fasten her into the kiddy swing.

It was quite a job juggling these kids in a park with so many other children and such potential for danger from falls and other accidents. But somehow I felt safe taking my eyes off Angie long enough to push her sister. Angie got through childhood with no broken bones, no stitches on her head, as active as she was. Incredible!

Angie is small of stature, like her father. I'm on the short side too, only five feet three. We used to joke about how we'd kill for a few more inches — more for calories to spread out in. She doesn't resemble me very much except that we're both on the small side. She has very dark hair and deep brown eyes like her Spanish ancestors and beautiful porcelain skin. As a child, she looked like a Mandarin doll. She was just gorgeous.

Angie was born in 1979 high in the South American Andes. Xavier was a political/military officer in the Foreign Service, and this was our second post. As a baby, she was swaddled by her nanny, and I like it that swaddling has come back into favor. From a very young age she excelled in gymnastics, a sport that generally attracts people of small build. A short, compact body has an easier time navigating all the moves in gymnastics. And maintaining your fitness in that short, compact body almost always requires great discipline in what you feed it.

We returned from South America in the spring of 1980. Angie wasn't yet one, Carlos was two, and within six months I was expecting Caroline. It was a busy time in our lives. Readjusting to living in the United States takes time. But mostly I was lonely. In July of 1981 I had three children under four and almost no one to talk to. All my family still lived in Massachusetts and I was very isolated from them. Mother came down to help when Caroline was born, but she couldn't stay with me for long. She still had my father to look after.

I quickly joined a babysitting cooperative in the town where I lived. This was a lifesaver for me. I made friends with other young mothers like myself. One of them is still a close friend after thirty-two years. We helped each other by babysitting for each other's children while we went to the dentist, or shopping, or just stayed home alone to stare at the wall.

Many times that's all I did. Sometimes I still craved the isolation that was my worst enemy. Being alone allowed me the freedom to indulge my food addiction, which I did but with less and less frequency. I was getting tired of it, the way it hovered over me like a dark cloud, beckoning me into the temporary nirvana that made everyone in my family invisible for a time. How I must have neglected them then! So for a while I started seeing another therapist and went into remission from the bulimic behavior. From then on I've abused food less and less, though there have been plenty of times over the years when I've given in to my addiction. I would rationalize, "It's just food; it's legal." But legal or not, food addiction costs our health industry billions of dollars every year. Michelle Obama has championed a very worthwhile cause.

Today I'm free of the compulsion to abuse food. But "once an addict, always an addict," I believe. Every day free of the obsession is a daily reprieve for me, and I never take my abstinence for granted.

One thing I felt very strongly about was raising the children in the Episcopal Church, as I had been. It had been years since I'd attended services, but I still knew all the prayers by heart and many of the hymns. I remember as a child and young adult feeling comforted by the rituals in church, just as my mother had been. So every Sunday Xavier and I took the children to St. John's on Georgetown Pike, rewarding them with McDonald's on the way home.

This routine every Sunday lasted for six years, until we moved to Greece. The children all went to Sunday school during the service, and Xavier and I enjoyed talking to the other adults afterwards. But for reasons I'm not sure of, we never went to church again, not as a family and not as individuals. Our marriage fell apart in Greece, so maybe that had something to do with it. But I failed to instill a spiritual foundation in the lives of my children. Ever since she was eight years old, Angie has been a confirmed atheist. This would haunt me a great deal later on.

From the early age of three, Angie loved gymnastics, and I used to drive far from our home, getting on the beltway at rush hour, with three little children, to get her to Mr. Youssefi's gymnastics class. Carlos brought his Legos to play with and I was still nursing Caroline. We sat on the sidelines watching Angie flip around with the other three-year- olds.

This continued for the next five years until we moved to Greece in 1987 and she would be in her prime in the sport.

School went well, but there was some serious dysfunction happening at home. In one of Carlos's early preschool reports, his teacher warned, "his aggressive tendencies need to be watched." So we channeled all that into sports: t-ball, kickball and soccer. He was on two teams a year. We thought we had found a healthy outlet for Carlos's energy. I didn't start to see the whole picture until much later on. But what I "saw" then was Angie coming to me complaining about Carlos kicking her or just generally being a bully around the house. I never witnessed this and I largely dropped the ball there. I consulted my pediatrician and he told me to "let them work it out." What I was unconsciously doing, unfortunately, was replaying the script from my own childhood where I learned from my mother to do nothing. And Angie (Lucy) for years struggled with feelings of victimization—and intense anger toward me (Mother) for not protecting her more.

But that's not the whole picture; it's not that simple. What I found out much, much later from my son—the layers keep peeling off the onion—is what motivated Carlos in the first place to kick his sisters and pull their hair. My son wasn't born angry; he was made to be. The girls liked to play in their room, which they shared, with their dolls and little ponies. Big brother wanted to play too, but they locked the door and wouldn't let him in. If I had had my wits about me I would have seen the pain my son was in, opened that door and encouraged it to stay open. I would have nipped that dangerous dynamic in the bud. I was the parent; I was in charge.

"What lessons were taught to the people who lived in that schoolhouse? What did I (Angie) learn about family, about right and wrong, about how to work difficulties out within the safety of the family unit? As a child there was no healthy resolution—"

My mother was the parent in 1954. She was in charge. Why didn't she pay better attention to the dynamic between Lucy and me? Why didn't she nip that dangerous dynamic in the bud while we were still young? If she had, I might have had my sister in my life.

But I didn't interfere. My daughters growing up were not close to Carlos, partly because of these unaddressed resentments. Despite all the parenting books I read and Parent Effectiveness Training I took, I wasn't a very good parent when I let things slide and I might have intervened more. I was very passive. What did I learn from my own mother? We pass on what was given to us. Yet there was no real malice in my life, neither growing up nor with my own children. And as I've come to terms with my parents and siblings, as well as myself, that is a crucial detail that makes all the difference and enables me to view everyone in my life with a kinder eye.

Our marriage started to strain under the weight of three little children and a lot of responsibility. Xavier was working long hours in a government job that didn't pay a whole lot. We fought often and loudly, sometimes with the children in the next room. How could we be so wrapped up in ourselves, so unthinking and unaware of what this might be doing to our children? Nevertheless, Xavier was a good and loving father to them. He read to them and put them to bed every night. He went to many of Carlos's many sports events, always toting along a book or magazine to read. There's no question that Xavier loves his children and has been there for them. But I was asking a lot of my husband so early in our marriage.

So I made my bed, and now I had to lie in it. I was in charge of the home, the packing, unpacking and traveling from country to country in the Foreign Service. I was in charge of raising the children, of enrolling them in school, of seeing the doctors and finding orthodontists to straighten their teeth. I arranged the birthday parties and the play dates, the shopping, the babysitters and childcare.

But how emotionally present was I to my little ones? I was not a happy woman. How emotionally present was my mother to me? She was not available to me either. I would learn many years down the road — as my mother did not — that happiness is truly an inside job.

This legacy of depression and addiction seeped into my family and exploded in a toxic way, claiming Angie many years later. Ten years into our marriage, by 1985, Xavier and I had grown apart and we were no longer happy together. By the time we left for Greece two years later, our marriage would be in deep trouble.

Angie's early years in Virginia — despite the growing family dysfunction — were uneventful. Surely the children must have felt confused and worried when they heard their parents frequently arguing. But they were young, very involved with friends and activities, and seemed resilient. I would see soon enough down the road how I was just whistling in the dark and should have been paying closer attention. But I was too wrapped up in myself — my pain, my loneliness, and my own fear.

Years later, through my recovery work in Al-Anon, I began to examine these fears that had held me back so much in my life:

> Fear dominated my life. Denial clouded my perception. I ignored reality because it hurt when I thought about it. When painful thoughts emerged, as they inevitably did, I quickly and anxiously shoved them away. It was as if my thoughts were my enemies, and as they approached, I turned and ran as fast as possible in the opposite direction. Instead of expending

my energy on living my life, I focused almost exclusively on avoiding pain, stuffing disturbing feelings, and keeping myself as numb as I could. (*How Al-Anon Works* 171-172)

Soon after school was out, in July 1987, the five of us flew to Brussels, Belgium, and made our way across Europe to Venice, where we took the boat to Greece. It was a wonderful and memorable trip, except in Belgium where Angie got lost in a museum. As we were leaving in the crowd we counted heads and saw she wasn't with us. It was closing time and they were locking up the building. Xavier and I turned around and banged and banged on the doors to let us back in. We screamed for Angie in a panic and she came running to us. The terror I felt must have paled in comparison to hers. Yet she didn't show any fear or anger at us for losing sight of her. That was one of the first times when I observed Angie reacting oddly to events that should have visibly upset her. There would be many times in subsequent years when Angie would fail to show emotion when it was more appropriate to do so. "But this was Angie," we all murmured to ourselves, "this was the way she was."

Though our trip began on this scary note in Belgium, our time in Venice was sublime. I have many pictures of us all, peeking in and out of corners in old churches and museums. The children loved feeding the pigeons in St. Mark's Square, and I have several pictures of six-year-old Caroline holding out crumbs to the greedy birds. I, too, wanted to make an offering to the gods to watch over my family and give us some peace and happiness in our new home across the Adriatic Sea. Would a change of scenery be the answer for Xavier and me to put our marriage back together? Could any outward change, comfort, distraction fill in the hollowness that had plagued me most of my life?

After a brief stay in temporary quarters, we moved into a beautiful house in a northern suburb of Athens called Politia. Angie followed through with gymnastics as a pre-adolescent, and when we arrived in Greece she joined the school team. I used to pick her up after practice at school, and there she was flipping on beams and doing back flips. The movements were so controlled. *What an amazing sport*, I used to think to myself, *and what incredible discipline these kids needed to perform these movements.* She and her best friend Jane spent all their free time practicing, at home and at school.

She was very good, a natural athlete, so I wasn't surprised when she was chosen, along with Jane, to represent the school at a competition in England in 1989. They didn't win, but it was a great experience for her to compete in a foreign country. When we picked her and Jane up at the airport, she gushed about the other kids who competed as well, about the "awful" English food, and about the rain. "My God, Mom, it rained every day!"

She and Jane batted jokes back and forth in the car, laughing about one kid from Romania whose tights split and exposed part of his groin. Angie was just ten, a pre-adolescent, and this seemed hysterical to her. I can still hear her guttural laugh as if it were yesterday. Gymnastics really took her to a place where she felt happy and competent.

Angie seemed happy during much of the time we lived in Greece, from 1987 to 1990. She was coming into her own and feeling very successful both in school and in her work in gymnastics. But she must have felt the void in our marriage, as her sense of security started to slip away. It was the last time I would see her really happy for a very long time.

Particularly in Angie's case, I've needed to cling to memories of her carefree days as a child. Only now do I recognize how bitterly angry and disappointed I've been with her throughout her addiction, partly because it's been such a difficult challenge for me as a parent, but more so because she has become the incarnation of the worst in me: lonely, isolated, compulsive and driven by addiction. Seeing this pattern carried down through the generations has burdened me terribly. But equally powerful has been my capacity to rise above the devastating effects of addiction: my parents', mine, and my daughter's, and move forward in my life.

It's been more than twenty years since separation and then divorce pulled the rug out from under my children. In 1990 the end of our tour was nearing in Greece, and so was the end of my marriage. It was a terrible time for Xavier and me, and surely for the children as well. But we decided on a trial separation before deciding on anything more final. Xavier was offered a brief, six-month post in Rome, which meant he would have to travel a lot. It would put the children and me in a holding pattern while their father and I decided how to proceed in our marriage. Then, in six months, we would all return to the States.

The kids and I, with our dog Oscar in tow, actually had some fun times there. I used to take them out to dinner on the Cassia del Norte and we always got white pizza, something I'd never even seen back home. I can still taste the crust—completely different from American pizza—must be the shortening they use in Rome. I tried to distract them as much as possible from the terrible disruption in their lives. But the loss they were going through was very real.

Angie's disease first manifested itself there, in Rome. Right after we moved there, she all but stopped eating. Angie was now eleven, but hadn't started menstruating yet. I laid out cereal for all three of the kids every morning, but noticed Angie only ate a few bites. I couldn't see what she ate at school, but on weekends it was just a bite of whatever sandwich I made for them. Dinners were the same, often preceded with "I have a stomachache, Mom." I wasn't sure what to think; I thought maybe she was starting to menstruate. She was also sneezing a lot, so I thought it might be a virus.

After a couple weeks of this, she started getting listless, and for a gymnast she was stumbling a lot. There were a couple of days when she said she was too weak to walk so I kept her home. I remember so clearly how I sat on her bed kneading the cramps out of her legs, with every stroke of my hands begging her forgiveness for taking her father away from her.

I took her to the embassy doctor for a checkup, and he talked to Angie privately in his office. Then he talked to me alone, where I leveled with him about the separation, as Angie had not. He said that loss of appetite was a common reaction for children to separation. He added that I needed to monitor her very closely and call him immediately if this behavior continued. Then we joined Angie waiting for us in the outer office.

He prescribed some vitamins for Angie and shook her hand. "Angie," he said, staring into her eyes, "I hope you'll listen to your mother now and do as she says. I know she loves you very much." My little girl looked very happy and almost relieved, I think, to have seen the doctor. She gradually started eating more and regained her strength. This was a (mercifully) brief episode of anorexia that foretold, perhaps, what was ahead.

Very social kids, they had a number of friends, so they were distracted and not doing too badly, considering their world had been turned upside down and they missed their father. All three children were doing so well in school and in various activities that it was easy for me to think that they were adjusting well to the separation. They weren't acting out or getting in trouble, and I was distracted with worry about how I was going to move forward in my life without a job or a husband. I was forty-two that year.

Angie, much to all our delight, even got picked by a movie scout to work in a small B-movie being made then in Rome. We were delighted. There couldn't be enough distractions, I thought, at this difficult juncture in her life. And this was a fun distraction for all of us. If only I'd seen then what I see now: that distractions were just that: focusing on something else sometimes to avoid painful realities which, if not dealt with in a healthy way, might, would, and surely did in Angie's case, interfere with a smooth transition to adulthood.

We would be leaving Rome in February. I wasn't working. Things were still in boxes because it was such a short tour. The five of us were in transition from an intact family to a broken one.

Stubbornly, I was more determined than ever to divorce my husband. I needed to be on my own, no matter the cost. On the one hand I was finally able to embrace my independence. On the other hand, I was sacrificing the security of my children to do so. By leaving my marriage I was free to embark on a career that would bring me much happiness and fulfillment. Opportunities for wives to work in the Foreign Service were very limited then. At the same time, my children lost their moorings. I've told myself that they've been better off with a happy single mother than with an unhappy wife to their father, as my mother had been to my father. But there is no right or wrong. How can I invalidate the happiness I found in the classroom and with my present partner of twenty years by saying I should have stayed married? We make our choices in life and we learn to make peace with them if we can. I spent years allowing guilt to manipulate me and weaken my footing as a parent, and that winter I was consumed with it. Angie was just eleven.

January 1991

Pounding the pavement in Rome, I was on a mission to get Angie what the movie company had promised her. *That production company promised to pay Angie $800 for her work in their frigging movie, but when it was wrapped up I never even heard from them.* I was livid, not because she needed the money or for any other reason than I wanted to see my daughter's efforts validated. I also didn't like being lied to. So I tirelessly schlepped all over Rome looking for their business office. *I can't do enough for Angie to try to make up to her for leaving her father.* I finally found it, hidden on a little side street. Well, they couldn't hide from this mom, as if this small gesture on my part, retrieving this money, would absolve me from divorcing her father. Entering the office with authority, my eyes locked on to the woman at the desk, flaming daggers ready to strike:

"Hello, Sra. Gluck. I'm Mrs. Romero, Angie's mother. You cast her in the film you just finished, and you promised to pay her $800."

"Oh yes, how are you? Have a seat, Mrs. Romero. I'm sorry. We've been so busy with production details, I haven't had time to take care of business."

"Well I'm here now," I asserted, sounding very businesslike.

It was a pretty bleak office, very dark and small. It looked like it was getting ready to close down, with boxes of papers all over and swift movement in the back rooms as though these people were going someplace. I'm glad I got there when I did; I got the feeling they wouldn't be there a week later.

"Yes, well..." pulling a huge checkbook out of her desk drawer. "How much did you say?"

"$800.00." I should have lied.

"Here you go," she said, hastily writing the amount. "Sorry you had to come all the way down here. We could have mailed you a check."

"Yes, well, we're going back to the States soon and you know how things get lost in the mail. I wanted this settled before we left the country."

"Oh sure, I understand."

Folding the check and storing it safely in my purse, I stood up and opened the door.

"Thank you, Sra. Gluck."

"You're welcome, Mrs. Romero. Have a safe trip."

Slam!

I will never forget how triumphant I felt, elevated off those cold January sidewalks. There have been many stops for me along this road to redemption, and this was one of the early ones that I remember. I felt so proud that I had gone to bat for Angie like this. And I was delighted that my efforts had been rewarded. I bounded into our apartment and waved the check in front of my daughter. Chocolate eyes as big as saucers, she squealed:

"Mom, you did it! You're the best! Let me see the check; is it made out to me?"

"No honey, you're a minor. It's in my name. But I promise you can use the money any way that you want."

"Good. You know what I want? All of Jane Fonda's tapes — every one — I want to start exercising with her."

"Oh Angie, are you sure that's what you want to get?" I wrinkled my nose with obvious disapproval.

"Yes Mom. And don't argue. I earned the money, so I get to spend it my way."

Yes, Ma'am!

Already, though not for the first time, I was seeing a stubborn willfulness—just like her mother—a proud but wayward determination in my daughter, not so much because she wanted the tapes, which was harmless enough. It was the fierceness in her tone, the refusal to bend or consider my opinion. I was remembering myself when I was twelve and how much I hated my mother then. I was afraid she might be turning into me! She had a need to supersede me, even erase me sometimes, so great was her need to control the uncontrollable, life and all its unfolding, disappointments, divorce.

One Year Earlier in Greece

Xavier and I had been struggling in our marriage for a number of years, almost since Caroline was born. In our case the pressures of three children close in age took hold, along with my husband's demanding career, and my own ever-present loneliness. But divorce, whatever the cause, is a sad occurrence. I refuse to place blame where none exists. We got married with hopes and dreams for a happy life, but we couldn't work together to see those dreams realized.

By 1990, while we were still living in Greece, I found myself spending more and more time with my friends outside of our home. Xavier was entirely consumed with his job as a political/military officer at the American Embassy. The children were still young but involved in school, friends and all their activities. Somehow I thought they wouldn't notice if other people filled the void in my marriage.

I had a close girlfriend with whom I spent most of my free time. Greeks are incredibly hospitable people, and dinner at Eleni's long table was always an event. There's nothing worse to a Greek than having dinner alone, and she always had at least five or ten friends drop by and join her and her husband at dinnertime. "Dinnertime" started at nine or ten in the evening and, after around eight courses, with cigarettes in between, I would thank her and stumble home at two in the morning. I never joined in, but she and some of our friends then went dancing at the various bouzouki joints around Athens, falling into bed around dawn. Where did Eleni get the energy? Then she got up and went to work at eight or nine in the morning. This was the routine for many Greeks I knew. And this is certainly why the afternoon siesta was so vital.

Eleni and I enjoyed a very close friendship, especially during the last year we lived in Greece. And though Xavier and I had grown apart, I wasn't tempted at that point to add to the disruption in my children's lives and complicate my own with another serious involvement. I loved my children. As much as I've messed up in my own life as well as theirs from time to time, that is the one thing that has always remained constant for me—like true north on a compass: I wanted my children very much. They weren't accidents. And I will always be there for them.

Still, that year I seemed to be transitioning emotionally into another phase of my life, and there's no excuse for such selfishness and neglect of my children. I offer none. But I was away from our home a lot, and the absence it caused in their lives reverberated for a long time.

June 1990

I had gone away to Crete for a few days with my friends, missing my children and feeling very guilty the whole time, even though their father was home. I couldn't wait to get back and try to make up for the time I kept robbing them of. As I opened the front door Oscar, our dog, ran to greet me. How I adored Oscar—we all did. He was the most wonderful companion. Angie, especially, bonded with him from the beginning. They did everything together. Maybe he became the parent/friend that she could trust.

"Hi kids, I'm home!" Listening for their voices, looking around, I waited, but there wasn't a peep, not a sound, just Oscar's heavy breathing. At least he was excited to see me. Did they know I was coming back today? Where the hell were they? "Anyone home?" I shouted. The big white house echoed with my absence, and my selfishness hit me on the head like a boomerang. They weren't home because they'd missed me so much on other occasions when I was also absent emotionally and physically. I hadn't been there then either. My children, these past few months, had learned to invest in other things, other people.

My food addiction had always been like a panther ready to pounce at vulnerable times in my life. Ever since I was a child I'd used food to numb me from any uncomfortable feelings — but not on this day. I felt very guilty, knowing that I had just spent some carefree days with friends in Crete while my children were at home without me. But I didn't fall prey to my weakness this time. I was too depressed to even think about food. Occasionally over the years my bulimia has been eclipsed by plain old depression, and lack of appetite is a common symptom.

We were about to leave Greece, and I would be saying goodbye to several dear friends, friends who had sustained me through my estrangement from Xavier. My future was a question mark; I wanted to be on my own with my kids, in a career that gave me satisfaction. Happiness was a distant dream. I just wanted to be independent for the first time in my life.

The kids came home at around four in the afternoon, all from various friends' houses where they had been busily occupied. *Maybe they weren't so unhappy without me around. My children — my three wonderful children,* I thought to myself, *I'm so sorry.*

"Hi, guys," I offered, cheerily, trying to cover up how miserable I felt. "How was your weekend?"

Carlos greeted me at the front door, "Hi Mom," with a quick hug and put Oscar on a leash to go for a walk. He was out the door before I had a chance to say anything.

"Oh fine," Angie responded, coming in from the garden in the back. "Tamara's getting a new cat. Where's Oscar?" she asked, looking around for our dog.

"Carlos took him for a walk around the block, honey. Tell me about Tamara's cat," I pushed, hoping she would stay and talk to me.

"It scratched me," she answered, without looking at me, walking out the front door.

"Where are you going?" I whined.

"I want to go catch up with Oscar," she called from behind the closed door

This was her refuge, her best friend. Oscar slept with her every night and would continue to do so until the day I put him down ten years later. Angie showered Oscar with all the physical affection she could not show others. She had a great capacity for love and demonstrated it on paper often. But showing any physical affection was hard for her and didn't come naturally. Now, when I needed her to absolve me for running off all weekend, she was unable to do so. I'd been too unavailable, too often, for too long. I was only just beginning to see the cost of my selfishness to my children.

Caroline had gone upstairs to see her father without greeting me at all. *My baby,* I thought to myself, *I've neglected you most of all.* Remembering the parent-teacher conference when her first grade teaher informed me that my daughter had lice. I was sick with embarrassment, suddenly aware that I hadn't washed her hair for quite a while. I took her that very day to get her hair chopped off, while she screamed as I held her. *My sweet little Cal, I'm so sorry. Where have I been for too long?*

I climbed the stairs, calling for my daughter. She didn't come to greet me. She and Xavier were watching one of our movies in the TV room. I was glad to see them spending time together. Unwilling to disturb them, I went to my room, lay down on the bed, and softly cried. I knew what I was doing, what I was facing down the road. I would be on my own finally, anxious to test myself. But I had such tunnel vision.

Later, Xavier came to our room. We faced each other with all the knowing between us, like a brick wall. We had no secrets from each other. He knew about all of my friends. He knew they had served a purpose in my life, that they had helped me deal with the loneliness in my marriage. He tolerated all my evenings with Eleni, perhaps, because he knew they were soon coming to an end. My husband was glad that we were leaving Greece and hoped I'd come to my senses and decide to work on our marriage after we left.

But I was resolute. I never wavered in my decision to divorce Xavier. Something had broken loose inside of me, a willful streak that would not be harnessed. This locomotive had taken off, and in my mind and heart there was no going back.

Even then, back in 1990, I knew I had neglected my children and was embarking on a course that would hurt them. But what I didn't know was how my failures would stalk me forever after and put the quality of my parenting at grave risk. Before I could ever deal from strength again and have a strong relationship with my children, I would have to learn to tame the monster of self-hatred in me that had shadowed me since I was a child.

Guilt is a terrible crippler. I had much more work to do, from the inside out, to learn to value myself enough to pull myself out of the mire I was in and reclaim my life.

Spring, 1991

Back in Virginia I soldiered on, working a day job and a night job, taking graduate courses so I could keep my day job as a teacher. All this so we could continue living in the town the kids had grown up in. They needed their friends and familiar places, and I so wanted to minimize the pain of the divorce on my children. We had returned to Virginia from Rome in February, the kids and I in a temporary rental and Xavier renting an apartment nearby.

The family room was downstairs, and I was mighty grateful not to have to listen to Jane Fonda while I was trying to grade papers and do lesson plans. Money was tight now, and luckily Angie was happy to work out in her regular clothes. I'm sure some of her friends wore leotards and leg warmers but she never pressed me to buy those things. She cared more about what was driving her on the inside.

"Angie, turn that off!" I yelled. "Two hours is long enough. You need to finish your homework and study."

"OK, Mom. I'm almost done."

She'd gotten all the Fonda tapes by mail and spent hours burning calories in front of the TV. I never saw Angie binge on food, as I had for years, like a starving animal. Maybe she did but like many food addicts, she indulged the compulsion to overeat in private. Angie was for a year or so an exercise bulimic: she burned extra calories off by exercising. Normal self-indulgence is one thing. We all overeat now and then and, if we are athletically inclined we might go running the next day or two to get back into our comfort zone. Those of us who don't run or support gyms might just eat less for a day or two to achieve the same results. And then there are those of us who, not tyrannized by the numbers on a scale, really don't care one way or the other. I'm very close to claiming membership in the third group. As my weight goes up or down over the holidays, or as I age into my mother's body, I care less and less about what I weigh and what size pants I wear. I know that being happy has little to do with outward appearances, and there's a lot of freedom in that.

On a scale of 1 to 10 Angie's mania was pretty high but burned out quickly. Exercise that crosses the line from healthy to sick, to compulsion, is a matter of degree, I suppose. But there's no negotiating with compulsive addictions. You either have them or you don't. Fortunately, Angie either got bored with it or just gave it up. But the weight obsession, the neurotic fear of fat, would shadow us both for a long time.

I've often felt that her drug addiction, right or wrong, had a lot to do with this obsession. You can't get fat if you never eat, and when you're using hard drugs, eating is often the farthest thing from your mind. I myself, in struggling with the same thing, have wished many, many times over the years that I'd had a stash of amphetamines around to propel me through a depressing day that all too often took control of me. But I never acted on that fantasy. As I continue to emerge a stronger and happier version of what I might have been, I must remember to thank myself for giving up hard drugs and saying no to that impulse. I'm an addict, just like my daughter, and saying no to willful self-destruction involves, among other things, loving something else more.

I loved my children more.   Most of the time…

Five years earlier in Virginia, before we had gone to Greece, Angie witnessed one of my forays into self-abuse.

May 1986

I had been co-facilitating a support group for young mothers at a local mental health center in Virginia, and much to my surprise my supervisor, Betty, tapped me for a statewide award, Best Volunteer of the Year. This was quite an honor. So she and I met at the mental health center early on a warm spring morning. The trip to Charlottesville took ninety minutes and the ceremony was at ten in the morning. But we had lots to talk about and enjoyed the ride.

In the year we'd worked together we'd become good friends. She seemed very proud of the initiative I was taking to help bring young mothers together to talk. I felt that there was a lot of isolation among those of us who chose not to have a job and stay home with our children. The local newspaper even wrote an article about it, picking up on the emerging controversy between mothers who worked and those who didn't. We needed a supportive setting to discuss issues that we could relate to. Betty was married but chose not to have children, and she couldn't really empathize. So I admired her all the more for embracing our little support group as she did.

Arriving just in time in the large auditorium we took a seat and listened to all the speeches about the value of volunteer service. I was in some pretty heady company there. Everyone was dressed to the nines, and I wore my best off-white Easter suit. This award was really the culmination of years of volunteer work I had pursued since I was thirteen. My mother, very much to her credit, got me into volunteer work from a young age — not only because it was her thing for which she won her own awards — but also because she thought it might help with my depression. Maybe, she thought, it would get me out of myself long enough to focus more on others with problems and less on myself. Her instincts were good, and I'm very grateful now for her efforts. But I guess at that time winning an award just wasn't enough. It would take many more years of therapy and recovery work for me to discover that I was OK and had value just the way I was.

When it was my turn to receive my award, Betty and I walked to the podium together. Our picture was taken holding up the award and shaking hands—mine were so sweaty I had to dry them off. We returned to our seats, and I don't remember what was being said after that. I should have been glowing with pride and a sense of accomplishment, but I wasn't. A dark ominous cloud very quickly took over my space, eclipsing the award winner who mysteriously evaporated.

Betty had to get back to work, so we didn't linger with the other award winners, many of whom had their proud family in tow. In the car I gave her some ideas about kinks she needed to work out when the group resumed in the fall. We batted back and forth some new topics they might want to discuss. I wouldn't be part of it because I had to go into language training for our upcoming post to Greece and I wouldn't have much free time.

The ride home seemed faster than the ride there. On my way to Charlottesville, I kept trying to shut up an inner voice that said I didn't deserve this. I felt a sense of dread and didn't want to get there. But on the way home I felt no such dread. By the time I pulled into my driveway, that dark voice had nearly taken over and completely obliterated the pride and self-worth this young mother should have felt.

Already exhausted from the long awards ceremony, I walked into the kitchen, trancelike, ready to do battle with the two voices inside of me screaming for attention:

"Maggie, you just got back from Charlottesville. You won a fucking award: Best Volunteer of the Year. Your supervisor picked you out of all the candidates. Whyinthenameofallthat'sholy can't you just sit back and feel good about yourself for once? You've earned this honor!"

I was often self-absorbed, overwhelmed with pain and guilt from my childhood, lingering depression, and low self-esteem. My dream of creating a happy family to fight these demons was not working out. I found myself fantasizing about having a career outside of the home and felt guilty about that. Why wasn't I happy enough with all that I had? Why did I continually want more? These distractions kept me from being emotionally present to my children.

"Shut up, you stupid cow! They might be fooled, but I know better. You're an incredible fraud and you don't deserve a goddamn thing. You're nothing but a fuckup, a miserable excuse for a mother."

Same ole, same ole, this was the same old troll beckoning me into that secret dark place. I put my hands over my ears, but why? The noise wasn't coming from the outside. I was so tired of doing this to myself. How many teeth did I have to lose before I would stop this? Vomiting destroyed the enamel on my teeth and this caused widespread decay as well as costly reparative work. Poor Xavier was spending a fortune on my dentist's bills:

"Well, that's exactly what you deserve, you piece of shit. Go ahead. Stick your head in the toilet if you think that will rid you of me. Ha! I'll be back, dahling."

I just couldn't let myself take in—ingest—the pride I should have felt. It was a huge honor, this award. But the troll would have none of it. He comes alive when I'm threatened with success; puts on his armor to do battle with my fragile self-esteem. So now I was home to face the life, the troubled marriage, the children who didn't ask to be born, the troll who still, sometimes, told me what to do. That day anyway, the troll won.

It was one o'clock, and I figured I had two hours before the kids got home from school. I'd have to do it quickly, though; it usually took longer, like six hours, for me to ingest enough guilt, frustration, anxiety, and self-hatred, followed by plenty of liquids, to be able to purge myself of all that shit and feel cleansed. "Cleansed"??? Jesus Christ, it's that very delusion that keeps us purging! We always think this is gonna be the last time, that we won't have to anymore. We'll get rid of all the bad shit that keeps popping up, like an uninvited relative, and afterwards we'll say no to the troll when he comes knocking. But on this day I didn't try to fight him off. And anyway, don't relatives keep coming back?

I got in my car and went to the nearest 7-Eleven I could find. I was on a mission. I knew what to buy: ice cream, chips, donuts, canned spaghetti and meatballs, candy bars, all the food I never allow myself to eat, and a quart of milk. Oh good! They have those honey-dipped donuts I never eat. Now I can!

THE DAM HAS BROKEN!

I would have preferred to go to the all–you-can-eat smorgasbord they have at the Indian restaurant down the road. That's great binging food because it's soft and comes back up easily. But I didn't have time for that. The kids would be home soon.

I was in such a hurry I dropped all my change on the floor waiting in line. Picking it up I thought about the insanity of letting myself enjoy "forbidden" food, spend ten bucks on it instead of on my kids, only to have it end up in the toilet. Well, this was serious addiction.

I knew a couple of bingers in college who threw up four or five times a day. That, I think, would be deadly. At my worst, back in my early twenties, I was a weekly binger. So I guess, like exercise bulimia, it's all a matter of degree. And now, after years of therapy and recovery work, I don't binge like that at all.

Racing back home, I was trying to beat the clock, getting all this crap into me and washing it down with enough liquids so that I could get rid of it before the kids got home. "Before the kids got home." I kept saying that as though they were the stop sign that would make me slow down and reconsider. Usually I did—usually I loved my children more. But on that day I didn't slow down.

Forces in my life were converging now and I wanted momentary peace from this endless struggle between Maggie and the troll. I am a food addict, a compulsive overeater, and though I had enjoyed long periods of remission from binging, today I was relapsing.

Good and bad, love and hate—opposing forces that meet us on every front in life. I needed the relief of numbness that food would provide. One donut wasn't enough; I needed more, and more, and more, then French fries, then ice cream, then—and it's always hard to know exactly where I crossed the line into profound discomfort—I knew I had to undo all the damage this food would do to my waistline. That's what bulimia is: "bull hunger," followed by purging of some kind. Vomiting was the quickest. That's where the warm liquids come in; they loosen everything up in my stomach so it comes back up like hot soup.

Ah! Sweet relief! I had my high, my hit, and even got rid of the damage—no consequences! Very few times in my life have I ever thrown up normally because I had the stomach flu or something. I always had to induce vomiting, and I shudder to think of the damage I may have done to my esophagus and intestines as a result of this. Not to mention the damage to my teeth. No consequences, indeed.

But today I couldn't stop this locomotive, even when I heard the front door close and Angie came upstairs but I told her to get lost, I was sick, and locked the bathroom door and she banged on it trying to get in and every bang was a thrust down my throat bringing up more guilt, frustration, anxiety and self-hatred.

When I was done, flushed the toilet, cleaned it, and sprayed air freshener, I calmly unlocked the bathroom door, hugged her and asked her how her day had been. This runaway train had come to a screeching halt, and didn't even notice that Angie was choking in the dust.

For too many years I've watched my child get swallowed up by the same addictions that crippled me. What could be a worse hell for a mother than to see her daughter become the worst version of what she might have become? When I married Xavier in 1975, in many ways he was an angel to me. My marriage to him and the three children I had in quick succession saved me from what I might have become: an unrecovered drug and food addict. And though it would take a number of years to get my food obsession under control, I never abused hard drugs again.

The end of my illness and the beginning of hers is the unbroken umbilical cord that has held us hostage to the disease we share. We mirror each other so much. And now, as she struggles on her own to face her demons, she wants nothing to do with me and angrily resents my attempts to demonstrate any understanding. It is her disease that wants nothing to do with me, not my daughter. It cannot allow my recovery to get close and threaten its survival. Its oxygen is isolation.

But nine years after banging on that bathroom door, Angie's anger found a voice.

Fall, 1995

The year her father remarried, Angie embraced his decision to move on with his life. I had begun a relationship with a new man two years before, and I'm sure she wanted her father to find happiness as well. She was very fond of her stepmother, who had no children of her own. The two of them were good friends for a number of years, until Angie's addiction drove a wedge between them. My daughter never communicated with me about the divorce, not in words. There were other ways to communicate her feelings. One way was to stop eating, five years before, in Rome; another was to get depressed from time to time; another was to riffle through Mom's personal papers where she hit pay dirt in Mom's personal journal.

This was a journal I had kept since 1970, the year I graduated from college. It was a largely chronological account of important events in my life from that year on. A few pages are ripped out of my journal so I can't read them now. But Angie read them. They were an account of my trip to Crete with my friends from Politia. I talked about the Samaria Gorge we hiked, the friends we saw, the fun we had. I moaned about how I would miss all my friends when we left Greece and continued at length about my need to divorce Xavier and gain some independence. "It tears me apart," I said, "to destroy my family like this." "But," I went on, "I need to live my own life, unencumbered by Mother's shadow. I want to find my own place in the sun now. It's time for me."

Opening my bedroom door after school, I was startled to see my daughter in front of my file cabinet, holding some ripped out pages of my diary:

"Mom, how could you be so selfish? You couldn't wait to get divorced!" she yelled, backing into the wall as I approached her.

"Angie, what are you talking about?" indignant and furious that she had snooped among my things. "What do you have in your hands?" My heart sank as I realized she had been reading my diary. *Oh God, no!* I stopped in my tracks.

The room became very small and airless. I felt sick knowing that Angie had read my private thoughts.

"You're awful, Mom. You didn't even try with Dad. It's your fault! I hate you!" she screamed, as she stormed out of my room with the diary pages and slammed the door. I heard her go into the bathroom next door, rip up the pages and flush them down the toilet. I was grateful that she had slammed the door. I needed time alone to catch my breath.

So now she can blame me for the divorce, I thought to myself, *as if things could ever be made so simple.*

This isn't the beginning of Angie's anger about the end of our marriage, but it's the first time it would be directed exclusively at me. This wound has festered on and off in Angie since that day, in spite of therapy for her and a number of interventions. And like her mother for so many years before that time, she would turn it inward against herself, crippled on and off with bouts of depression.

In any case, as painful as the divorce would be for Angie, it was not the cause of her illness. She had the seeds of addiction in her already, passed down through me. It has been a great relief for me to realize, like a welcome breeze on a still sea, that Angie's illness is not my fault.

Angie appeared to bounce back from this eruption with me. For the next five years, before she moved out and her drug addiction came into full force, we all continued living in our home in relative harmony. Still, there were problems. The year before her father remarried, in 1994, he had been living in Rome on assignment, and Angie became visibly depressed. I remember her talking on the phone to him: "Dad, I miss you. Please come home." Angie shed no tears but was clearly in need of her father's presence in her life. This worried him terribly and he arranged to have himself reassigned to the States. I will always be grateful to him for that. However we may have mismanaged our marriage and caused our children to suffer, this is a man of great substance who loves his children well. It was a sacrifice for him, but he has never regretted coming back for Angie. We immediately started our daughter in therapy every week with a woman she would continue to see for a number of years.

Angie was happy, or so it seemed, now that her father was back home. He married Roxanne in 1995 and they lived nearby. But she could not stand the high school she was attending. Back in Greece she and her friend Jane had listened to heavy metal music, and she was getting into alternative culture, skinheads and tattoos. This was not to be found much at her high school, so she begged me to let her finish her few senior courses at an adult education center nearby. I told her if she could maintain a B+ average, I would allow it. So she did, and that last year before graduation she applied to college for acceptance in the fall, relieved that she wouldn't have to go back to cliques, cheerleaders, and the pain of being an outsider. I knew what that felt like—I'd felt it my whole life—so I let her finish high school as she chose to.

Kids coming back to the States from overseas often have problems adjusting to the change in culture, especially during the teen years. And my children were also coping with our divorce. I know plenty of other children in the Foreign Service, though, who seamlessly moved from country to country without any problems.

But my kids didn't have an easy time of it. Carlos did well in school and had a few friends, but he kept to himself a lot and I felt his loneliness. He wasn't close to his sisters, in spite of the closeness in age. They were very different. Both girls attached themselves to music and a culture that was pretty dark, and I allowed them the freedom to pursue it. My mother would have sent me away to boarding school. But, as you might guess by now, I was determined not to be my mother.

The pendulum swung quite a different way in my household, or so I thought. The more I tried not to be my mother, the more her influence surrounded me. I could be just as oppressive as my mother. I felt I was giving my girls the freedom to be, but I snatched it away in an instant if I expressed any disappointment. Later on in Angie's addiction, terrified at my inability to control the uncontrollable, I would emerge as my mother's voice incarnate, pushing Angie further away from me just as my mother had done all those years ago.

All three children had part-time jobs as soon as they were old enough. They were really good kids, in spite of their family problems. They saw how hard I worked and they never asked me for an allowance. Angie was working in 1997 in a bookstore, and I remember what she said in her essay to get into college. Among other things she said, "Nothing could have helped me appreciate the value of a college education as much as working two years in retail." They must have liked what she wrote; George Washington University accepted her and, though I had to take out a loan to help pay the tuition, that's where she chose to go.

Predictably, though, she only lasted there one year. "Too mainstream," she complained, so she transferred her credits to George Mason University the following year. Angie did very well in college; she was on the Dean's List a few times. She loved to write and was very talented, so she chose to major in Journalism. One of her part-time jobs was as an editorial assistant.

I have to say this because of the painful irony it embodies: Angie was "the good daughter." Caroline had green hair when she was fourteen and almost dropped out of high school in 1999 when she was a senior. She was the family rebel, not her older sister. She has never been under my thumb like I was with my mother. She is fiercely independent, and that's a good thing. I'm very proud of Caroline.

But she took up a lot of my energy then with all her rebellion. It was easier to turn a blind eye to Angie since she behaved so well and so responsibly. I worried about her, but most of the time she went out of her way to function on a very high level. She saw her therapist faithfully every week, though I'd wished she could have opened up to me more. I longed for closeness with Angie, since I'd missed it with my own mother. When at times she seemed sad I used to go sit on her bed with her and prod her to talk to me. She always kept the blinds closed in her room. I could smell that awful patchouli oil she and Caroline used to wear. She just lay there sometimes staring at the ceiling. Oh, I used to do that too, for hours. Years ago in my twenties I sat so long I watched the shadow of the sun move across the pictures on the wall in front of me. Then there was no more shadow and I knew the sun had set.

"I'm here, Angie," I pleaded. "Please, tell me what's on your mind." My mother had never reached out to me like this. She was too preoccupied with her own sadness in her own bedroom. Angie always closed up like a clam, and so I left her alone. I rationalized, "Oh well, she has her therapist to talk to." I wish now that I'd pushed much harder to get inside her head. I might have managed better if I'd had more information.

Angie worked at one part-time job after another, saving her money in the bank. I bought her an old car so she could drive to school and she never abused the privilege. Friends were important to her, but she remained focused on school and work. Angie was endlessly thoughtful to both her parents and grandparents on special occasions. And the list goes on.

If I was surprised by my daughter's drug addiction in 2001, this is why. Later on once her addiction had taken hold of her, I would be incredulous at the dysfunctional behavior I was seeing. It's as though she had become possessed. She had problems, but I thought I was helping her deal with them responsibly. There were no visible red flags. She didn't stay in bed every day and pull the covers over her head. She diligently saw her therapist every week, facing every day with discipline and good humor. She never missed her classes and she never quit her jobs. Her grades were excellent. Maybe—and this is important to recognize now—this was the beginning of the denial that would hamper me throughout Angie's addiction, preventing me from dealing with her illness intelligently and effectively.

Angie was a good daughter. But please, beware of the complacency in those words. Clearly, she hid her pain very well. Clearly, much was lurking beneath the surface that I did not see. And if I ache with the vacant promise of all the "woulda, coulda, shouldas," it's because I know that even if I had known what was coming down the road, I couldn't have stopped it.

The Dream

I see the wolf
In the shadows of the night
With its back arched
looking ready to fight
With eyes like steel
And teeth stained red
It's sharp ribs stick out obviously wanting
to be fed
It tilts its head toward the moon
And lets a long loud howl
It gives me a look
Savage and foul
It runs toward me
And I gasp with fright
As it tears me apart,
bite, by bite
I sit up in bed
Ready to scream
But then I quiet down
It was only a dream

ONE

*"'But I don't want to go among mad
people,' Alice remarked.*

*'Oh, you can't help that,' said the Cat; 'we're
all mad here. I'm mad. You're mad.'*

'How do you know I'm mad?' said Alice.

*'You must be,' said the Cat, 'or you
wouldn't have come here.'"*

(Carroll 67)

Good Morning, Lucifer

There it is again, I muttered to myself, *carelessly parked in the fire lane, daring the local police to ticket it.* I raced inside to get the key I had secretly made to rescue her from another ticket. In the kitchen making coffee, the hem of her long red kimono picking up dirt from the floor, she glared at me in disgust as I, exasperated, held up the car key for her to see.

"Oh go fuck yourself, Mom. No one asked you to leave your little love nest to move my car."

Pow-Pow.

"Angie, it really hurts me when you speak to me that way, " staring at her plaintively, as if I could awaken a long-buried morsel of feeling or affection she once had for me. Angie was unmoved, ignored my comment and brushed past me as she went back downstairs to the privacy of the basement.

My partner, Gene, and I took turns staying at each other's house on weekends. This was a weekly ritual, moving the car. I came home from Gene's early in the morning on purpose so that I would beat the cops on their rounds. I don't know why I bothered; she had a stack of tickets in her car that she had no intention of paying. If it weren't for me, she'd lose her car. Even with me, it's been towed more times than I want to remember. But if she loses her car, maybe she'll stop going to campus to finish up her last two courses. Nor would she be able to get to work.

She needs her car, because she's too spoiled to think of the alternative, and I, like a fool perpetuating that destructive notion, was in a position to rescue her. So I did, over and over and over again, unconsciously enabling her to continue the irresponsible behavior that was claiming her, enveloping her, consuming her. Before I knew it, she would be running from meth, to cocaine, to heroin. She was waving a red flag in front of me, and I chose to take the path of least resistance: take care of the damn car myself.

Then there was the silver. If it wasn't nailed down, it was gone. I came home from two weeks with my mother, only to find a lot of my silver gone. A beautiful Chantilly service for twelve, handed down from my mother. With serving pieces worth, well, enough to a pawnbroker to buy a few more hits.

I was sitting in the dining room with my head in my hands. She came upstairs from her basement refuge, and I told her that I'd been robbed of much of the silver Nana had given me. Without batting an eyelash, she said she probably knew who had broken in to the house and stolen it. I bought that, hook, line, and sinker, had the locks changed, and said no more. Out of guilt, I suppose, she retrieved a couple of serving pieces from the "Pawn Shop" which somehow she knew about, and I gratefully thanked her. Gratefully thanked her!!! If I didn't know then, it was slowly to dawn on me: my daughter was gone, hijacked by a disease that was killing her slowly and sucking all those close to her down a black hole. As long as she was living in my house, I was at war with her illness, and it was winning hands down.

Simply put, I didn't have the courage to confront her with what was obviously a continuing addiction problem. She had two courses left to complete her B.A.!!! I didn't want to rock the boat. Funny how the most well-meaning parents can rationalize the most foolish behavior—or worse. I thought a college education would open doors for her, the right doors. It couldn't have been more irrelevant by the time she turned twenty-two. She was already a full-fledged drug addict, morphing, to my horror, into a complete stranger.

Angie had always been very thoughtful to both her parents. I have drawers full of birthday and Mother's Day remembrances. Angie and I were close, connected in a strange way, a way that I would understand much later; and even though she was first at George Washington, then at George Mason University, she chose to live at home. It wasn't just to save money; she could have taken another loan. She should have wanted to get away from me, but she didn't. I should have encouraged her to get out on her own, but I didn't. She didn't move out until she was forced to when her father decided to sell the family house the year before, in 2000.

That was a busy year: her brother was finishing college, her sister drove to San Francisco with her best friend, and Angie, without her sister or a choice, moved into her own apartment in D.C. She wasn't quite twenty-one, which is old by many standards. But she left because she had to. Also, the same month the house sold and we all moved out, I had to put down her (our) beloved dog, Oscar, whom we'd had from Greece for thirteen years.

I was beyond sad. I sobbed nearly every day for months, before he died. Have you ever listened to Gustav Mahler's 9th Symphony, the one he wrote immortalizing his dead wife, Alma? It's a very emotional piece of music. That was my breast-beating ritual for weeks before I put Oscar down that summer. It was a form of anticipatory grief—a terrible, terrible self-indulgence—accomplishing nothing but robbing you of the time you have left together.

To be honest, that summer of 2000, I was grieving more than our beloved dog. Leaving that home of ours that we'd lived in for fourteen years, when we weren't overseas, was hard. Back in 1986, Xavier and I had fought in a nasty bidding war and won—to give our children this lovely home—and to give our family another chance. We wanted to breathe life into our marriage, as if a bigger, lovelier house could carry that burden.

So leaving that house nearly a decade after our divorce seemed like another, more final divorce decree, seemed like another letting go for me, even though both Xavier and I had moved on with other partners. It was another concrete example, signed, sealed and delivered, of my failure to shield my children from the pain of our divorce, even though I know now that we cannot and should not shield our children from life's pain—a potent teacher. For a while I worked at two jobs so that we could keep it, and though the kids seemed to get through high school OK, it still felt like a terrible loss when we sold it. It was the end of an era, in more ways than one.

On a rainy day that spring, Angie was sitting in the family room downstairs staring out of the window, and she called me to come downstairs. She had something to tell me, so I went down to join her on the sofa.

"I've decided to move in with Heather, Mom. She needs a roommate."

I was stunned to hear these words. She was twenty-one, a grown woman. What was the big deal? Suddenly I felt the oxygen leaving the room and I felt a weight on my chest. I reached out to touch her, but she quickly got up from the sofa to go upstairs.

"Oh, Angie! Are you sure? I moaned, following her upstairs. "Gosh, honey, I know it's probably time, but I can't imagine us not being together!"

"It's time, Mom." She was resolute and showed no emotion. No regret, no "I'll miss you, Mom."

Looking back, I think Angie knew exactly what she was doing and where she needed to be: as far away from me as possible. I never witnessed any drug use in this home, but that didn't mean she wasn't experimenting elsewhere. And whatever demons may have been beckoning her at this pivotal time in her life, if Addiction had found a vulnerable victim to seduce, she didn't want me to know about it.

I went to my room and shut my eyes. I was crestfallen. I'd lived with her for twenty-one years and now I had to let her go? What was I thinking, anyway? She should be moving out on her own. Did I think she was going to live with me when I relocated after the sale?

I'd bravely waved goodbye to Caroline as she drove off to San Francisco the previous winter, refusing to make a big fuss, thinking this is what parents are supposed to do: let their children go. And Carlos already had an apartment lined up in D.C. right after graduation. I wasn't sad about that at all. The biggest grief of all that year was that my three children left the nest—all of them, within six months of each other. Now, I know I'll never get a "Mother of the Year" award, but my three children were quite simply the joys of my life and I liked having them around. As flawed as I was/am, I was and still am the best mother I can be. I'll shout that from the heavenly rooftops when my time comes so the angels will hear me and make room.

But Angie leaving my house, my company, somehow felt like I was losing a part of myself. I didn't understand why I felt such cold fear releasing her to the world. Much later I would distance myself long enough to understand the terrible connection we shared, and I'd understand why it was so hard for me to let her go. Deep down, though I didn't see it then, I knew we were mirror images of each other. I was afraid for her.

It's possible Angie stayed home because Oscar was there. He slept in her bed with her every night. The day before Carlos and I walked him to the vet for the last time, she came to say goodbye to him. She didn't cry or show any emotion. But that was Angie; she kept her feelings to herself. I have never understood why Angie is that way. When we lost her in the museum in Brussels that summer, why didn't she cry and show any fear? Maybe from a young age, when her feelings were sometimes ignored, she learned to fear them or worse, shut them off. When I was growing up in that schoolhouse by the lake, I was in so much pain that I learned to turn my feelings off, like a light switch. Maybe that's what Angie had done since she was little. And when feelings did emerge, whether happy or sad, I numbed them with food or drugs, just like my daughter.

Maybe losing Oscar set her off—I don't know. I guess I'll never know where, or when, or why. Parents don't look for possible disasters with their kids. Children symbolize hope, the future. Their parents don't dream about tragedy; they envision good times and grandchildren—a happy ending to their own lives. But parents should never do that to themselves; it's such an awful setup.

That summer was her Nana's 90th birthday and Carlos, Angie and I journeyed to Massachusetts to celebrate with the rest of the family. We had a wonderful time with all the aunts and uncles and cousins. Lucy and I both wrote poems honoring our mother. And Angie did a beautiful rendering of an early portrait of her grandmother. My mother and Angie had always been especially close. While my other children were busy with friends and activities during summer vacation, Angie often chose to spend this time with her Nana.

This would be the last time my mother would see Angie in all her innocence. My aunt and uncle lived by the sea not far from where I grew up. Angie and I enjoyed an outing sailing with them before we all drove back to Virginia. Angie wrote a beautiful thank you letter to them when she got home. She was still my daughter then—my daughter, like a ghost that would slip away in the night before we had time to recognize the disease that was claiming her.

Her first year of living independently seemed uneventful at first. I often went to see her in the apartment she shared with a very nice girl. I took her furniture from her old bedroom so that she would feel at home in her new digs. But there were signs that she was changing. She had never had many boyfriends that I knew of. She wasn't at all promiscuous. Then one Sunday morning I arrived to find a "friend" of hers on the sofa, clearly feeling very much at home. I was later to discover that he was a bartender at a watering hole and drug hotspot in Adams Morgan. Well, she was on her own. And by now she was twenty-one. I didn't have much leverage.

In the spring, only two courses short of her graduation requirements at George Mason University, Angie was allowed to walk with her class, cap and gown and all. The fact that she was happy to do this at all spoke to us. But it distracted us, as well, from facing what she was doing in the evenings. Again, and always, she went to a lot of trouble to cover up behavior that she knew would alarm us and might threaten an intervention. Addiction is a powerful disease and, like cancer, it wants to survive.

"Hey, Mom, I want you to meet my friend Shelly. She got me through statistics sophomore year."

"Hi, Shelly, nice to meet you. Thanks for helping Angie. Is your family here today?"

"No. They had to work. No big deal for them anyway."

"Oh. Well I think it's a big deal, so congratulations from me! It was nice to meet you, Shelly, and good luck."

Xavier, his wife and I all dressed up for our second child's college graduation. It was spring 2001, and we all viewed this ceremony as a symbol of hope that Angie was willing and anxious to embrace her adulthood and take on more responsibilities, like so many other young people.

But at the end of the summer, she asked if she could move into my basement. Her roommate was buying a condo and their lease was up anyway. Later on, when I watched in horror as the tragedy unfolded in my own house, I wondered about the truth of that. I thought maybe the roommate saw where Angie was going and asked her to leave. No matter. She was in my home now, and the war was about to begin.

There were a number of red flags screaming for my attention. One was the dropped Milton course. It was totally unlike her to be that irresponsible and give up on something she had started. And then, a far clearer statement, there was the homemade concoction left in the basement for me to find. On my way downstairs to the laundry room I couldn't believe my eyes. One of my mixing bowls was full of some off-white substance I didn't recognize. She wasn't home when I found it, but I moved it up to the kitchen near the garbage disposal, ready to toss in the morning, so she'd see it when she came home.

At 4:30 a.m., Angie exploded into my bedroom while Gene and I were asleep:

"Mom, whatthefuck! How dare you mess with my stuff downstairs! Don't you ever touch my stuff again, youfuckingbitch!"

She looked raw, animal-like, with blood-shot, wild eyes. I was half-asleep; I hoped I'd been dreaming. Angie slammed the door and my hand mirror, tempting fate on the edge of my dresser, fell to the floor and cracked. *Uh-oh,* I thought to myself, *seven years bad luck. OK, I guess I'm still asleep. This can't be happening! What planet am I on? 'Scotty, get me outta here!' Who is this horrible bitch?*

Gene went downstairs to check on her, as if there was anything he could do to stabilize this toxic, nightmarish situation. He came right back upstairs, trying to comfort me, the only person he might be able to influence. I remember like it was yesterday how I pushed my face into my pillow, praying to God to put an end to this horror. Little did I know then in the fall of 2001 that this was just the beginning of facing down my daughter's — and many of my own — demons.

Oh, well, no more sleep for me. I freaked out — she freaked out — and thankfully moved out, temporarily, to live with her pusher. A half-hour later, I went downstairs to make coffee. Loudly stomping upstairs from her basement hideaway so I'd take note of how mad she was, she brushed by me without a word or a look, stony-faced and resolute. Carrying a garbage bag of clothes and shoes, she slammed the front door as she left. I went to the window to see if she was parked in the fire lane she had always parked in, and for once I was glad because I could watch her for a little longer as she drove away. Two feelings I would spend the next decade learning to reconcile: complete and utter hatred for this stranger who was living in my daughter's body; and total and complete surrender to love for my child.

Angie was in a very bad place, and tumbling faster out of control. She was a "tweaker," a sleep-deprived meth addict, and she was extremely abusive and paranoid. I was so afraid I would get in her way and she would hurt me. She would have no memory of it anyway. That's what's so frustrating and frightening about this changed behavior. If you confront them when they're (relatively) sober, they deny it or don't remember anything. If you confront them while they're high, you could wind up dead.

By December I'd had enough "Fuck you's" and "Get out of my face's." I knew I couldn't have her in my house any longer. It was a war zone. And I was developing physical problems, chest pains, from all the stress.

My niece invited me and Gene, Angie and Carlos over to her house on Christmas Eve. How could I tell her that Angie doesn't even live with me now, that I had no idea where she was living? Did I really have to accept Linda's invitation? Why did I have to keep up a brave front? Couldn't I, please God, just go to sleep and wake up on New Year's, Happy New Year! It was all just a bad dream? No, I saw little enough of my brother's daughter, and I needed to put my misery aside long enough to help her celebrate the holidays with the family she had close by.

Carlos accompanied Gene and me, but Angie was only an occasional visitor at the condo, and she never even responded to my invitation. *That little bitch*, I thought to myself. Linda, her husband, and three children eagerly greeted us when we arrived. Like I had done over twenty years before, she left Massachusetts by marrying a man whose work would take her away. We both felt lonely for family over the holidays.

The Christmas tree lights in Linda's living room were a blur to me, and I couldn't taste the food she kept offering. I was obsessed with my absentee daughter and where she might be. *Where was she living now? Was she still with that miserable creep? Whatinthenameofhellwasshedoing?*

Startled — and feeling invaded — by the dreaded question that I would have to answer:

"How is Angie, Aunt Maggie? What's she up to?" Linda asked as her six-year-old swooped up onto her lap. Molly was adorable, the apple of her mother's eye. She was a towhead, like her mother, but she was very much her own person, even at age six. I admired that, how she could assert her independence at such a young age. Angie was a six-year-old once, and I used to swoop her up onto my lap at family gatherings.

I remembered a family gathering in June 1985:

"Bopi, come here. I want to show you my awards from school."

My father and mother had driven down to Virginia to visit us. I had made a picture album of the children with special events of the year and all their school awards. Angie wanted to show her grandfather all that she had accomplished that year. My poor father had such painful arthritis as he hobbled over to the sofa and sat down.

"OK, Angie. What have you been doing with yourself, you little monkey?"

Angie plopped onto my lap where I was holding the album open to show Dad the pictures:

Beaming broadly, Angie gushed, "This one's of me at gymnastics practice doing flip-flops on the floor. And this one is me hitting the piñata at my birthday party last year. Mom said we could have another piñata for my birthday in August. And this one is after Carlos's piano lesson, where I was pretending I could play like him!"

"Angie," my father enthused, "you're quite something, do you know that? But now your poor old granddad is tired and needs to take a nap. I'm going downstairs for a little rest."

"I'll help you down the stairs, Bopi, so you won't fall."

Angie loved both of my parents very much. She was so intuitive. It was the last time Angie would ever see her grandfather. He died of a massive coronary three months later.

Never in my wildest dreams could I have imagined that beautiful child becoming a drug addict. But she is. And right now she was asserting her independence too.

"Oh, she's fine," I assured Linda. "Finishing up her courses at Mason so she can graduate. She has a good job doing college counseling at Phoenix. Online universities are really getting big now. Maybe she'll keep at it after she finishes up. Anyway, she sends her love. So sorry she couldn't make it tonight."

Liar. I was such a liar.

We had a pleasant enough time with Angie's cousin. Carlos chatted excitedly about his job and his apartment in D.C. We drank some punch and sampled the Christmas cookies Linda had just learned to make. My mother, her grandmother, had given her the recipe. She thought I might remember them from my childhood Christmases. Gene said I should try one; they had just enough nutmeg to be spicy without being overbearing. Ignoring him, I got up to walk around and admire Linda's decorations.

Momentarily dazzled by the glitter of the Christmas tree, my attention was drawn like a magnet to all their family pictures placed around the room. Then I pictured my condo all decorated for Christmas and my family pictures all over my baby grand piano, the one my mother had bought for twenty-five dollars in 1955. There was a picture of my mother and me taken on Christmas in 1965. She was smiling broadly and I looked utterly forlorn, wearing a bathrobe she had made me: pink felt with an empire waist and an olive green ribbon at the bodice, zippered up the front and fastened with a huge snap. It was long and flowing and covered my body nicely.

I remember that robe so well because I wore it like a beacon on both Thanksgiving and Christmas at Terraces for a couple of years. It defined me in many of the family holiday pictures. I refused to get dressed, even with company coming over. Mother must have given up trying to get me to keep up appearances. I was resolute and determined to literally advertise how depressed I was. But nobody ever said anything. Mother did take me to a psychologist once. But after interviewing me the doctor said I was fine. That was what my mother wanted to hear, so no further interventions were pursued, not until I underwent intensive therapy later on when I was in my twenties.

Remembering that picture, how could I have known that such sadness would echo down through the generations to this night thirty-six years later? Now I was feeling that pain reach across time and strike me in the heart through my daughter. How could I be losing her like this?

I hear my mother's critical voice from so long ago. I can see her face — her thin, passionless lips, the way she wore lipstick, and how she despised the way I wore it, dark red, on my full mouth. I tried to be everything my mother wasn't, to give my children the freedom to be who they wanted to be and not use them as puppets to live out my unfulfilled dreams. But I may have gone too far in the opposite direction. Maybe I should have reined them in more.

Linda's two other children trotted back out from their rooms to dutifully give us reports of their accomplishments in school and out. I turned to rejoin them in their excitement, remembering my own three children not so long ago, full of promise and hope. I was grateful that Carlos and Caroline were doing very well. But I agonized over Angie's drug problem. I hoped my niece would never have to face addiction in one of these beautiful children.

In my family all of us were expected to behave in a certain way in life. Failure was not an option. If problems did occur, they were swept under the rug. And that's where I spent most of my youth suffocating. I felt like a burden to my parents in some ways, until I was finally married and someone else's responsibility.

So leveling with my family, here or in Massachusetts, about Angie, was something I wasn't able to do. I would not have enough recovery yet to know that Angie's drug addiction wasn't a failure, and it wasn't my fault. In my fantasy, unrealized at that point, leveling with my mother might go something like this:

"Mama, I have such sad news to tell you. Angie has gotten into drugs," not "Angie is a drug addict," which to me sounds more decadent and final. "She's been struggling for a few months now and we're all devastated by what's been happening."

"Oh, Maggie, I don't know what to say," she answers, her eyes filling with tears.

"There's nothing to say, nothing you can do. We're all still in shock about it. I certainly never saw it coming. Caroline was the one who worried me. And then as soon as we left the house in McLean, and Angie started living on her own, she started seriously using drugs. We're all just starting to put the pieces together, and we'll do anything we can to help her."

"Like what? What can you do?"

"I'm not really sure. Honestly, I still can't believe this is happening to Angie. I wasn't prepared for this. But we'll just have to take it as it comes and do our best to help her."

"Of course you will. Oh darling, I'm so sorry,'" she said, offering me a big hug. "I can't believe this is happening to my Angie," she said, tears falling down her cheeks. I grabbed a Kleenex from the box and gave it to her.

"**Your** Angie," I intoned wistfully. "She always has been your favorite, hasn't she?"

"Oh no, dear, I don't have any favorites. But she and I always had a special connection."

"I know, Mama," slowly going upstairs to bed. "Maybe we'll all have her back again once she gets the help she needs. Good night. I love you."

No, I never had the courage to tell my ninety-one-year-old mother about her granddaughter. My sister Lucy was the first one I told, and the only one for quite a while. She was very sympathetic when I told her about all the verbal abuse, the drug mixing in my basement, and all the bizarre behavior. She advised me to kick Angie out.

But I couldn't wait to get out of Linda's house. How I hated all the deception! At this point in my daughter's disease, no one in my family except my sister knew what was happening to her. I was still hoping that it would go away—Poof—like a virus gone astray. I loved my niece and she loved me, but I needed to be held and comforted. If Angie had had cancer, I'd have been held and comforted. The mother of a drug addict is kept at a distance and (I imagined) avoided, afraid that it might be contagious. A friend of mine calls addiction "the modern leprosy."

Shortly after we got home, Angie barreled through the front door and crashed on her sofa in the basement of the condo. Not a word to me—nothing—not "Sorry, Mom, I couldn't make it." Or "Sorry, Mom, I tried to make it but got hung up." I thought to myself, *At least try, Angie, to appear normal, try to appreciate that you have family here that you just blew off. At least try to feed my fantasy that this is just a phase you're going through and you'll snap out of it.*

I imagined that my own mother nearly forty years before also had fantasies that I was just going through a depressive phase and would snap out of it. At least, that's what the psychologist told her. But I didn't snap out of it; my depression got much worse, and I needed a lot of help before I would get better. So would Angie, I supposed. But I wasn't nearly clear-headed enough at that point to know exactly what to do. I still felt that her drug addiction had come out of left field and I wasn't prepared for it. And anyway, I was starting to feel afraid for myself.

But I was tired, sick of her rudeness, and I didn't want to deal with her. At the same time I felt grateful that she was safely ensconced in the basement, considering the alternative. So I left her alone to sleep and I went to bed as well, looking forward to Christmas morning.

I tiptoed down to the basement of my condo to wake Angie and ask her to join us for gifts. Nudging her shoulders, I got no response; there was no movement. *Oh my God! Is she breathing? Oh Christ! She might have been OD'ing right here last night while I thought she was sleeping and I calmly went to bed. Oh my God, what have I done now? What have **I done now?***

"Angie, is there something I should know?" I said meekly, politely, as if I thought such a mild delivery would be rewarded with a mild, innocuous answer. What I was thinking, of course, was that I'd have to disturb the neighborhood tranquility of Christmas morning with ambulance sirens after I made my call to 911. In blind red-hot panic, I was afraid she had pumped enough drugs into her system to stun an elephant and *JesusChristwasshedeadoralive* and I put my face next to hers to see if she was breathing and *yes, thank God she was!*

"Angie, wake up, it's Christmas, honey!" I repeated my earlier question, just as meekly and politely, as though I were appeasing the gods for granting her a reprieve. Barely stirring, she mumbled angrily, "I just wanna sleep, Mom. I'm really tired. Leave me alone." I was relieved that she was still breathing, but sick in my heart to know that she was just coming off a meth high. *Merry Christmas, Maggie*, I whined.

Meth addicts can go for days without sleep sometimes, and then they need to crash, recoup their energy and start the cycle all over again. I went back upstairs, tiptoeing around the house, a minefield waiting to be activated by just the wrong look or comment. Most of the time I felt like a scared rabbit.

Angie came and went like a phantom between the holidays. She was a body, yes, but nothing else resembled my daughter. Her face was still healing from the burns she had gotten from freebasing crack cocaine back in October. She lost all her beautiful eyelashes then and had been wearing false ones ever since. How bizarre: false eyelashes at age twenty-two. And the eye drops — always the eye drops. She ate not at all as far as I could see, nothing from my refrigerator anyway. She was painfully thin. But, of course, meth took away your appetite. That was the point, one of them, anyway. All those years ago when I took amphetamines, I delighted in the same side effect. Life was repeating itself and I was in a time warp observing myself at the very same age. God, it was so painful.

We barely spoke. Sometimes she mumbled "Hello," but mostly she just needed a place to crash and get her clothes. Why wasn't she living with that creep, her pusher? I was glad she wasn't and at the same time I'd wished she were. Every day was a surreal pageant, dancing around with this stranger. The terror was so disorienting that I lapsed into denial sometimes and pretended it wasn't happening. But that was easier to do when I was working. I was on a break from school now and I couldn't escape from it. It was right in front of me.

As New Year's approached, I couldn't bear it anymore. Did I snap? I hadn't even joined Al-Anon yet, but years later I would hear a saying at meetings: "In Al-Anon we learn to trade a wishbone in for a backbone." Amazing! I was ready to cross these frightening waters before I even had the support of the group. But I would flee, in subsequent years, to higher ground all too often, unable to navigate effectively. This was going to be a journey as much for me as for Angie, I soon found out. And like most journeys there would be many bumps in the road.

On December 28, 2001, I told her she had to move out. She had a week to find a place to live. Standing across the dining room table from her, I felt safer with the table between us:

"Angie, you need to move out. I won't have you living here any longer."

Those words must have activated a button in this drugged-out robot because all of a sudden she showed some normal human emotion:

"Come on, Mom, you aren't serious!"

"I'm dead serious. You've got a week to look on Craigslist and find a room in a group house. With January first coming up, it's a perfect time to be moving."

"Is there nothing I can do to change your mind?"

Was I imagining it, or was her voice tinged with a pleading tone? Well, if it was, it didn't work.

"Nothing, Angie. You brought this on yourself."

I didn't go on and on with a litany of reasons. I didn't have to. She was still conscious enough to know full well what she was doing. And furthermore, she knew her mother. This was a logical consequence for her outrageous behavior. She had pushed me to the limit and now, voilà, there we were.

It was still so early in her addictive disease that I wonder how I found the courage. I had learned over the years to value and take care of myself most of the time, though I still had a ways to go on that front. But letting her abuse me and steal from me was not good self-care. I had overcome many challenges in my life. But this one—this one tested me differently.

It wasn't just me vs. life anymore. Now it was me vs. my own daughter. And being an addict myself, *it became me vs. me.* With every lash of the whip at her, I felt the pain on my back too. I had no idea then that in trying to help Angie go into recovery I would need to reach for my own too. Of course I wanted us both to win. But it would not be so simple. Addiction is cunning, baffling, and treacherous—and not just for the addict but for the family as well. The deeper Angie sank into this black hole the more I would need to recover myself from the effects of addiction. At first, more often than not I followed her into that hole: in the form of ignoring healthy boundaries, blaming myself, and catering to the needs of an addict. Walking away from her and kicking her out of my home seemed so counterintuitive.

Yet it was instinctual at that point, self-preservation. I felt like a moth turned into a butterfly for the moment. I felt like I was taking charge, as I should have. I felt like I was making the right choice, and definitely giving Angie the message that she'd better shape up or lose her family. I had no idea at that point that an addict deep in the disease couldn't care less about family.

Oh, how this butterfly would flutter and die in the years that followed, as I backtracked over and over again, trading in my courage for equal doses of martyrdom.

Still, she found a place right away, and made sure I heard her talking on the phone to her pusher about how she had found a place to go and wasn't she smart to be so resourceful so quickly? So she went, again, without a choice. I changed the locks and breathed a sigh of relief—for a while.

I remember sleepwalking down the halls of my old school, telling myself, "I have two children. I have two children," forcing myself to focus on the two kids I had left. Back then, more than a decade ago, it was just unthinkable that my daughter was throwing her life away like this. Angie had been such a good daughter. She had such promise, so many gifts. I saw her in any number of leadership positions; she had such incredible presence, such command in a crowd. *Angie,* I thought to myself, *don't you remember at Nana's birthday the way Uncle Bill and his friends circled you and serenaded you? You were such a star that day. You loved it!* And she was bossy, opinionated, fearless, reckless and brave. She could be a CEO!

But now something else was in charge, something else was, like a thief in the night, robbing her of herself. Angie wasn't in charge anymore, though she couldn't admit it. Without recovery, it was just a matter of time before she ended up institutionalized or dead. I couldn't bear to watch this. So I buried her in my mind from time to time. Somehow—don't ask me how—it brought me comfort to pretend she'd never been born.

I used to pinch myself every once in a while and ask myself if I was still alive. Like, how could I be alive and well if she were suffering so much that she needed to pollute herself over and over again with dangerous drugs? It wasn't right that I was still healthy. My survivor guilt was starting to crush me. I went to see a cardiologist for an echocardiogram, and the results were good: no heart condition, just stress-related spasms. "You must have been under a lot of stress," my doctor said.

Stress, uh-huh.

Roller Coaster Ride

From January to August Angie only called me once. Two weeks after she moved out she called and asked when I would be home so she could get the rest of her stuff. She knew I had changed the locks and she needed me to be there. I told her to come by after school the next day.

I was in the kitchen making coffee when she rang the bell. *Will she be glad to see me, hug me, and tell me she's sorry?* I mused, smiling. I opened the door, hoping that our time apart had mellowed her. She brushed right past me and raced down to the basement.

I didn't have time to formulate Plan B. I had been brewing her favorite kind of coffee in the hopes that we could sit down and talk. Five minutes later she raced back upstairs with a garbage bag full of stuff, brushed past me again without a word, and slammed the door as she left. She never even looked at me. I was heartbroken. Here was an opportunity for us to communicate and she wanted nothing to do with me. Twenty-two years of raising this person, loving her as best I could, have come to this. She was erasing me from her life. Addiction was her new parent.

At some point in the spring she left that group home she had found on Craigslist and moved in with her pusher. The girls where she had been living gave me this man's number, and I called there a few times, just to make contact.

"Hullllo?"

"Hi, is Angie there? Could you tell her her mother's on the phone?" I didn't have a stopwatch, but that creep kept me waiting for five minutes.

"Uh, she's kinda busy. Call back in a coupla hours."

"Never mind," I said, grinding my teeth. "Just tell her I called."

I was at home in Arlington, trying to grade papers and plan for the next day. I imagined the dump she lived in, dirty rooms with nothing but bare essentials: beds and drugs. There wasn't enough food there to attract cockroaches. Junkies didn't eat much. I think she was still just using meth orally. She'd always been terrified of needles. She had really small, hard-to-find veins, so I didn't think she was mainlining anything.

She never called me back, even after I showed up at the door, but I guess no one was home when I did that. Somehow I got her address and I used to drive there and literally stalk her, waiting to see her come out and grab her, shake her, and remind her that she still had a mother who loved her, *sopleasefortheloveofgod, Angie, snap out of this and come home!*

One time was on a teacher workday in April. There were no students that day but I was still expected to put in eight hours in the building. I worked there till lunch and then said screw it. I had better things to do. In my fantasy, I would drive to Angie's place, park my car, knock on the door, she would answer, the look of joy and relief would melt my heart, she would fall into my arms and beg me to take her away from there. Away we would drive, never looking back.

Parked across the street, I awoke from my reverie, stunned by my ever present need to be my daughter's savior. *Did I push her to this by kicking her out last January?* I asked myself. *Maybe if I had let her stay and tried harder, she'd still be with me.*

The voice of reason kicks in to knock some sense into me:

"Tried harder to do what, Maggie? This isn't your illness. It's hers. She's the one who needs to try harder."

I lose patience with the voice of reason. Sometimes he wants to forget how complicated I am, just to make his job easier:

"No, asshole, it's mine too. Don't you know me at all? Why do you think this has been so hard for me? Watching her drown cuts me right down the middle. Half of me wants to go with her and the other half needs to survive."

But she never came out. Maybe I had the wrong address. So I turned on the ignition and started home, circling four, no five, times around the block hoping each time I'd see her looking out a window, or leaving the building. After a while I gave up; I needed to get back home, and out of her orbit. Still, I had a phone number, so she was allowing bridges; she hadn't left her family completely. At least that's what I wanted to believe. And so I clung to hope.

What I know now, twelve years later, is that what I did or didn't do mattered very little. Angie had a monkey on her back—a gorilla—and only she could wrestle him off. Loving her as I always have, it has been heartbreaking to watch her try, and to know that I haven't been able to help her do the hard work of her own recovery.

When she called at the end of August about wanting to go into rehab, I was so happy! But time was of the essence. Her pusher had started to beat her up, and so she fled to a sofa at a friend's house. But she couldn't stay there long.

"Mom, I'm really scared. Sam freaked out yesterday and started pummeling me. I'm covered with bruises and I'm just sick of all this. I'm so frightened. I think he wanted to kill me. I want to go into rehab and try to deal with all this. Cathy said I could come sleep on her sofa until I find a place to go. That's where I am now. Please help me, Mom. I can't take this anymore!" she sobbed.

My first and only thought was that I must rescue her from all this madness, believing as I would time and time again that I had the power to do so.

"Oh baby, of course I'll help you! Just stay put at Cathy's. I'll get on the phone as soon as we hang up and find a place. I'll call you back as soon as I know anything. Bye, baby. I love you!"

"I love you, too, Mom. And thanks."

But I was woefully unprepared: I hadn't done my homework; I didn't know where to send her. I had only joined Al-Anon six months before and I didn't understand the program anyway. One of the key concepts in this program of recovery is the idea of detachment. This means learning to distance ourselves emotionally from our loved one enough so that we could start acting on our own behalf more—and not reacting so much to the lies and manipulations of addicts while they're using drugs. I couldn't accept that at all. I had miles to go before I would be able to remove myself from the equation and detach from my daughter.

I looked in the Yellow Pages, of all places, and found a facility about two hours away. I picked her up at Cathy's and drove her to the rehab, which, thankfully, had a bed available. This would be the first of several new starts for my daughter, and we were all, in that moment, so full of hope and optimism.

Rehab was an old converted motel out in the middle of nowhere. Good thinking; patients could leave but there was nowhere to go. What a desolate place it looked like, with grass that hadn't been mowed outside, crumbling asphalt walkways, peeling paint, and a screen door that was falling off its hinges. This is what I got for looking in the phone book and making a hurried decision.

Eyes half closed, she staggered out of the car and we entered the building. I checked her in and took care of all the financial arrangements. I guess they weren't going to wait to get paid at the other end.

"Goodbye, honey. Don't worry about your car. When you finish here we can go get it at the impound lot. Angie, are you listening to me? I'm trying to save your car! What would you do without it?" I yelled at my drowsy daughter.

I must matter, I must be important, I must not be irrelevant, I hammered away at myself.

In that moment, her car was the last thing on her mind.

"I'm tired, Mom. I just want to sleep," she answered me wearily.

"Well, maybe they'll let you do that."

It seemed like she couldn't wait to get away from me; I know she just needed to lie down and rest. But I hugged her tightly, and told her she'd be OK. I loved her, and would be back on visiting day. "Goodbye, baby. You'll be all right."

It's worth noting here that of the four rehabs Angie has been to this one, the one she herself wanted, produced the best results in her. Why? Because she wanted it—as plain and simple as that sounds. She wanted it because for the first time in her disease she felt her life was in danger—not from drugs—but from the life and the people that accompany them. A few years down the road, no longer a stranger to the danger that went with this way of life, three more rehabs would be placed in front of her, like roadblocks: "Choose, Angie, do this or die." And to her credit, I suppose, she chose to go where we wanted to send her. "Where **we** wanted to send her." That's why they didn't work. She wasn't ready to make that commitment again. She was just Alice tripping from one place to another, when all of a sudden this bulldozer broke through the ceiling and screeched, "Angie, come with me. I want to save you!" And "curiouser and curiouser" she cracked, "Oh, what the hell, I need a vacation from all this anyway."

Carlos and Angie had never been close, but he nevertheless loved his sister and was anxious to show his support in her recovery. So he and I along with Xavier and his wife made the two-hour journey to visit Angie on visitor's day. This was the first of our family missions to support the daughter/sister we so dearly loved and had helplessly watched descend into terrifying waters.

The ride was quiet. Xavier played a lot of tapes so we wouldn't be able to talk much. And what could we say? All I could think was that Angie would snap out of this. She would get it right away; I was sure of it. How could this be happening anyway? I was certain I had been dreaming and would wake up from this nightmare. *This sort of thing happens to other people's children,* I assured myself.

Angie was a Foreign Service brat. She was born in South America and moved easily from country to country, or so it seemed. When we lived in Greece, she competed in England with the gymnastics team. When we lived in Rome, a scout picked her to be in a movie. She was a shining star, and her outward accomplishments duped me into thinking she had a bright future. Oh boy, was I ready to take the credit! Ten years later, when she was twenty-one, I was completely unprepared when she started tumbling into the hell of drug addiction. I should have, but I didn't see it coming. Oh boy, was I ready to take the blame.

Approaching the entryway, we scanned the ten or so young people chain-smoking on cheap metal chairs, looking for Angie. Then she came out to greet us, all smiles and grateful, I think, that we wanted to be there for her. She looked rested and had put on some much needed weight. She'd been sober for two weeks, and hopefully was becoming clear-headed enough to evaluate her life better.

As we walked in I was assaulted by the smell of laundry and Clorox at the same time, the smoke from outside invading the building through the open windows. We all sat down in a small auditorium with other family members and friends who were there for the same reason. Looking at each other, we didn't need to say anything. We looked so sad. We all had one thing in common: we loved an addict.

Oh God, here we are. What a nightmare the past year has been! But I'm still here — we all are — to support Angie. I've started to get help in Al-Anon. And it makes sense, what they teach us. I just can't let go, though. I feel like so much is my fault. I was so often neglectful of Angie. How many times did I zone out on my kids? And between work and graduate school, I was barely home right after the divorce. If only I had a second chance to do things over. But I don't and I'm just gonna have to try to be strong for her. We'll get through this together; I know we will. I didn't raise my daughter to throw her life away like this.

So much of what I felt and said to myself back in 2002 was a stage of my recovery. At the urging of a counselor at work, I had agreed to join Al-Anon in January of 2002. And I was a very hard sell when it came to the principles they taught. I was not at all ready to detach and let go, as they advised. I was up to my eyeballs in codependence and feeling responsible for what was happening to my daughter. It would take years of recovery work to let go of my attitude, my clear misunderstanding of how addiction worked. My guilt gave her illness power over me. It kept me enabling her, pandering to her needs, protecting her from the consequences of her choices. It wanted to survive. I hadn't yet been able to separate Angie from her addiction, and so all I was doing to help my daughter was really giving oxygen to her disease. It was simply too painful at that point to accept that my daughter had been taken over by a Monster, and only she had the power to exorcize Him.

The director of this facility looked and spoke like a guard at a concentration camp. A muscular, big-boned woman, in her mid-fifties, she wore a dull gray suit and sensible pumps. Nurse Ratched without the uniform. Her voice was equally intimidating as she explained to all of us the daily routine and schedule that everyone was expected to follow. She was 100% no-nonsense; there was nothing soft about her delivery or her expectations. The patients were there for thirty days to play ball by the house rules. It was up to them to benefit from their time there and make it count towards their recovery. This was the easy part, the beginning. The hard part would be applying what they'd learned in the real world—one day at a time.

This rehab facility based their program of recovery on the Twelve Steps of Alcoholics Anonymous, a spiritual program for living that most rehabs across the country use. The Al-Anon groups that I was increasingly involved with used these same Twelve Steps. Many top-of-the-line facilities add individual therapy, horse therapy, exercise programs, and gourmet food. This place was not top of the line and Angie complained about the fattening, high-carbohydrate food that she had to eat. She was afraid she'd gain weight. Another thing Angie hated was dinnertime at 4:30. She got hungry again by 8:00 p.m. and the kitchen had been shut down.

After addressing the families, the director invited the four of us to walk around and tour the place. This didn't take long; there wasn't much to see. We saw the room she shared with another girl. Walking into the kitchen, I noticed the huge vats of institutional food they were serving.

I saw Xavier and his wife chatting with some other parents in the main hall. When we were back in the car I asked him whom he had been talking to. He said he thought he had recognized another of the parents from work, but he was wrong. They kept talking, anyway, and commiserated about Angie and this man's son. His son was a heroin addict and this was his second time at this rehab. Xavier told me, breathing a sigh of relief, that he was glad Angie hadn't gone that route.

"I'm sure we've nipped it in the bud, Maggie."

"Oh yes, I'm sure she'll snap out of it," I answered, even then doubting my every word. "We've nipped it in the bud, Maggie." *Is it **our** problem to fix, Xavier?* I thought to myself. But I didn't challenge him in that moment, as I would dozens of times in the years that followed. He needed to believe that his parenting had counted for something. He needed to believe that she would survive this. But we would both learn, though not at the same time, that our parenting efforts when dealing with a drug addict were largely irrelevant. Angie wasn't being a rebellious child. She was sick.

It was a beautiful sunny day in September, so we all went outside to sit down, but the chain smokers had reclaimed the cheap metal chairs. Grabbing one kid by the shirt, Angie implored:

"Franklin, I'm out. Pleeze lend me a couple. I promise I'll pay you back. Oh, these are my parents by the way. Mom, say hi to Franklin."

"Hi, Franklin."

"Sorry, babe, I'm almost out. Try David."

"Fuck you, Franklin," she hissed. Then, remembering that I was standing behind her, she changed her tone: "Oh, sorry Mom. Forgot you were here."

Carlos stepped up to hug his sister. "Angie, we've got to go. But I'm glad we came. I hope you're gonna be OK. Take care."

Angie didn't say anything as she accepted his hug. But I saw the look in her eyes. I couldn't quite put my finger on it—a cross between relief and doubt. I'll never know exactly what was in her mind. But in the years that followed, she would betray her brother more than once. Despite his love and support for her, she would fall prey to the monster Addiction over and over again, and their relationship would be sorely tested.

Xavier and I looked at each other. We didn't like the snapshot of our daughter that we'd just seen. And anyway, it was time to leave. So we all hugged and said goodbye. I told her I'd be back in two weeks to help her move into the group home where she'd be living.

For a while we made small talk in the car riding back. Then we grew silent, lost in our own thoughts. This hadn't really been fun for us. We got an eyeful, and then some. This was our first experience visiting a rehab facility. It wasn't the belly of the beast; Angie had already been there. This was a chance for her to come up for air, to start breathing again, a chance to slow down, sober up, look in the mirror and make a decision.

Or not. At least her month away gave me a chance to breathe, and make a decision of my own. I chose to work a lot harder on my own recovery from the effects of loving an addict. It would be an uphill battle for me, with many slips and falls. But I felt energized to save us both. Higher up the hill I would learn, though, that I would have to make a choice—the hardest choice of my life.

For the first few months out of rehab Angie seemed to be doing very well in the group home. She was responsible about going to work and paid all her own bills, acting like the twenty-four-year-old adult she was, and she was very thoughtful about keeping in touch with her family. One Saturday I got a welcome call from her:

"Mom, meet me after work so I can take you thrift-store shopping. I just discovered a new vintage place in Takoma Park. You'll love it! Then maybe I could treat you to dinner."

This was my girls' and my favorite pastime: digging through used clothes and finding gems. My mother grew up in the Depression, and she taught me how to spot quality merchandise at thrift stores. I was very good at it by now, and so were my girls. It's not that we couldn't afford to buy new clothes. That wasn't the point. It was the treasure hunt we loved. And we still do it whenever we see each other. I can't bear to part with a pair of jeans that I bought with Caroline in San Francisco. They swim on me now, but I hate to let go of my memory. That's what they represent.

In December 2002 Angie accompanied Xavier, his wife, and Carlos to Miami for her cousin's wedding. I didn't go but I saw the pictures that were taken. She wore a beautiful red Chinese dress. I'll never forget how gorgeous she looked in the pictures, smiling as though she didn't have a care in the world. Angie has beautiful hands — artist's hands — and her nails were painted the color of her dress. She has tremendous grace about her. But then she was a successful gymnast for ten years. She still had thick, dark brown hair, and heavy bangs that emphasized her beautiful brown eyes. The hair is thinned out now, from vitamin deficiencies. And she has a big scar on her forehead, from a bad fall she took. She pulls her hair away from her face now because the scar prevents her bangs from falling properly.

I miss her bangs the most.

Another memory, from Takoma Park in December 2002, warms me as I look at my wall of treasures. When Angie came out of that first rehab, she made me the most beautiful gift.

"Mom, I'm not quite finished with it. I just have a few more flowers to cut. You'll need to find a 17-by-22-inch frame to mount it on. Sorry it's such an odd size. Guess I wasn't thinking. I copied it from one of my Chinese art books. I hope you like it!"

Right now it's hanging in my room for me to see. Over the years I've taken it on and off the wall, hidden it in a closet, too painful for me to look at. Maybe it's a sign of my recovery. Now I can leave it on the wall, look at it, and appreciate all the work she put into it. This was her way, I believe, of telling me she loved me and she was sorry, not for getting sick, but for what that sickness drove her to do to me. She never, ever, was able to express her feelings easily with words. So she showed me, in countless ways, as she did once in December 1993.

"Where the hell is that $300 I put away for safekeeping? If you kids want any Christmas presents, you'd better help me find it now," I shouted, panicking at the thought of losing my hard-earned cash. I was so scattered sometimes. I was perfectly capable of misplacing it.

"Found it, Mom! Don't you remember when you hid it in this book? Well, here it is. Aren't you glad I'm as honest as I am?"

"Yes, Angie, my darlin girl, I am. And thank you!"

Years are passing by, and sometimes it's hard to remember her as she was. But when I look at the tapestry she made, I remember:

Angie had a fascination for all things Asian—Chinese, Japanese, it didn't matter. She loved the grace and flow of much of the artwork. She copied a simple series of flowers. But she did it not with paint or pencil or pen; she cut out every pistil, not completely detailed, a few sepals in place, the rest scattered, all the ovaries in different colors for contrast, every leaf, in varying sizes and colors, every stem, and glued it all together on a piece of gold cloth. It looked just like the picture in her book.

I treasure this gift she made. The tapestry is twelve years old, and sometimes a petal comes unglued and I have to put it back on. I should put it under glass to preserve it. I wish we could put our children under glass — to keep them safe.

I would soon discover, though, that no matter what I did for Angie it would never be enough to protect her from the illness that was consuming her.

Many people are not strong enough to battle the terrible force of addiction on their own. Application of the Twelve Steps had proven successful over and over again since they were put together by a couple of alcoholics and their friends back in the late 1930's. Addicts need help; some say they need spiritual help. Our society is full of naysayers — skeptics who eschew these programs that are found in every major city across the country, and in big cities, in many of the churches, meeting three or four times a day. There's a reason for the popularity of Twelve-Step programs: they work for many people. So I promised myself I would try harder now. *Angie was worth it.* **Angie** *was worth it?*

There is no one place on this journey to pinpoint where I discovered that I was worth it. I knew what a flawed human being I was. I was aware of my mistakes along the way — big ones and little ones.

But as I was starting to embrace the principles found in these Twelve Steps I was reacquainting myself over and over again with my own humanity and feeling my self-worth solidify with roots into the earth. None of this growth in me would have occurred if Angie's illness hadn't pushed me onto this path. And I would always — still — reckon with the survivor guilt that has challenged my right to be happy while my daughter still struggles with addiction.

There are many who view Twelve-Step groups as cultish and unattractive. There's such a powerful stigma in our society against addiction in all its forms that, I suppose, families of addicts suffer from guilt by association. Early on in my recovery my sister, Lucy, once said that it must be nice to have "those people" to talk to. But as she's watched me grow and change these past few years I think she's developed a healthy respect for the Program.

To this day, though, Lucy has never discussed with me the dark side of our father, the alcoholic. Maybe she never saw his dark side, as I did. To her, he was the best father in the world, and I have no need to invade that sacred place where she holds him in her heart. In fact, I agree with her. He was a very loving man who passed on many gifts to his children and grandchildren. Yes, he was sick, and he died too young because of it. But just as I have forgiven my mother for any ways she may have hurt me so have I lovingly accepted my father's illness. And in learning to forgive my parents and others who have wounded me in my life, it has become easier for me to forgive myself for my own shortcomings.

I, being an addict, a daughter of one and a parent of one, have found myself quite at home among these seekers of peace and serenity. I've been in the right place for twelve years now, and I cannot begin to tell you the gratitude I feel for the wisdom in this simple program that has helped me to look forward to the sun coming up every day—and to embrace my life in its entirety.

Because of their proven power and worth, A.A.'s Twelve Steps have been adopted almost word for word by Al-Anon. They represent a way of life appealing to all people of goodwill, of any religious faith or of none. Note the power of the very words! (*Al-Anon Alateen* 13)

THE TWELVE STEPS—AS I UNDERSTAND THEM

1. We admitted we were powerless over alcohol—that our lives had become unmanageable.

I admitted that my loved one had a problem that I could not fix, and when I tried to fix it, my own life often went out of control.

2. Came to believe that a power greater than ourselves could restore us to sanity.

I let go of my need to be in charge, my wish to control, and considered turning the whole problem over to a "power greater than ourselves:" a tree, or God, or our group fellowship.

3. Made a decision to turn our will and our lives over to the care of God *as we understood Him.*

Those are not my italics. I got to choose anything to have faith in, as long as it's not me. My best thinking—chaos and confusion—got me here in the first place. I needed help from someone outside of myself to carry my burdens.

4. Made a searching and fearless moral inventory of ourselves.

I stopped obsessing about my loved one long enough to put the focus back on myself, look in the mirror, and admit to my own strengths and weaknesses.

5. Admitted to God, to ourselves and to another human being the exact nature of our wrongs.

To really own the flaws that I faced in the previous step and hold myself accountable, I needed to share them with my higher power as well as someone else. "You're as sick as your secrets."

6. Were entirely ready to have God remove all these defects of character.

Having braved the stormy waters of Steps Four and Five, I became ready to let go of all the things that had limited me in my life and tried to become a better human being.

7. Humbly asked Him to remove our shortcomings.

I couldn't change a lifetime of bad habits and bad attitudes on my own. I needed to let go of my self-reliance and ask for help.

8. Made a list of all persons we had harmed, and became willing to make amends to them all.

I went back over my life and tried to remember the people I had hurt. I took a deep breath and considered contacting those people and apologizing. Or I thought about changing the behavior that caused a need for amends.

9. Made direct amends to such people wherever possible, except when to do so would injure them or others.

I sought out those people and apologized. If they were dead, I wrote them a letter and burned it. But I didn't, in an effort to clear my conscience, reveal information to someone that would only prove hurtful and serve no purpose now.

10. Continued to take personal inventory and when we were wrong promptly admitted it.

I kept looking in the mirror and when I realized a mistake I made, I tried to rectify it. If I messed up with someone, I admitted it and apologized. On a regular basis, I cleaned house.

11. Sought through prayer and meditation to improve our conscious contact with God *as we understood Him*, praying only for knowledge of His will for us and the power to carry that out.

I kept in touch with my higher power; I talked to him. Some say that's praying. The point is that keeping up a relationship with this other being was a constant reminder that I was not in charge, and I needed this reminder. The second part is tricky: how do I know if what I did was His will or mine? I still don't know the answer, but my sponsor told me that if I really, really want to do something but don't, if I sleep on it, at least that gives God some time to get in. In other words, acting on impulse is often a willful act—mine. The acronym EGO (Easing God Out) could apply here.

12. Having had a spiritual awakening as a result of these steps, we tried to carry this message to others, and to practice these principles in all our affairs.

When I thought I'd finally understood these guidelines to recovery, I felt free to talk about the Program to anyone who was interested. And I tried to live the Program through my own example. (*Hope* 367)

Most people have rules that they try to live by: a certain moral code that they may have picked up from their parents or others as they grew up. Religion grounds many people in rules for living that give them a welcome sense of security. And though the Twelve-Step Programs are not religious, many of their principles are found in any number of organized religions—Zen Buddhism, for example.

But my friend Shigeko reminded me that while much of the Program philosophy sounds like Eastern thought—accept what is, don't resist, live in the moment—it is nevertheless very linear, very "Western:" (Step One, Step Two, Step Three, etc.) She and I have been going to the same meeting in Virginia for years, and I appreciate her wisdom and perspective. But the best piece of wisdom, I think, is the Serenity Prayer, which is a blend, I think, of Eastern and Western philosophy:

> "God, grant me the serenity to accept the things I cannot change, courage to change the things I can, and wisdom to know the difference" (*How Al-Anon Works* 79).

There are so many things in my life over which I have no control: the weather, road rage, barking dogs. Really, the capriciousness of events that surround us is astounding and is perhaps the reason why many people, myself included, need a lot of daily structure to feel grounded and secure. A sound mind, good health and a sense of well-being only add to that state. But when illness strikes, all sense of security and control flies out the proverbial window.

My daughter falling ill with drug addiction threw my life into turmoil, and I spent years flailing around like a decapitated chicken trying to make sense of things and gain a sense of control. My life was becoming very messy because I kept trying to influence the course of an illness that had nothing to do with me. Turning my attention to other areas where I could have had an impact would have been more constructive. I know I must continue to accept the unpleasantness as hard as it is because if I don't—if I fight tooth and nail to get my way—I'll just make myself crazy. I've kept trying to help Angie because I care so much, but it's a losing battle if the change is beyond my reach. Our addicts may indeed find recovery—and we all pray that they do—but if they do, it will be through their own efforts and commitment, not ours.

The big sticking point, however, for anyone who loves an addict is where and when and why and howinthenameofallthat'sholy can I ever let go? It's a process we all go through in different ways and at a different pace. There is no right or wrong way. The Twelve Steps have provided me with a useful program for living and given me the guidance I've needed to navigate through the difficulties in my life.

Life Had Become Unmanageable

Many parents will tell you that they experience a great sense of calm, peace and hope while their children are safely tucked away in rehab. And I was no different. I was so sure that the trials we had been through previously were the worst of it, that there was no place left to go but up. I still had much to learn about the relentless nature of this progressive disease.

We weren't a wealthy family; I remember as a young wife draping sheets over my body until July 4th to save on air conditioning because doing so felt cool in the humidity. But we were comfortably middle class. Angie's father scrambled to keep her on his insurance, a situation that was never properly resolved. I think we went out of pocket close to twenty thousand dollars that first time to pay for rehab.

But then the creditors started calling, while Angie was there. And I, inexperienced as I was, caved in to every one of them. I wrote several thousand dollars worth of checks to various collection agencies — out of fear — trying to wipe her slate clean and give her a fresh start. Months later she would tell me, and angrily without an ounce of gratitude, that paying off the creditors was an admission of guilt, and so forking over all that money didn't really help her at all. She would still be fighting low credit scores and creditors forever.

Eyes on fire, "Why didn't you wait till I got back to handle the creditors, Mom?" she screamed at me. "Don't you realize that paying them off just validates their claim? How could you be so stupid?"

Half in shock from her attack on me, and ever slow on the uptake, tears filling my eyes, I stammered, "I don't know, Angie. I was scared for you. They were threatening legal action, and you would soon be getting out of rehab. I didn't want you to have even more to handle."

If this was her attitude several months after being in rehab, I had wasted my money. I realize now that I was trying to force solutions and control outcomes, as they say in the Program — lessen the consequences and pain for Angie — and in the process teach her nothing. This is something we must all fight against.

From *A Guide For The Family Of The Addict And Drug Abuser,* a Nar-Anon pamphlet:

> It is appalling how the drug abuser controls the family, especially the mother or father or husband. The individual uses drugs again and again. The family screams, yells, begs, pleads, prays, threatens or practices the silent treatment. It also covers up, protects and shields the person from the consequences of his using. If the drug dependent continues to act like a little god, it is because the family helps to preserve this illusion of omnipotence. In the preservation of this omnipotence neurosis (the attempt to play God) the user has two primary weapons.

> The first weapon is the ability to arouse anger or provoke loss of temper. If the family member or friend becomes angry and hostile, his ability to be of any help to the user has been completely destroyed...When those close to the user react in an angry, hostile manner, he feels justified in his former using and has an additional excuse to use drugs in the future.

The gods first make angry those whom they wish to destroy, and the drug user has a long experience of acting like a little god.

The second weapon is the ability to arouse anxiety on the part of the family. Thereby they are often compelled to do for the user that which can be done only by him if the illness is to be arrested. In their mistaken efforts to help, family members find themselves repeatedly protecting the user from the consequences of his actions, covering up, protecting, giving him a place to crash...

I joke at my meetings about how I could have bought a house in California with the money I've spent on rehabs for Angie. It's not a joke, of course. I could have spent the money on my other two children—or myself. Though I don't regret sending Angie to all those rehabs, I do regret my single-minded obsession with her, often neglecting my other loved ones. And several years down the road I would acknowledge this to Carlos and Caroline and ask their forgiveness. But first, I would have to learn how to forgive myself.

Months passed, and by April 2003 she started distancing herself from us; I was getting worried. And sure enough, that group home had turned into a coke den. *God, where **were** you?* I asked, looking up where I thought God lived, and wondering if He had any mercy left for my child. I would learn further down the road that God's mercy had nothing to do with addiction. But, for some people, it did have a lot to do with recovery from it.

High on coke with a new coke boyfriend, and two months pregnant, she landed on my doorstep, but without the coke boyfriend. She hadn't called me and I was surprised to see her at that hour. She was supposed to be at work at six o'clock. Opening the door, I said, "Hi, honey. What's up? Aren't you supposed to be at work now?"

She came in and hugged me like she hadn't hugged me in years. I hugged her back, so grateful to feel her warmth, remembering how not so long ago she had hated me and wanted nothing to do with me.

"Mom, I can't live there anymore. They're all using cocaine and I've been using, too. I've tried to stay clean, but I just can't be around people using drugs. I'm not strong enough yet. Can I come back here and live with you?"

"Of course, honey. And I'm so grateful that you're reaching out to me now! Tomorrow's Saturday, so I have all day to help you get your stuff and get settled back in the basement. Sit down. Let me make you a cup of coffee."

Sitting down at the kitchen table together made it feel almost like old times. This was my mother's kitchen table that I'd had for years. I was looking at the initials my kids and their friends had carved into it years before. "AR – 8/96." "CR + DS. 7/98." Those had been such innocent years, it seemed to me. My kids had seemed fine. They weren't getting into trouble. Since then, they'd finished high school, the girls were in college, and Carlos had finished college three years before. I just wasn't prepared for this. But I was determined to tackle it with Angie and see her through. How I would see it through with her, however, would not be helpful and would only teach her to avoid responsibility.

"Mom, there's something else. Please don't freak out, but I'm pregnant. I'm just a couple of months, but I took a test and I know I am. I can't have a baby now. I want an abortion." Her eyes were pleading—I think she was on the brink of tears but, as always, Angie found it almost impossible to give free rein to her feelings.

"Well of course you can't have a baby now. And no wonder you've been so stressed out. We'll take care of this as soon as possible."

I never saw anyone switch gears so quickly. Like night to day in seconds, she breathed a sigh of relief, got up from the table and started making herself a sandwich.

"Thanks, Mom. Thanks for helping me. And thanks for letting me come back here to live. I know things will work this time. I'll keep my job, and I'll sign up for those last two classes I need to graduate."

What would any mother do with money in her pocket and a pregnant, repentant daughter who promised to fly straight from now on? Yeah, I took her to the abortion clinic, and it was over. But what was Angie learning about responsible behavior and accountability? Not much, because I kept getting in the way.

I felt I had to keep managing her life, which was so clearly out of control, deciding what was best for her, and never, God forbid, letting her feel the consequences of her bad choices. Angie and I were in parallel universes—both of us making terrible decisions. I was reacting so badly to situations as they came up. I really needed to change the way I behaved with my daughter. Sadly, it would take me a long time to let go of my need to control and let her face herself in the mirror—alone.

There were other ways far more invasive to me that Angie violated my trust, yet I still let her get away with it. After she moved in with me, she stole my identity—twice. She was such a whiz on the computer, and I was so clueless. She ordered a credit card in my name; she had my social security number, so it was easy. Then she tried to use my debit card to get money.

That's when the bank called me. And she was so clever: she came to my school and confessed everything. She knew I would be grateful for the intimacy/honesty. And I was, so I let it go. But before I let it go, the footwork I went through to change my bank account number, get new checks, inform all my utilities people, etc., of the change, was incredible. That was when I set up a fraud alert with the credit card agencies for seven years. *Oh God,* I moaned, *what if I forget to renew it? I'll be vulnerable again! And inside my own family! I don't feel safe anymore.*

Years later in one of my support groups in New Mexico, a friend shared how she had to lock everything up in her house. She'd lock the jewelry here, the silver there. She had a different key for every place, and one time she was so flummoxed by her son that she lost all the keys! We laughed together at that one, grateful that we still could laugh. This is what it comes to for many of us parents. We erect walls to protect ourselves, keeping the addicts out. And then, of course, we feel guilty about doing that.

Angie was stealing valuables from my home again, just as she had been two years before, in order to sell them for drug money. It was safer, she thought, to steal from me than from a store. She already knew what an enabler I was; but she was still a thief. And even though her addiction pushed her onto the wrong path, she still should have paid the consequences if she was going to learn and mature.

They will work us, manipulate us, and use every tool in their arsenal to get what they want if they're still using. Parents are so vulnerable, and they're walking a fine line between helping their child recover, and enabling them to continue using. We learn eventually to sit frozen in inaction, to do nothing. We learn to let our addicts be accountable for their own actions, and hopefully learn from the consequences (eviction, jail, death). But it's that last consequence that holds us hostage, keeps us doing for our addict all that he should be doing for himself. We say to ourselves, "As long as he's alive, he can recover." True, but when will we ever get rid of our God-like parental power, thinking that his recovery is all up to us?

It was all very well for me to be down in Virginia, waging my battles every day with Angie living in my house, desperately seeking some kind of relief from my suffering. But there were other people in my life, friends and family, who wanted to know what was going on. I imagined my sister screaming at me over the phone:

"Maggie, **do** something!" How can you let her kill herself like this?"

I responded in my mind, lacking the courage to say the words: "Lucy, until you've walked a mile in my shoes, shut the fuck up."

I never had such a conversation with my sister. I was only imagining the outside world knocking on my door—and judging, always judging—just as I had felt judged and condemned as a child.

On a visit to his son in a treatment center, David Sheff listens to a program counselor's words:

> If your child had cancer, the support from your friends and family would flood in. Because of the stigma of addiction, people often keep it quiet. Their friends and family may try to be supportive, but they may also communicate a subtle or unsubtle judgment. (152)

What does this subtle judgment look like? Needing to keep cousins and other relatives in the dark because "they weren't compassionate." At least my relative acknowledged that compassion was called for, but why then couldn't they be told? Because instead of kindness and understanding, there would images of bag ladies, prostitutes and homeless people, from whom many instinctively turn away. It's unattractive, it's scary — and it might have been them. It's not something people enjoy looking at. So best to keep it in the closet, I suppose. I can't change society's attitude toward drug addiction just for my convenience. Hopefully in time society as a whole will view drug addiction with a kinder eye.

I was, nevertheless, so sure that my family, who knew nothing of my daily struggles, felt at times that I was being heartless and worse, irresponsible. Perhaps this feeling goes back to my childhood where a lot of our family dysfunction was focused on me. This family of mine, my family of origin, was also watching in horror as this was unfolding. They had known Angie, too, growing up, and they were as saddened and shocked as I was that this was really happening.

But yes, there was a world outside this nightmare, this hurricane called Angie, and I wasn't able to insulate myself from it all the time, though I wished I could have. It made my pain that much harder, having to lie to my family, not being completely honest with them. Just as I had been growing up, I once again felt so isolated in my own family. And it wasn't just my family I lied to; my friends and colleagues received half-truths, whatever information I dared disclose without shocking them to death. At this point in the struggle, I still couldn't separate myself from my daughter; I was deeply, deeply ashamed, and felt that her addiction was a reflection on me as a parent. We were both, after all, addicts, another truth that very few people knew about.

In fact, I was still so joined at the hip with her that, in the beginning during the brief periods when she was in recovery, I used to claim at meetings that our mutual recoveries were intertwined. I remember saying, "I have no doubt that her recovery goes along with my recovery." My Program friends just nodded their heads in support, probably wondering what the heck I was talking about. It would take a number of years and much Twelve-Step work to rid me of that notion.

Self-blame has reared its ugly head through this ordeal all too often. At that point I was still too connected to her. And I couldn't yet let go of my inflated sense of responsibility. I know that she was making bad choices that I wasn't responsible for. Yet I think my guilt over all the times I had failed her as a young child kept me stuck in a deep hole. These unresolved feelings have put me at terrible risk over the years in managing any number of relationships. But guilt surely compromised my effectiveness as Angie's mother. I overcompensated and indulged, easing my anxieties, but helping her to mature very little.

I was a consummate enabler, a word that is becoming very familiar to families now that addiction is epidemic in our society. I paid for her abortion; I didn't have her arrested when she stole from me multiple times; I placed one safety net after another under her so she would avoid the painful consequences of her actions. This was not good parenting — not at all — though so much of what parents should do to produce responsible adults is counterintuitive.

We all want to protect our children from pain. However, helicopter parenting and over-protectiveness, from what I've seen, produces more anxiety in our children, not less. I asked a friend of mine who's going through the same battle with her son what her take was on this: "We are a burden to our addicted children," she assured me, "until we finally embrace our own recovery. While we are busy getting well ourselves, the addicts don't have to deal with so much of our oppressive anger and judgment." So when we finally let go of them, the addicts themselves become freer of their own anxiety and guilt, at least toward us. They have plenty of their own to carry.

Enabling — helping — and the stigma of it all surrounding us like a masonry wall, isolating these families from "normal" people. There was so little compassion, so little understanding, and therefore so much blame heaped upon the parents who raised these hapless people. And why did I blame myself? If there is something to the gene theory, then it shouldn't be a surprise that one of my three children succumbed to the disease.

So, for a couple of years, Angie lived with me — shenanigans and all. She had a very good job, never totaled the car, and kept her drug usage under wraps. So I shouldn't have been surprised when she managed to get pregnant again by that same coke boyfriend, and this time she was so oblivious that she didn't realize she was pregnant until she was very far along. There was only one clinic in D.C. that would take care of this problem, and it cost several thousand dollars, probably to pay for the anesthesia. Though it was little comfort to me, she and the coke boyfriend did insist on splitting the cost and paid me in advance. At least they were shouldering some responsibility.

Driving to the abortion clinic, we spoke not at all. My mind kept wandering to happier times, such as Halloween, 1984.

"Angie, Carlos, come get your costumes on. We're late for the party."

I had worked so hard to put together these costumes myself, instead of buying the ready-made ones. I had a creative streak in me that wanted to get out. Once in a while it was fun to play with it.

Carlos mumbled, "I don't want to be a bumble bee, Mom. I look really stupid. My wings keep falling down. I want to be an Indian."

Angie, looking from me to her brother said, "You can wear my Indian costume, Carlos. I don't mind."

There was a time when my daughter was kind and loving, and not so long ago. When I last saw her there were glimpses of the child I raised, though the drug addict keeps erasing her. Even then as I prepared to endure the unendurable for any parent, I needed to remember Angie as the loving, innocent child she once was.

Parking the car in a nearby lot, we walked briskly in the cold that February day in 2004 and entered the clinic. It was nice and warm inside. I appreciated the warmth and hoped that it would be warm where they were taking my daughter.

"Angie Romero?"

Angie jumped up to acknowledge her name, smiling widely as if she were collecting an award.

"Hi, how are you?" Angie said, as if making small talk would make it all go easier and faster, as if this nurse who she hoped would oversee the procedure would understand and not judge her. *Please don't judge me*, I imagined her begging.

This was my fantasy. I needed to think she was sorry for what she was about to do. I needed to think she still had a conscience, that she felt badly about letting things get so out of control. I needed to believe she was begging for absolution. And maybe, no certainly, since I was an accomplice in all this, I was begging for absolution as well. Did my daughter really seek to be forgiven? Did she care at all? Would she be changed, reformed by the procedure she faced? Would I?

"I'm fine, dear. You can come with me now."

Together they disappeared as the door closed. I didn't let myself think about what was happening on the other side of the door. I needed to get out of there, so I went for a long walk, as cold as it was. I walked and walked, it seemed for miles, not really looking at anything. I was just letting the pain in my heart work its way down through my legs and into the sidewalks. Let the streets house my pain. I'm sure they'd seen plenty of it.

I felt so complicit in what was happening. I wasn't an uninvolved bystander. I drove her to it, helped pay for it, and fed her after it. I added this guilt to what I was already carrying, compounding the remorse I already felt. And though I didn't know it at the time, I was moving into very dangerous waters myself. Hell, I was already there. I realize I'd been sucked down into the belly of the beast again. I couldn't see the forest for the trees, I was so enmeshed in my daughter's difficulties, and still so crippled by my own regret about not managing things better that I think I zoned out as well, not on drugs but on paralyzing grief.

Angie came out of the room, looking relieved, and said she wanted a meatball sub. We left the clinic right away and raced against the cold to reach the car. We stopped at the sub shop and she wolfed it down as though she hadn't eaten in days. She probably hadn't.

"Take me home, Mom. I'm really tired."

"Are you all right, honey? Can you take some time off?"

"No, I'm fine. I'll pick up a shift tomorrow."

No tears — flat — emotionless. No "Thanks, Mom, for getting me out of trouble." And why would she? Angie is very smart. Maybe she knew even then, as I'm only seeing in hindsight, that far from "getting her out of trouble" I was only helping her dig herself deeper into the hole she so desperately needed to climb out of.

What had happened that cold day in February, and what was so heartbreakingly horrid, was that she had given birth to a 26-week-old fetus that was disposed of. My grandchild! Nowadays, babies that small can live, and I know of a few who have.

What had happened on the other side of that door? Did they put a mask over her mouth and put her to sleep? Or did they give her an injection? Did they just give her twilight sleep so that she was vaguely aware of what was going on? Then what? Did they somehow induce labor so that this tiny little baby slithered out on its own? Or did they have to pull it out with forceps? What did they do with these little babies? I didn't want to know. I didn't want to know. Is there a special place in heaven for these little innocent beings? I believe so, with all my heart.

So once again, Angie had had an abortion. Once again, I'd placed a safety net under her so that she wouldn't suffer the consequences. But what I couldn't protect her from, what no one could save her from, was the guilt that was piling onto her small frame, relentless and punishing. She kept using afterwards, as any addict will tell you, because of the physiological need in her for more dope. But I also believe that there was still enough of my daughter left in her, the child I raised to have a conscience, to feel the conflict and enormity of what she had just done. She kept using, I truly believe, in order to quiet that voice inside her that was growing louder and louder, telling her she was a worthless, murderous, human being.

In a letter I wrote to my daughter a few months later, I appeared to be at the end of my rope. I pointed out much of her dysfunctional behavior, from throwing away parking tickets to driving without a license. I asked her in conclusion:

"What does all this say about your level of maturity, and what changes are you willing to make in your attitude and your life in order to live more like a functioning adult? Because until you make some changes in your behavior, you will depend on me too much for all the wrong reasons, and if I allow it (your dependence) without limitations, part of you will continue to hate me for it."

And so part of her did—and has—hated me all these years for not allowing her the dignity of living with her own choices. Yes, she screamed for intervention and help. And yes, too often we gave it to her. But if I had known then what I know now: that cushioning her falls, no matter how deadly, simply kept her in suspension—held her in the air like a doll—and prevented her from touching ground with her own life, I would have behaved differently. Our over-protectiveness relieved our anxiety, but failed miserably to help her mature. She wanted us to say yes but she needed us to say no—the oldest parenting rule in the book. Well, it didn't come with a manual, we often hear people say. I was a divorced, guilt-ridden single parent, so grateful to be needed, so sure that my redemption would reside in her recovery.

I would find it several years later, not in Angie's wellness, but in my own.

Slipping Away

In May of 2004, Angie did finish her courses and graduated from George Mason University with a B.A in English/Journalism. It was anticlimactic for all of us at this point, after all we'd been through, but still we were glad. It was right then that I should have eased her out of my house to be more independent, but I didn't. I was busy with work and grad school; I think I wanted to keep her around to keep an eye on her. And we had so much work to do to repair our relationship. I was reluctant to see her go.

Nevertheless, I knew my bird needed to test her wings. The following October, I set the boundary: by January 1, she had to live elsewhere. And on that day, Gene and I walked down to the basement and made good our word. She was prepared, and had found a place two miles away. I was very happy. She was on her own but close enough for us to see each other easily. It was almost too good to be true.

I would discover over and over again in the months and years that followed that when something is too good to be true, it usually is.

From January to May, we were both in heaven, or so it seemed. It was a transition period, of course, with Angie living on her own for the first time in two years. Given her addiction history, was it wise to think she could manage on her own? At the time Gene and I felt sure that it was time for her to be independent of me. She had earned her college degree. She was in a good position to get a job. Isn't that what good parents do— encourage independence in their children?

I have friends in the Program who have chosen to keep their addicted children living at home with them. "Children" who were forty, fifty years old. This is one of the hardest choices parents make: do we keep them home— assuming they are sober and don't abuse the privilege— or do we push them out the door? There is no easy answer. Every case is different. At the time that I encouraged Angie to live on her own, I felt like I was doing the right thing.

We were in frequent communication by email. We talked about her job search, car concerns, and I was starting to wonder if she had attention deficit hyperactivity disorder. Some of her behaviors pointed to this: her sleeplessness and restlessness. Later on in her drug addiction we would wrestle with the possibility that Angie was bi-polar. When I asked her if she had attention deficit hyperactivity disorder she agreed with me and started seeing a doctor about that. But because she was a meth addict, I also thought she might be manipulating doctors to get another ready— and legal— supply of her favorite drug.

Four years later, when she went to rehab in Palm Springs in 2009, she would be diagnosed with ADHD, and Focalin was prescribed. When I heard about this I thought to myself: *Never once was there any mention growing up of her having attention deficit hyperactivity disorder. There was never any disturbing behavior noted on her report card, much less a diagnosis like this. Is it possible that this was an adult-onset version of the same? Or had she found a way to get another form of amphetamines?*

At that point in her disease I was grateful for explanations and possible solutions, whether it was medication or not. I would often wonder in these years of Angie's addiction what came first: an underlying mental disorder, previously undiagnosed, that might have led her into the dangerous practice of self-medicating; or was it her drug abuse that led to this mental disorder? This confusion frequently arises when trying to understand addiction in the people we love.

But for now, this was a blessed period when Angie was functioning well, and her father and I hoped that she was truly in a period of recovery, doing whatever was necessary to remain there.

She was on her own again in her own place, happily painting it in her favorite colors with the help of her new neighbors. She had a job, a car, paid her own bills. She went out and got a rescue dog, a lab named Sebastian, and loved him dearly, just as she had loved Oscar. I used to meet her in the dog parks that spring on nice warm days where she took him to run around. No matter where Angie was in her illness, she always surrounded herself with animals, just as I did when I was growing up in New England. There's something about the unconditional love of an animal that is very comforting.

She used to sit in her living room and crow about her improved life: "I bet you never thought I'd make it to this place, after all I put you through, did you, Mom?"

And I gratefully agreed. If this was the best she could do for verbal amends, I'd take it. She flew up to Massachusetts to see her grandmother for the long Memorial Day weekend. In so many ways, she seemed to be on the mend, and making amends, to the people she loved.

That spring of 2005 I earned my M.A. in Teaching at George Mason University, and she and her brother loyally attended the ceremony. I turned around in the auditorium and saw her there with my son. I felt so proud not only of my achievement, but that Angie had turned her life around, and seemed to be happy in her recovery.

But when the program was over, and we started to file out, I saw that she had already left, and I felt a sense of foreboding, one of many that I would have in the years to come. That dark cloud began to cover the sun once more and once again, unbelievably to me, she began to tumble back into her addiction.

I don't know where she met Joe, but he was a meth addict and he kept her high and happy. I tried to keep out of it, but she lived close to me, and I used to stop by sometimes to say hi. The signs were there: her mailbox jammed with mail that hadn't even been picked up, unpaid bills, and overdue notices for rent. She wasn't answering her phone or returning any messages. It was like she had dropped off the face of the earth.

I needed to finish and present my final research project in July. The school year was winding down, but I still had to get through exams and writing conferences. The turgid air in northern Virginia was stifling, and all I could think about was getting away from the humidity and hiking in the southwest that summer. This was Gene's gift to me for completing my Master's. I couldn't wait to bask in the sun of New Mexico and hear a performance at the Santa Fe Opera for the first time.

But I had to go see what she was up to. Her apartment was only two miles away from the condo. I parked on her street and was relieved to see her car, so I knew she was home. Running up the stairs, I tripped over a cat and sent it screeching down the steps. I knocked on her door but there was no answer. I knocked again — again, no answer. Music was playing, so I knew she was home. If she'd answered her phone, I could have told her I was coming. But I was determined to see her so I banged on the door.

Finally she came and opened it, a cigarette hanging out of her mouth while she zipped up her jeans. Without waiting for an invitation, I brushed past her and approached the bedroom, but stopped in my tracks. Joe, her boyfriend, was lying on the bed, prostrate, his long legs hanging off the end. He was so out of it I don't think he knew I was there.

"Mom, come back here," she hissed, frantically beckoning me back into the living room where she was standing. "This is not a good time."

"It's never a good time, Angie. You've been avoiding your father and me, and I want to know why."

"Mom, I know you're worried. Joe's really trying to kick the stuff, honest. Me too. We're detoxing right now. That's why it's not a good time."

"Not a good time…" Summer of 2005 was upon us, and Angie had been struggling with serious drug addiction for four years. First it was methamphetamine, then cocaine, and now meth again. There had been two abortions, countless betrayals, one rehab, and brief, blessed periods of sunshine between the clouds, not to mention the accomplishment of earning her college degree. The highs and lows were exhausting me. But I was so sick of it all and frankly really angry with my daughter for not trying harder to work on her own recovery. She had so much going for her; it was such a waste.

"I can't deal with this, Angie. You know what you need to do, forchrissake—just **do** it!" Pausing to take a breath and looking back toward the bedroom, "And get rid of that creep on your bed," I hammered.

I turned and left the apartment, slamming the door. I was furious—and terrified. It was so overwhelming after all we'd already been through, to be watching her in the middle of another relapse. Had Angie learned nothing from all her suffering so far? And what about me? Was the teacher still teachable?

Her life started to go to hell again, while I clung to my recovery in Al-Anon. To celebrate my Master's, Gene and I went to New Mexico in July. But my heart was heavy knowing of Angie's latest relapse. I had been in this awful place before. I had been filled with hope only to see it smashed over and over again by the power of addiction. I have an image of myself grabbing her by the throat and screaming out the words, "Angie, stop this! You're killing yourself!" as if choking her into unconsciousness would make a difference.

I had had such high hopes for Angie when she moved to her apartment and began living independently. Forcing her to do this had been hard for me. On the one hand, I had a daughter who was emotionally challenged and a drug addict. On the other hand, she said she was in recovery and anxious to embrace her independence from me. It was what I desperately wanted to hear, so I believed it.

But it didn't work out well. By June she was with another methamphetamine addict and getting hooked again herself. I tried to lose myself in the beauty of New Mexico over the summer, but I was sick with disappointment.

Angie's father and I, feeling increasingly helpless to influence our daughter, arranged an appointment in the fall with a psychiatrist we knew, and Angie agreed to a meeting for all of us together. Xavier and I were doing what we could to intervene and expose her to the help she needed. But she was just going through the motions to please us. Her behavior got much worse and she started to isolate from us once again. We knew what that felt like: it was like screaming at our daughter through a glass soundproof wall. But we were learning to stop screaming. We knew we needed to let her go.

She sent me an email toward the end of October complaining about her landlord and how her neighbors were in the process of suing him. She had become expert at deflecting attention away from herself and her own behavior.

This may have just been setting us up for what would happen a couple of months later.

Oh, I was so angry, so terrified, and so sad to watch my daughter continue to slip away like this. The slow-motion living of putting one foot in front of the other, going to work, loving, making love, just carrying on with the rhythms of life was hard many days. But I was increasingly involved in my program of recovery to help me face the challenges in front of me. When I remember the years of depression that paralyzed me as a much younger woman, I'm so grateful for what I was learning in Al-Anon and incorporating into my life. I was getting better slowly. But I still had a long way to go.

By December 2005, she was evicted, packed up all her stuff into Joe's truck, and fled to his brother's house nearby. I got a call from somebody (my number must have been on a bill or something) whose house was in their getaway path, saying that a big box of stuff had fallen out of the back of the truck into the middle of the road and would I please come get it. Personal stuff, family pictures, bills, letters to Angie from friends in Greece that she had held onto for ten years.

"Fallen out of the back of their truck, and would I please come get it?" Would I please rescue her yet again? Well, of course! Didn't I have this coming to me, after all? Just like a mindless lab rat I set about to stand by her, and rescue her, and make it all better for her, once again. As Gene said to me many times prior to this, "Things are gonna get much worse, Babe, before they get better." And they did. My God, how they did.

Gene and I drove over to this house and picked up a laundry basket full of letters and bills. No one was home, or they didn't want to be bothered. They left it all on the porch and Gene and I swooped it up and put it in the car. I took it all home and looked at the kind of things Angie, through all this turmoil in her life, had chosen to keep among her belongings. Her B.A. Degree in English/Journalism from GMU; her certificate of appreciation from University of Phoenix; many of her letters from Nana, birthday cards from her father and me, her brother and sister; letters from Greece and many others from friends she'd had since she was five years old. Why had she kept them with her all this time? I believed it was because there was still a part of her that had not yet been corrupted by drug addiction. And whether this was wishful thinking or not, it governed my reactions to events as they continued to unfold.

I was on such a fast moving train that I was dizzy with the drama of it all, and very much caught up in it as well. I was addicted to my addict; I felt important because I was needed (translate: used, like an ATM machine). When she got pregnant, why did I make it my problem? When she broke the law, why didn't I let her face the consequences?

When my kids were young, I used to pride myself on my parenting. I took Parent Effectiveness Training classes, and joined preschool coops so I could participate in what was going on from a very young age. Oh boy, did I think I had my mother beat! I was going to do it right this time! And for all those years even after the divorce, they were really good kids. I thought, because they seemed OK, that I was a good parent. I measured myself against them. I think many parents do that. So now, when my skills were sorely tested, I was falling apart. It was as if I thought that if I let her fall down that rabbit hole, without trying to stop her, that I deserved to go with her too. And I did, a bit later on, when my heart and my nerves gave out, and I was finally, at long last, on my knees.

Angie didn't last long with Joe, who stole her car and beat her up. She left him, and ended up on a friend's couch. But two years after the second one, Angie found herself very far along in yet another unwanted, unaware of till it was too late, pregnancy. *How can this be happening again, for the third time? I asked myself. Because she was a drug addict and unconscious most of the time, dummy.*

Angie's MO has always been to wait till the eleventh hour when, if she weren't rescued then and there, there would be disastrous consequences. This was the last week when the abortion clinic would take care of her problem, so if she was going to get another abortion, it had to be now. Either she was so unconscious from drug use that she really was oblivious, or she finally felt movement down there. That's when she sounded the alarm for her father and me to rescue her. Xavier and I caved in again—out of fear—we didn't yet have enough strength or faith to allow her or ourselves to learn from the consequences of her actions. But she went to the clinic by herself; we called in the credit card. I couldn't bear to walk into that hellhole again.

Later on we would learn how to let go—just let go— and have faith that life was unfolding as it was meant to. But we weren't there yet. We still had so much to discover about resilience, not Angie's, but our own. We still had so much to learn about the nature of parental love—how it tears away at us like ravenous birds until finally we realized, out of self-preservation if nothing else, that the only road left to us was to pray "for the grace to release our addicts with love and cease trying to change them" (Nar-Anon 3). But it would take still more trials before we would be able to surrender our will to save our child.

I don't know how my daughter processed all her abortions, but I can tell you that I was beyond shocked, beyond grief-stricken, numbed by it all, and in denial about how seriously disturbed my daughter was. I didn't let myself think of what this was doing to my girl; I was just putting one foot in front of the other and hoping and praying that this would be enough, that this would end it, that she would come out of this coma and be herself again.

Selfishness is recognized as healthy in the Twelve-Step programs. We learn a lot about self-care and focusing on ourselves, not to remain self-centered but to get away from blame and learn self-reflection and accountability. But there would be many slips and turns on my road to getting to this place.

The following year I would continue to inject myself into a journey of self-discovery that was Angie's alone to make. Instead of becoming selfish in the best sense of the word and focusing on my own growth and betterment, I would persist in seeing myself as Angie's savior, denying her what little dignity she had left in managing her own life. What I didn't realize then was that it didn't matter what I said or did. I hadn't yet accepted that Angie was in the grips of a progressive disease, and that she alone had the power to battle it. It would take much more recovery work for me to find the humility to let go of my oppressive involvement and let my daughter live her own life.

I still wasn't willing to let Angie return to living in the basement of my condo. I didn't trust her or her recovery at that point. It was too soon. So the next few months were a blur of friends' sofas and drug hotels. Driving her to one of these hotels near Dupont Circle in D.C., I felt no regret. This was a good thing. I had been so traumatized by having her live with me before, with all the theft and verbal abuse, that I felt it was intelligent self-care to keep her at a distance. Some ideas from the Program were sinking in—at least sometimes.

"It's the big house on the corner, Mom. The room is nice. As long as I go to a meeting a day, I can stay here. I just have them sign this paper at the meetings."

It was a well-kept-up old Victorian house; it didn't look like a crack den.

"Do they serve any meals, honey?"

"They lay out coffee and donuts in the morning, but I just drink the coffee, which sucks."

"I'll call you in a couple days and we can have dinner together."

"OK, Mom. Love you. Bye."

Always the same desolate feeling when we parted company; would I ever see her again? Would she go to her NA meetings, only to be seduced yet again by the power of her addiction? She was so changed, so wounded. Drugs are powerful killers, and usually they destroy our mind before they destroy our body — but not always. Angie was such a stranger to me in so many ways now. But I still stubbornly clung to my wishful thinking, to my faith that she would choose recovery and fight to get her life back.

Well, the drug-free honeymoon didn't last. The trouble with NA meetings is there are often lots of using junkies there just looking for contacts — and new drug buddies. So she made a new friend named Hope, with a house, a car, and lots of heroin. If you were Angie, with enough remorse to sink a ship and equal amounts of shame, this would be just what the doctor ordered.

Hope's house, I soon discovered, was a small, two-room dump right next to the beltway in Takoma Park, Maryland. I went to visit them before Gene and I left for a backpacking trip in California. I don't know what it is about drug addicts. Do they need to be surrounded by chaos or are they just hopelessly oblivious? Angie grew up in a tidy home that was cleaned regularly. She never went to bed without a shower. Who was this person?

Two guard dogs, sentinels of this strange domicile, scared me half to death until my daughter pulled them away. There was no path to walk so I climbed over furniture and strewn clothes to find a place to squat.

"Where's Hope, Angie? I'd like to meet your friend."

"Oh, she doesn't feel well, Mom. She needed to sleep this morning."

This morning, this afternoon, probably all day, I thought to myself. I knew as I sat there in my daughter's presence exactly where I was and what was going on: Angie and Hope were living in a drug den and they were using drugs. Such clarity — such utter powerlessness. I had a choice right then and there: drag her into my car and kidnap her; or leave her to the life she had chosen. It was 2006, five years into her addiction, and I knew that any intervention on my part would be nothing more than a band-aid on a serious wound unless she, heart and soul, wanted to recover and give up drugs. I was powerless to change her — I was powerless over her addiction.

So she latched onto Hope for a while, until they got evicted for nonpayment of rent. Angie parachuted into a furnished place in Adams Morgan where I went to see her that fall. It looked nice; she had her computer, and began to discover easy ways to make money.

I didn't even speculate at that point. The anonymity of computers allows any number of creative adventures. She told me, when I asked her, a few things I would approve of, but mostly she said she was doing online editing, an easy lie for me to swallow because it was her college major. I would discover later on how she was using her computer to support herself and, as if my heart hadn't been broken enough already,

I would find out that my heart could be shattered many more times, and I would still come back for more. When suitcases full of evidence crashed into my living room along with my strung-out daughter and a terrified pit bull a year later, it would be clear that Angie had been getting into online sex, and not all of it online.

When I was growing up in that schoolhouse all those years ago, there was a big problem in my family that no one confronted, and so I started to question my own reality. *Am I the only one who sees this problem?* I asked myself. *Well, no one else seems to see it, so I guess it's not there.* People around you are lying, so you start to lie too. This is what I learned there as a child. Eventually I got my head on straight and by the time I started raising my children it was important to me to raise them with a clear moral code. You can only imagine how Angie's fall from grace — drug-induced as it was — has been hard for me to witness. Watching the moral deterioration of one's child would be hard for any parent. But it seemed doubly hard for me because I still had so much old guilt of my own to resolve, my own moral code to strengthen. Steps Four and Five in Al-Anon have been a lifesaver in helping to free me of past wrongs and move forward in my life without this baggage.

When I was very young growing up in New England, I carved my own little home out of the woods near my house. I said "house," because it wasn't a home to me a lot of the time. My sister and brother were not close to me, Daddy spent a lot of time in the basement, and Mom cried in her bedroom. I wasn't a happy camper growing up.

In one of my bank accounts, the security question that I have to keep changing to keep one step ahead of my daughter who keeps trying to rip me off is "What was your favorite place growing up?" And my answer varies so she can't hack in, but it's always something like "in the woods."

Gene and I used our summer vacations from teaching to explore the national parks all over America. Being outdoors in nature is where both of us were happiest. It was a tremendous relief for us to get away and lose ourselves in the natural beauty surrounding us. That year on vacation, I was in a pretty good place, thanks to my ongoing recovery in Al-Anon. The following is a journal entry for July 2006:

"This day was so cool. Carlos checked up on me at the Apple Store to see if I'd really go to the workshop! And of course I did go, learned a lot, and am determined to become more independent computer-wise. Poor kid, he's probably worried I won't be able to cope without him when he leaves for Austin, but I will. I'll be fine. And Gene's no dummy, either. He has a lot of common sense and a far better temperament than I do. I've noticed in recent months how I tend to panic— not a good thing. I know I've been losing a lot of my steadiness in recent months. Maybe I'm just getting older, maybe my struggle with Angie is wearing me down, I don't know. Anyway, today I have a little peace about Angie, just let her go. I don't want my grief over her to destroy me. Leaving for California in a week to hike, camp, see Caroline, and revel in the earth's beauty while it's still there to witness. Yes, God, life is good to me. I'm grateful!"

Gene and I had a wonderful trip, but we always did when we got away from the city and into the country. We went to Yosemite National Park in California. I don't recommend going there in the summer, however—too many people. Some campers pitched their tent about an inch away from ours and yakked and played music well into the wee hours. I don't remember why curfew wasn't enforced that night, but the next morning we knew we had to get out of there. So we packed up and decided to hike down into the backcountry. Backpacking is hard work even for young people. We were not so young anymore and I was a little nervous. In a picture someone took of us at the end of this trek, we looked like death, with grim relief all over our faces. By then, Gene had a stress fracture in his leg.

The hike to Mono Meadows was at first a steep walk down hill, which is in some ways harder than going up. We had everything on our backs: tent, sleeping bags, kitchen, food and water. All that weight on our knees straight down and then snaking down along the winding trail was painful. But we finally reached a beautiful meadow worth all the effort. Jumping from one log to another, we found a place to sit in the tall grass to eat our lunch and just lie down and rest. We marveled at the lupine spreading across the meadow, moving with the sun, in colorful bloom. Crossing the meadow, balancing ourselves on logs part of the way, we followed the trail further down into a valley where we pitched our tent later in the day. After breakfast the next day we followed an incline to Mono Creek and the ridge beyond where we viewed Mt. Star King. To Gene and me, taking the extra time to hike into the backcountry of this magnificent national park was like viewing a secret garden not seen by everyone. We basked in the quiet, the lack of noise and stress from the world we lived in. The simplicity of it was humbling and refreshing.

We were refreshed for a few days until our food supply ran out and we knew we had to trudge back up the mountain. So we loaded ourselves up once again with everything we had brought down with us. But two things were noticeably missing: three days' worth of food and water. And speaking of food, Gene can't stomach freeze-dried things; he always drags whole grapefruits, steak, and fresh vegetables when we go hiking or backpacking. No wonder he got a stress fracture!

We went up a fairly steep incline, stopping to catch our breath as we turned each corner. I had quit smoking four years before. But Gene was still pushing the envelope with his Camel habit and he felt the effects of it hiking. I was not happy on our way up; this was too hard for me. Finally we neared the trailhead where our car was parked. Other back packers coming down the same trail cheered us and clapped; that made us feel good. We knew we had accomplished something difficult and we basked in all the congratulations. Then, collapsing in front of a tree where someone took our picture where we looked like death, we rolled our eyes at each other and said "Never again! Flat hikes from now on!"

The following year, if you can believe it, Gene and I would climb another mountain, in British Columbia, this time with twice the climbing distance. I think I counted twenty-five hairpin turns on our uphill climb there, aptly called switchbacks. We were getting older now and really feeling it.

But we'd had a good run in the wilderness for almost twenty years, catching it before it disappeared into a memory. I was in the woods again and this time with a loving companion. How fortunate I have been to go back to my childhood refuge and start seeing my life with a different lens. When we got on the plane to return, we were ready to face our lives and challenges back East.

Autumn, my favorite season, came and went too quickly. Gene and I were busy teaching high school every day, and I was continuing my recovery work.

"When the student is ready the teacher appears," we are told. I was slowly making progress, but I still had a long way to go. This student still thought she was the teacher.

Another Joe entered Angie's life, and they decided in December 2006 to move to Richmond, though we didn't know exactly why. Around Christmas, Angie's father got a frantic call from the owner of the apartment she had sublet in Adams Morgan. "Help! The TV and all the electronics have been stolen! How can I get them back?" He and I just sighed, "Oh God, it never ends. When, dear God, is this ever going to end?" Now we knew why they left in a hurry. But we didn't see the whole horrible picture—not yet.

Hiding In Plain Sight

So, Joe and Angie lived together in Richmond. She was working in a hotel food chain, and he was a gardener. Right. She told me what I wanted to hear, and I didn't question it. Just like I used to lie to my mother when I was growing up. I was busy working, I never gave up hope that she would turn her life around, and she was so convincing when I talked to her. Sometimes, they drove up to northern Virginia to see friends (translate: to score), and one of those times, on my birthday, she had the most beautiful roses I'd ever seen delivered to my school. Every once in a while she threw me a crumb—this was a chocolate mousse—just to keep me around. She was good, very good. She really knew how to work me.

Toward the end of January 2007, I took Gene and all my kids down to Miami for a long weekend. Xavier's whole family lives there, and since the divorce they had hardly seen our children at all. To their credit they treated Gene like one of the family and never once made me feel awkward for having the chutzpah to bring my partner to meet them. I was pleased in particular that Caroline had flown in from San Francisco. Her godmother is Xavier's aunt, for whom she is named, and the godparent/godchild relationship is very sacred in Hispanic culture.

We had a great time staying in South Beach. I took the girls to a spa so we could all have massages. We ate well at a few very nice restaurants. And of course we all trekked inland in my rented car to visit Xavier's family. At a lavish barbecue they set out for us, Aunt Gigi, a prison corrections officer, looked Angie right in the eye. By now, they had learned bits and pieces of what had been going on for the past five years:

"So, are you behaving yourself?"

"Yup," Angie replied, as pure as the driven snow.

"How do you know when an alcoholic is lying?" is a frequently heard saying in Twelve-Step rooms. "His lips are moving. "

There was another incident back in South Beach that I found suspicious but didn't make an issue of because my kids and I were having such a good time together for the first time in years. On a shopping spree with my girls, Angie just disappeared for a half an hour. She has a mania for shoes, just like her Aunt Lucy, and so I took her to a store for a new pair. She found a few that she couldn't choose from and asked if she could go out and have a smoke while she decided. I said "Sure."

Ten minutes later I went out to get her but she was gone. Too quickly, I panicked and fumed. I saw Caroline walking toward me and breathed a sigh of relief.

"Hi, Babe, have you seen your sister?"

"No, I thought she was with you."

"She was, but she slipped out to have a smoke and just took off from here. I guess she didn't want the shoes."

"She'll turn up, Mom, relax," she said, ever the laid-back hippie.

"Turn up from where? How am I supposed to find her in this town?" I whined, my stomach doing somersaults.

See what happens when I panic? All sense of reason departs. Fair weather slips away as the sky darkens. I see a twister in the distance and I know danger is close by.

"You need to chill, Mom. Why don't you call her on the phone?"

With that question bringing me back to reality, I agreed.

"Now why didn't I think of that?"

Caroline had been living in San Francisco since 2000, before all this trouble with her sister had intensified. And I know that as close as they had been growing up, my girls had really grown apart these last few years. Certainly it's hard to bridge a 3000-mile distance. But it was much more than that. I think Caroline needed to keep her distance. It's been very painful to watch her sister turn into such a stranger, and she knew sooner than I did that she didn't have the power to help Angie. So in many ways she was out of the loop — and therefore wasn't as sensitive or aware of the possibility of relapse, much less how to deal with it if it happened.

I waited a couple of minutes and then called Angie on her cell phone. No answer. Now I really was scared. Not liking the bad vibes I was sending out, Caroline went next door to get a snack. Another ten minutes passed while I wore a groove in the sidewalk and finally I saw Angie sauntering in my direction as though she didn't have a care in the world. Walking briskly toward her, I shouted too loudly:

"Angie, dammit, where have you been? I was frantic with worry!"

"Sorry, Mom, I realized I left my phone in the room so I went back to get it."

"Then why didn't you answer when I called?"

"I left it there to charge up cuz it was dead."

"Oh well, at least you're back. Let's go meet your sister next door and get a smoothie."

Crisis averted, sort of. More like glossed over and ignored. We went back to the grandparents, aunts and cousins for a delicious brunch the next day and to say goodbye. I had thought of everything, I thought, to make this the best trip possible. The only thing that could have made it better for my in-laws would have been if Xavier and I had still been married and I had come with him instead of Gene.

I made sure our flights out of Miami were conveniently at the same time, and after returning the car and racing Caroline to her gate, we all prepared to board our own flight back to D.C. I had a terrific sense of accomplishment, the way you feel, say, when you bake a cake and it comes out perfectly. No uneven layers, it looks great. You don't know how it tastes, but it looks perfect.

Yet I had a strange feeling in my gut, like an itch I couldn't scratch. Something had happened there but I couldn't put my finger on it. I had no idea at that point that Angie and Joe had become heroin addicts, and the wreckage they had left in D.C. before they moved to Richmond would soon make sense to me. Months later she sneered at me for being such a clueless idiot. On our shopping spree when Angie went AWOL for thirty minutes, she had ducked around a corner to take some suboxone. If she hadn't brought some of that drug to deal with her cravings, she would have been climbing the walls in withdrawal, each day becoming a worse nightmare than the one before. I suppose I should be grateful for that. It certainly would have ruined our visit.

The spring flew by and I threw myself into work. I was a guest lecturer to student teachers at a nearby university, and I had been taking on one student teacher after another in my own high school classroom. I loved mentoring young people who sought work in teaching. As underpaid as it was, I'd always felt that this was a very noble profession and one that I was proud to be part of. It gave me tremendous satisfaction to know that I was a valued educator and that all I had learned from nearly twenty years of teaching could make a difference in someone's life.

Making a difference – I've always been driven to fulfill those three words, now more than ever. The more powerless I felt around Angie's addiction, the more I threw myself into teaching and helping my students. I have never in my life, before or since, felt so engaged and fulfilled professionally. This was probably one of the most productive periods in my career, a career that would come to a screeching halt only one year later. I admit that her living farther away enabled me to feel some distance from her illness and detach more. There were no crises to deal with, so I breathed a sigh of relief for a little while, trying to live my own life.

I had my own challenges to face and the biggest one was my mother, now living in a nursing home in Massachusetts. I went up to see her about four times a year, always wondering if when I drove away it would be the last time I'd see her. She was ninety-seven now and terrified of dying. Years ago I wondered if she was afraid of meeting up with my father and getting what was coming to her. I wonder if any other family members felt that she drove him to an early grave. But I don't feel that way now. Alcoholism took him from us way too soon. Knowing what I know now about addiction, I never blame my mother for events that were clearly out of her control.

I had acquired a long-abiding faith years earlier, when my friend Beth Murphy died in Guatemala where Xavier and I had been living on his first Foreign Service assignment. I believed that when we died our souls left our bodies and went somewhere else. I was sure of it.

I was asked to identify Beth's body at the morgue and when they pulled open the refrigerated drawer, I looked over my shoulder as if to ask, "Are you sure you have the right person?" What used to be "Beth" was gone now. I was certain then that when our bodies give out something of us – our soul or our essence—escapes from our corpse and moves into another space.

Jill Bialosky notes, after seeing her deceased sister Kim in her casket, "If you've ever seen a person embalmed in a casket, you have no doubt the soul has fled" (24).

Every time I visited my mother, I told her not to be afraid. I assured her that, since my soul would also go somewhere else someday too, we would meet up in the stratosphere somewhere. And we'd get a second chance to be mother and daughter. Only this time we'd get it right! I always got a laugh out of her with that. I know I raged against my mother for years. But she was so burdened with guilt about so many things, and I knew what that felt like too. I will be forever grateful that I was given the grace to forgive her and make peace with her before she would die two years later.

Another challenge for me was managing the inevitable collisions between Angie, her illness, and the rest of my family. The following month, Carlos came to my condo to get some of his things as he was preparing to move to Austin, Texas to complete his MBA at the University of Texas. He is a very handsome young man, with his father's deep brown eyes, but taller and with some of my features and lighter coloring. He is very artistic and spent much of his childhood creating comic strips of his own, often sharing them with his father and me in birthday and Christmas cards. And he kept a prized collection of Marvel comics that he had been collecting for two decades.

"Mom, I'm in the basement," Carlos yelled upstairs. "Where is that collection of comic books that I left with you when you moved here? I want to take them to Texas."

"I don't know. Probably wherever you left them. While Angie was living there I hardly ever went downstairs."

"While Angie was living there..." The words caught in my throat as soon as I uttered them. "While Angie was living there…" My stomach did a flip-flop and I suddenly felt nauseous. I was remembering my mother's beautiful sterling silver pieces Angie had stolen and pawned, just to pay for her habit. I'll never forget how violated I felt, and how deeply in denial I had been to believe, as Angie had assured me, that someone else had broken in to the house and stolen them.

Omigod. Carlos! I thought to myself in a panic. *I never thought to lock the comics away from her, even after she had stolen from me.* Now, another missing item, another reminder of the lengths she would go — and the family members she would wound without a second thought — to fund her addiction. My heart sank. I knew before he did that Carlos wouldn't find them where he had left them.

"Are they valuable, Carlos?"

I listened to an ominous silence, frantic drawer and door slamming. The breeze coming in though the window was blowing papers all over the kitchen counter. I went to shut the window, turned and braced myself as I heard him pounding back upstairs two steps at a time.

"What's the matter?" I asked, knowing the answer. I faced him and saw the rage and frustration in his eyes. For a few moments he was speechless, incredulous that his sister could betray him like this. Then he exploded:

"That fucking bitch! She sold them!"

Helplessly, I apologized for letting this happen to him on my watch. He trusted me to take care of his things. And now he felt used, just like I already had over and over again. For the moment anyway, he was in a strange and unfamiliar place that nothing could have prepared him for: now I wonder if he knew, however briefly, what it felt like to hate his sister.

In recovery, we learn to profoundly adjust our expectations, hard as it is. We raised one child, and now we have another. We are all too aware of the change that drugs have produced in our children. A parent wrote in *Sharing Experience, Strength and Hope* a very revealing statement, something I could have written myself. It is a key to understanding my story, my mother and father's stories, and my daughter's painful struggle:

> I expected my children to be perfect, to always do the right thing. I tried to control them by giving them direction and making them do things in a way that I felt was correct! When they didn't, I could not handle it.

> I could not accept their drug use and I felt that their behavior was a reflection on me. I was embarrassed for myself and scared to death for them. I became so distrusting of my children that I showed them no respect. I would meddle and invade their privacy looking for any excuse to challenge and confront them.

> When I came to Nar-Anon, I learned that my interference and my attempts at controlling them were actually standing in the way of their recovery. I learned to let go of the control I never had in the first place. (29)

Weeks were passing by and I was growing suspicious that I wasn't hearing more regularly from Angie. I knew in my gut that they had moved to Richmond hurriedly for a reason, and if they were running away from something, they were probably using drugs too. I called the hotel chain later in the spring where she was supposed to be working, and of course they had never heard of her. This was another kick in the gut, another knowing what was right in front of me, and I could do nothing to stop it. She was a runaway train in the grips of her addiction, just like her mother had been many times before her.

When I called Angie in Richmond, she said they were in the middle of moving to a better apartment and not to come down right away. I guess that bought her a couple of weeks. Short of being in China, she knew she'd have to face me sooner or later.

I drove down to see them when school was out: hardly any furniture in this new place. Moving toward a closed door across the room, Angie warned me,

"Don't go in the bedroom!"

OK, I thought to myself, *what's she hiding now?* So I changed the subject.

"I'm starving, Angie, what's to eat?" I asked.

There was nothing to eat in the whole house. I drove two hours to see her, and after twenty minutes of being polite, she went to vomit in the bathroom and asked me to leave because she was feeling really sick. Uh-huh. Now I was remembering like a bad dream that lost half hour when Angie disappeared in Miami six months earlier. Now I could see with my own eyes what was eating her alive like a nasty virus. Heroin addicts don't always die from overdoses. Many die from starvation.

I said goodbye, I love you, take care of yourselves. I'd gotten very good at bravely moving forward with my life, doing the next right thing for myself, leaving her to manage by herself, even though I knew she was on a suicide mission. Five years in the Program were starting to sink in. But not fast enough. I would have to grow a lot more hair on my chest before I would be able to let go of trying to save her and surrender to the all-powerful disease that was consuming her.

I drove home and a few weeks later flew to the Pacific Northwest to climb a mountain. Somehow I thought if I worked my body really hard, I could knead the pain out, like kinks in a muscle. It was a great trip, but very taxing. Gene had been to British Columbia before and had always wanted to climb Mt. Garibaldi. They said it would be tough but we would be rewarded with a pristine turquoise lake for our efforts. And we were — but not before snaking our way up the trail with too much weight on our backs, huffing all the way. To lighten our load we ate our hamburgers — a big mistake — because we ran out of food before we came back down, got very hungry, and had to ask people for extra rations as they packed out. Really embarrassing for a couple of "seasoned" backpackers!

Anyway, I cried all the way up and sobbed all the way down. The only thing I kneaded out of me was my infernal pride to head up a mountain without planning better. A week after I got home, to rest and unwind, to get ready for school, Angie exploded into my living room with a dog and suitcases full of costumes and dildos.

Oh, God, no, this wasn't happening. **THIS WAS NOT HAPPENING!** *My girl was not entertaining men for a living. I don't know this person. Something has taken over her body and transformed her. Angie,* **my** *Angie, no longer resides in this walking corpse, this skeleton. She doesn't live here anymore.*

Gene took the dog to the animal shelter. Everything happened so quickly, and we weren't prepared to adopt this pit bull. But I was very gratified a week later to get a call from the rescue league where Gene took him. They had found the dog a home. I still donate to the rescue league in Alexandria every year as a way to thank them.

I threw the contents of her suitcases away, as if throwing it all in the garbage would make the reality of it go away, make it never to have happened, make it a bad dream that's happening to someone else's child. I'm haunted by the face of my daughter, so not my daughter, so lost. What a miserable thief this horrible disease is, how it hijacks those we love. She has been hijacked, no question. But if our children get cancer or diabetes, do we feel the same way? No, of course not. They have a disease. How sad, they're sick. Why, then, do we instill addiction with human qualities? Because in our society it's still something that we think we can (must) tackle as if it were human. And until we rid ourselves of that delusion, we'll be right where I was: fighting like a tiger to save my child, and gradually losing my mind.

I poured Angie into my car, drove her to the hospital, and committed her to the psych ward. She wasn't obligated to stay, but she did, for two weeks, when they put a lot of pressure on her to leave because that's all they could offer her without insurance. The first night I stayed with her, holding her down while she was detoxing, screaming, "I want the lights to go out! I want the lights to go out!" And if she hadn't been safely ensconced in the psych ward, I have no doubt that she would have put her own lights out.

While she was there, Gene sat with her at one or two in-house meetings. Xavier and I soldiered in to see her every single day, with her favorite food, and smiles, and earnest talk about how she could start over any time she chose to. On one such visit, I asked her about the contents of her suitcases.

"It's all perfectly legal, Mom."

Collecting myself and keeping calm, I asked myself if I was living on another planet, or was using your body to earn money an illegal act? No matter. It didn't matter to me because this person who was glibly telling me this was not the person I had raised. This person had no moral compass whatsoever.

And from this moment forward I knew that I was dealing with a split personality: two people, my Angie, and this fucking, hair-brained addict. I wanted to kill the addict, murder her in her sleep, and watch my Angie rise like a phoenix from the ashes.

As Angie's deadline at the hospital was approaching, we were all scrambling to find a place for her to go, because she wasn't coming to **my** house. She knew she had crossed the line too many times and didn't even try to manipulate herself back into my home. As luck would have it, there was a drug rehab residential facility right across the street from the hospital. She called to apply and they really kept her waiting for a reply. When they accepted her, I was overjoyed. Not only was it dirt cheap, she could stay there indefinitely, a year if she wanted to. My faith was being restored; I knew there was a God and he was answering my prayers. Angie, two miles from my house, safely in rehab for a year!

Xavier and I took her shrimp, and visited often, along with the one or two friends she had left in the whole world. It was a gorgeous autumn that year, warm and sunny. I felt so happy, so hopeful and free of anxiety. She was right where I wanted her to be, doing what I wanted her to do. We used to sit together on the back porch, chatting about the "bad old days," as if they were far behind us. Little did we know what she was planning.

Then, two weeks into her stay there, on another beautiful day, I went to see her so we could go for a walk. I knocked on the door:

"Hi, can you tell Angie her mother's here?"

"Excuse me, let me go find the director."

"Thanks, I'll wait out here."

Looking stricken, the director greeted me at the door. "Mrs. Romero? I'm sorry, but Angie isn't here. She just packed her suitcase and left. We don't know where she went."

"What? You just let her leave? Why didn't you call me?" I yelled.

"Mrs. Romero, her stay here was voluntary," she answered. "She could leave any time she wanted. And we had no authorization to call you. She's not a minor. I'm sorry."

Numb with pain, worry and disappointment, I turned around and made it back to my car. Funny thing about getting kicked in the stomach multiple times. You stop feeling the pain of it. Numbness sets in and somehow, if you're lucky, you get from Point A to Point B without any serious damage. So instead of feeling the pain of losing her yet again, I felt an incredible sense of relief. I told my friends in the Program that it felt like a weight had been lifted from my shoulders, that I was "finally off the hook." If ever I was to accept that I was powerless over her and her addiction, it was now. I was free of her and the worry and the anxiety and even some of the guilt. I didn't know whether she was dead or alive, but I felt free and unencumbered for the first time in months. Isn't that strange?

While she was at the rehab she eventually fled from, they had taken away her phone. That was smart, cutting her off from pushers and the like. But they had computers, presumably to help the residents do job searches, etc. Well, there were a million other things you could do with a computer, and Angie knew them all. It wasn't hard for her to find her latest drug buddy, Joe, and a friend of his rescued her a few blocks from the rehab, waiting on the corner with her suitcase.

But my respite was short lived. The phone rang two weeks before Christmas, and I knew she was still alive. At the sound of her voice, I was drawn back in to her world, her illness, and her drama. I didn't even think to take a step back from it all, so strong was my codependency at that point.

"Hi Mom. Doc thought I should call you and let you know how I was. Do you want to come down and see me? I'm on a farm in Fredericksburg."

"Oh, Angie. I'm so grateful you're alive and safe! We'll come down first thing on Saturday."

Why didn't I just hang up and say the hell with her? Because she was my daughter, somewhere closeted inside that addict's body, and no matter how much I raged at her endless betrayals of self and those she had once upon a time loved, I couldn't turn away from her. She was my child. She didn't ask to be born, and I know she didn't choose to be sick. I would go to her, on a tranquil farm two hours away, to try yet again to reach her, in some way, on some level, while she could still be reached. As long as she was still above ground, I told myself, she had another chance to start over. I was her mother. I would rescue her. **This time**, I would save her from herself.

This was my mindset when we went to see her: stubborn, stupid, willful lab rat that I was. After all that we had been through, together and apart, you would think I would have learned. I wanted to think we were both still teachable, still capable of redemption. And so I continued to seek it, my own, but I was looking in the wrong places. I thought I could only find it in her recovery.

I would find it, eventually, a little farther down the road. It was deep inside me, I discovered, all along.

What I didn't see then, and only see now years later, was that all the energy I poured into my attempts to save her were terribly misdirected. It said a great deal about me, but it said nothing about her. If she were ever going to beat this thing, she would need to do the necessary work on her own. We could help her access the tools she needed, but she needed to pick them up with her own hands and use them.

SANCTUARY

Doc was a retired physician with a specialty in addiction. Joe the gardener used to work for him trimming the trees on his property. He and Angie needed refuge, and Doc opened up his home and his heart to them. He eventually convinced Angie to contact me to let me know how she was. And so, one cold Saturday in December, Gene and I drove down to the farm to see her. She showed us around, seemed to be well. But she had become an expert at keeping her usage under wraps. We met Doc, a wonderful and trusting man, and were so relieved to know she was living in that place under his care. I think he was nearly eighty years old.

He and his family had lived on a big old historic property for many years. It had a very interesting history. It was built in 1859, the year before the Confederacy was born, and Robert E. Lee breakfasted there the morning of the Battle of Fredericksburg. On the National Register of Historic Places, it was a Greek Revival mansion covering over 6000 square feet. There were ten fireplaces, two kitchens, eight bedrooms, high vaulted ceilings, and beautiful marbleized woodwork. All this was on over 18 acres right next to a national park. It was very stately, recalling the gentry of the Old South.

But Doc's children and grandchildren had grown up and moved away years before. Now they were spread out all over the country. I think he was lonely for his family. His wife was living in another one of their homes closer to the Shenandoah, but she came to Fredericksburg for visits on occasion. Her room still looked occupied, her dressing table full of powders, creams and family pictures.

Doc had been living there, he told us, to organize all his papers and other belongings and prepare to pack up. The property was being sold to the city as a historic landmark, and it was time for Doc and his family to let go of this magnificent property that had housed so many happy memories. But at Doc's age, that's a lot of paperwork to sift through. Joe was from the area and used to work for him a lot on his property. The two of them actually shared a considerable history, and Doc took Joe under his wing from time to time. He tried to help him with problems that were piling up in his life as a result of his drug addiction.

Joe's friend had recently rescued Angie from her second rehab, and when they showed up in Fredericksburg Doc gratefully took them in. Maybe they could help him with all the sifting and packing. He really needed a secretary. I asked myself, *Is he really going to trust Angie and Joe with all this?*

Gene and I got a tour of the house, one room after another. At first glance, the place looked a little decrepit, especially the infrastructure, with exposed pipes and wires. Much of the paint was peeling, and the place seemed very "tired," like a geologist's "competent" rock. The place wasn't about to fall down, but parts of it could easily crumble—the stoop off the servants' kitchen, for example. Doc's office had the dug-in look of fifty years of keeping records, patient files, medical journals, and treatment centers. It was an overwhelming sight, and I knew he needed a lot of help preparing to move. There was a musty odor everywhere, wet greenery and almost a chill in the air. But then it was December and I'm sure he only heated part of the mansion to save money. Still, the place seemed a little dark and eerie, with Confederate ghosts lurking in every corner.

Doc and Gene and I chatted amiably about the mess these two kids were in. He had years of experience with addicts and was not in the least bit ignorant about what he had brought into his home.

"Maggie, I'm so glad Angie was willing to call you. I really felt you needed to be brought into this. I'd like to try working with the two of you together, maybe every other week, to see if we can make any progress together. But, and I have to emphasize this, nothing we do will amount to anything if Angie and Joe aren't willing to give up drugs and the life that goes with it. It may well be that they're just resting between sprees."

Startled by his frankness, as well as his willingness to lay himself and his home open to such a possibility, I managed to stutter:

"Oh God, you can't be serious! I can't believe my daughter would come into your care only to hurt you. I just can't believe she could be that ungrateful! I have to believe she's gonna take advantage of this opportunity."

"Well, let's hope for the best," he assured me, but with reservation.

His skepticism threatened my growing hope with every pause, every breath he took. I could feel it, and I wanted to slap it out of him. I was so worn out from five years of watching my daughter disintegrate into this person that I hardly recognized anymore. The child in me, the mother in me, the human being who begged God, Buddha, and all the powers that be to free my child of the addiction that was strangling her, this person placed a lot of hope in this dear man, and it was a terribly unfair burden to place on his shoulders.

Doc's goal in accepting them into his home was to talk to them, reason with them, inspire them, and pray with them, to help them ultimately want to reach for recovery. But even that, he emphasized, their reaching for recovery, was up to them. Like the rehab Angie had recently run away from, there was no deadline. Angie and Joe could have stayed there indefinitely, or at least until the property was ready for sale. This place offered free room and board, a tranquil setting, living in the care of a man who trusted them to want to get well. Gene and I drove home that day with so much hope in our hearts. I wrote Angie a long letter and sent it right off to her:

December 15, 2007

Dear Angie,

Affirmation: "Today is the first day of a new, healthy relationship with my mother." Did you take this into yourself today? I felt very grateful after I left Doc's. I think I understand why you finally called me two weeks before Christmas. I believe that you love me very much. And it is that very capacity for love, if you allow yourself to embrace it and work with it, that will be your savior and higher power, long after Doc and I and everybody else before you have died.

Gene and I had a great time discovering Fredericksburg after we left you. He's an incredible Civil War buff and was fascinated to talk to Doc and see where he lives. I'm glad he came with me. And of course he wanted to see you too.

Angie, you've been lost to us all for a long time, and it goes way back. I think it started in Italy, but maybe you can trace it back farther. Rather than going back over every incident in a letter, maybe it would be better if I share my recollections with you in person. And vice-versa: I want so much to listen to what you have to say.

I know that rebuilding your family relationships will take time. But Nana doesn't know anything about your struggles; she just misses you. I know she'd love to get a call sometime.

I'm glad I have my own program in force as well. It protects me from the addict. I don't need to steel myself away from you, Angie, if you are clean. As I said on the phone, I won't have a relationship with you if you are using. But as long as you stay in recovery, I look forward to spending time with you and supporting a loving relationship with you. You're my daughter; you can't imagine how the loss of you has affected me, or how the return of a healthy you to our life would bring me joy.

I look forward to coming down once or twice a month to work with you and Doc, and just spend some time with you. It's long overdue. I think it would be helpful for you to hear about some of my life, which is such a mirror of your own, if only because I was able to overcome terrible sadness as a child, get over much of my pain, and grow into a mature adult, with all the joy and misery that most people have. I know I'm getting older, but I'm so glad I survived because I've enjoyed a very full life. I hope you will too.

You can't imagine how much I love you and how much I appreciate Doc for supporting you. See you on the 27th.

Angie never responded to my letter. But I didn't fret about it. I was just so glad to know she was sleeping on a bed, eating meals, and in the care of a good man. Doc and his whole family had a New Year's Open House at the end of the month and Gene and I drove down to Fredericksburg to celebrate with them. I felt so grateful that they had opened their hearts to my daughter. They were very, very good people.

I made Christmas cookies in eager anticipation of their party. We were so full of peace to know where Angie was and who was overseeing her progress. It seemed almost too good to be true: she was in a comfortable setting, watched over every day by an addiction specialist. I didn't have a front-row seat anymore to watch her, which was just as well. I could detach.

But I could still see her if I wanted to. Then I remembered that the rehab she had just run away from was also too good to be true: close to my home, very inexpensive, and with no deadline. But I didn't want to think about that.

It was a lovely warm day for late December. When we arrived, first Angie and then Doc and his family greeted us at the door. She seemed very proud, as if to say to me, "See, Mom? Look where I am! Look how these people have taken me into their home; aren't you impressed?" But she seemed very content, and she knew I would heartily approve of her newest surroundings. Doc's wife took Gene and me on a tour of the third floor that was unoccupied. Doc confined his activities to the main floor and the three of them, Doc, Joe and Angie, were living in the servants' quarters on the right side of the mansion, using the huge servants' kitchen for meals.

We had a lovely couple of hours eating and chatting with visiting neighbors who would be saying goodbye to this family once the property was sold. Angie showed me *Broken*, the book Bill Moyers' son, Cope, wrote about his addiction. Doc had lent it to her and she devoured it voraciously. I asked her if I could borrow it and she said sure. She said it helped her to read recovery stories. That was music to my ears. Every time I saw a glimpse of the daughter I raised it gave me hope that she'd come back to her family someday.

Everyone gathered outside to see us off. But there were two small things that bothered me as I mused about our visit on the way home. One was that Joe didn't make an appearance at all. When I asked Angie why, she said he was too shy, but I didn't quite buy that. The other was the look I saw in Doc's daughter's eyes as we said goodbye. It was a wary look—very wary—as if she didn't trust what was going on there with her father's new charges.

But again, I brushed aside my suspicious thoughts. At no point in this five-year ordeal had I ever felt so confident, so hopeful, so sure that Angie was going to beat her addiction. I was at the top of the roller coaster ride. What a high I felt, forgetting momentarily that what goes up must come down—and the higher the climb, the farther the fall. I had no idea on that happy day that I would soon be falling into a deep dark tunnel of my own, where everything I had learned about being a loving mother and my own recovery would merge—and meet in a head-on collision.

As soon as I got home from the party, I wrote her another long letter and sent it right off to Fredericksburg.

Dear Angie,

Well, maybe I'll move toward Anna if you get militant about it, but for now this is the name I have known you as. And unless you instruct me otherwise, this is the name I have called you for nearly 30 years.

About the enclosed $20: I guess I'm rationalizing and enabling you to some extent, but maybe I'll support your birth control regime for the time being. It's not a lot of money while you're getting back on your feet, and it's a way for me to ensure that that aspect of your life is free from worry. PERIOD. If you ever end up pregnant again, you'll know, that I know…etc. etc. etc. no excuses; you will pay for the consequences.

Doc has emphasized that there needs to be less negativity in our communication. I'm well aware, Angie, of my distrust of you, of my veiled threats or whatever, which I trust will diminish in time, as our time together increases, as our friendship grows, adult to adult, with all the stresses and disappointments and JOYS that accompany it. I want to relax with you. But be patient. It will take me some time. The effects of addiction on the family are devastating.

Back to birth control, Doc said he would look into a cheaper way. $45/month seems like a lot of money for that nowadays, even without insurance. But, anyway, that's why you are getting a day job.

Angie, dear, you were racing with me when we talked. Maybe that's the bipolar, I don't know, but you need to slow down. If you see it in writing from me, maybe it will reach you: you are just fine the way you are; you don't have to get a Master's! That's ridiculous; there are many good jobs you can get without one. Your brother was making a lot of money without one. And why do you need to make a lot of money anyway? You just have yourself to pay for—no spouse, no children, no drug habit. You're putting yourself under a lot of unnecessary pressure thinking this way.

You forget, and your disease, cunning and baffling as it is, wants you to forget, how your first priority is to get well from addictive disease, which means too many things for me to list here, but one of the things is to keep things simple for as long as it takes for you to be able to handle things more complicated, like working and going to school at the same time, or even going to grad school at all. Personal things, too, may get in the way of the simplicity you need in your life. Angie, it may well be that you can't have it all right now. You have financial debt and perhaps bankruptcy issues that you may need to deal with. You may not be able to hold down a job, qualify for insurance (which you need for mental health and medication), and go to grad school at the same time. That can come later, much later, after you have secured a place on this earth. Don't you know that there was a time when I wasn't sure you'd be here by Christmas? By the way, did I thank you for staying alive?

I love you so much, and I love Doc for helping you. This man and his family, his trust in you and the possibilities for your future, have been a GREAT GIFT. Honor them.

See you the weekend of the 12th or 13th.

While Angie was in Fredericksburg, I really stepped up my attempts to reach her. For one thing, I had an address to mail things to. For another, I thought she might be reachable while she was in Doc's care. But I see in so many of my communications, like these two letters, a dreadful tendency to condescend to her. I still clung to the illusion of control and I wanted her to do things my way.

'Honor them, Angie, honor them.' I know what I meant when I said those words to her, reminding her of the moral code I had raised her with. But how she would react to them was a different matter.

Many of my letters to Angie throughout her addiction were pages of barely veiled anger and disappointment. Since she was so sick I didn't have the heart or the courage to be more honest with her. She saw through the mask anyway. My letters demonstrate how deeply entrenched I still was in needing to fix and control her. I needed to back off and let her find her own way. I kept hearing my mother's old (imaginary) voice in me: "You can't let go of her, Maggie. That's not love. You can't just stand by and let her self-destruct!"

It's no surprise that she never answered these letters. Angie was well into her twenties by now and I should have known better anyway. I really needed to do more of what the Program was telling me to do. Even in my own journey of self-discovery, no one could have told me that I was OK. I had to believe it myself. I've had a lot of therapy over the years, but none of them worked as well as the Twelve Steps to bring about change in me. And I so wished that Angie could find something in life to give her faith in her own worth — go back to the first twenty-one years of her life — and remember all the things she excelled in and how much ambition she once had for herself. I too wished she could access the love of her whole family. It was such an impotent thing now, I realized, though I once naively thought that my love could pull her away from all this. But there was a masonry wall between Angie and recovery: rough, forbidding, high and difficult to scale. Addiction crippled her with destructive "solutions" to the ache in her soul.

Lately I've been reading a few books on suicide: Jill Bialosky's query into her sister's suicide (84); and Judy Collins' heartfelt story about the addiction and suicide of her only child, Clark (111). Both of these authors consulted with the late Dr. Edwin S. Shneidman, a well-known suicidologist. His word, "psychache," resonated with me. From watching Angie grow into the addict she has become as an adult, I can see how that term would apply to her. If ever there was an aching psyche, it was hers, so in pain and so unable to express that pain effectively to those she loved. I often feel that drug addiction and the pain that accompanies it is a form of suicide, slow and relentless, if left untreated.

My father made attempts here and there to give up gin and tobacco. When he had his gall bladder removed the nurses made him cough into a bag, and he was so disgusted with what came up that he stopped smoking for a while. But he never completely set aside his self-destructive behavior. It was like an old friend who reminded him of what he'd often felt as a child from an uncaring, abusive father: "You're not good enough, not important enough." As a young man working in the family business, he met and fell in love with my mother, who spent a good part of their marriage echoing his father's disappointment in him. Where do the seeds of addiction take root? It's the old chicken and the egg confusion. Was my father predestined to become an alcoholic? Or was he made one by the emotional abuse he endured? And if the latter is true, then how and when was I an emotional abuser of my own daughter?

But Twelve-Step recovery gently steers us away from questions like that; we can't go back and do things over. And

I'm only human. I sometimes ask myself what I did wrong or what I missed seeing. Then I remember that addiction is a disease: "I didn't cause it, I can't control it, and I can't cure it." And like a gentle breeze blowing away the clutter of remorse, I let go of those thoughts and embrace my life again, free of responsibility.

In any case, whatever she chose to do now, I needed to leave her alone to do it. I knew better than to scream and wail in the night to God and all the graces that protected the innocent to save my daughter. Whatever the roots of addiction are, whatever holes were missing in her that this opportunistic disease filled in, I didn't have the power to combat them. And I just had to let go of the struggle, or I would disappear down that rabbit hole with her.

Came To Believe

I guess none of us knew at that point what we were dealing with, but we were soon to find out. In January my birthday came and went without a word from Angie, and I felt that same familiar cloud descending into my carefully protected space, threatening my well-being. When she was herself, she always remembered this day. So now I knew that something was very wrong.

Doc called that weekend of the 12th, telling me that Angie and Joe had taken off without a word. I'll never forget how I felt when he told me this. That same familiar hollowness returned, as if I'd been gutted on the spot. And as to Doc, I was speechless with shame, after all he and his family had done for them. A couple of days later, Angie called from Richmond, asking me to pay for one night in a hotel before they went back to Doc's to apologize.

They went back to Doc's all right, but not to apologize. Doc called to tell me that someone had broken into his house, stolen his credit cards, and taken his truck. Apparently they had been sleeping in the chicken coop, in January, waiting for the best time to make their move. *'Sleeping in the chicken coop?'* I moaned to myself. *Oh, God, what had she come to?* He called the police, and they were picked up pretty quickly in Baltimore.

The policeman who arrested them told me that Angie tried to get away, screaming, "I'll kill myself if you arrest me!" They were both taken to the jail in Baltimore. Joe was locked up on the spot for grand larceny/car theft; Angie was released to the psych ward in a nearby hospital. She had no priors and got off the hook. The very sympathetic policeman who arrested my daughter gave all this information to me over the phone. It was a Tuesday night, and I needed to get to my parents' Al-Anon meeting. I was leading that night. I'll never forget how I was feeling: hollow again, but wooden; it was almost surreal, sort of an out of body experience.

This wasn't happening! My daughter was getting arrested? I kept saying to myself.

"Mrs. Romero? Mrs. Romero? Are you still there?" the policeman asked.

Then he advised me, "Let it go, Mrs. Romero. There's nothing you can do for her now. Let the legal system handle her."

Sure, but they'd have to find her first.

I didn't have time to go into rescue mode. After one day in her second psych ward, she called a friend who lived in Baltimore to come get her out. Poor, hapless friend, she had no idea that she was releasing Angie to the wind. This time my girl truly was gone with the wind: no word — no contact — nothing.

After Angie's arrest, I felt myself start to dissolve. I was a sugar cube with hot water poured over it, and I was melting. It was January 2008, and I started to feel my insides harden, or soften; I'm not sure which. I could barely swallow food, my bowel movements changed, my taste buds had totally changed, everything in me changed, I couldn't watch the shows I used to watch. I would lie in bed for hours at a time staring at the wall. I lost a ton of weight. At school, I watched in horror my hands uncontrollably shaking. I would space out in the middle of teaching a lesson. One of my students noticed and asked me if I was OK. What the hell was happening to me?

I spent the long holiday weekend up in Massachusetts with my mother in her nursing home. "How is Angie?" she queried. Bless her heart, for the past three years we all lied to her, told her that her granddaughter was living in California. How could I break my mother's heart and tell her the truth? What was the point now of disclosing to my mother truths that would only further break her heart and open a can of worms she wasn't well enough to deal with? My mother was ninety-eight years old, and was soon to meet her Maker. Leave her to her illusions, we all agreed. During my time with her, I sat on her bed and did the strangest thing: I wrote the first twenty pages of my life story. I felt driven right then and there to write down things I had been putting off for years. It was an incredible adrenaline rush.

Then I flew back to my life and my job and admitted to myself that I was having a nervous breakdown.

It was a perfect storm of family pressure, heartbreak and despair at that point in my life, and as hard as I had tried to function under the weight of it, I couldn't any longer. I was too ashamed to tell my colleagues that I was falling apart. The stigma of mental illness is so great in our society, I was afraid my principal would ask me to go home and rest then and there. But at the same time, if I stayed in the classroom, I knew that I couldn't do my best. I was doing my students a disservice if I stayed. So I decided to retire at the end of the year. It was one of the hardest decisions I've ever had to make because I loved my job and I was a good teacher. But there were a lot of young people waiting in line for me to retire, so I applied for early retirement, effective in June.

That first winter after her arrest, I was so fearful for her, and also for myself. I was still pretty fragile after my breakdown. I was really afraid that she would knock on my door, and I didn't want to let her in. I had heard in the news how addicts when they're high sometimes kill family members without a second thought. I was more than afraid— I was terrified—of my own daughter. If there's a special hell for parents, then I was in the thick of it, and had been for too long. No wonder my nerves were shot. This is when I got an alarm system for my condo. Then I left a manila envelope with fifty dollars and the names of shelters nearby taped to my front door. My neighbors must have thought I was crazy. Well, I was, sort of. But I was recovering very well, and before I knew it, I took the big Angie envelope off my front door. I knew she wasn't going to come, and I wasn't afraid anymore.

I couldn't leave my job in the middle of the year. I loved my students too much, so I determined to hold on till June. I saw a therapist and took medication, Zoloft, for clinical depression. It would take a few months for my nerves to stabilize, even with the medication. But I weaned myself off of it within a year, so determined I was not to be dependent on mood-altering drugs. My doctor tried to talk me out of retiring. He knew that I needed time to make sense of things before I made any life-changing decisions. But I was adamant, just like I had been years before about divorcing Xavier. I still had such a black and white mentality sometimes, like many compulsives. I needed to choose one side or the other, without considering something in the middle, certain shades of gray. Binge on junk food or starve—that's how I used to behave without any recovery. But now food had become nothing more than a way to nourish my body. And I'm so very grateful for that.

And I was about to have a little fun, for a change. I was a foodie about to go on a honeymoon. Over the years

I've learned to control my weight by eating the right foods, healthy foods like vegetables and lean meats, as well as getting a good amount of exercise. Well, as I said earlier, my taste buds had changed. I could no longer stomach a rice cake or a salad. Maybe this was my body's way of putting on some of the weight I had lost, but now I was attracted to bagels and butter and cream cheese. Gene, who never gets up this early, faithfully and sleepily came downstairs every morning before I went to school to make sure I had eaten my bagels and butter and cream cheese. I was very touched by the way he took care of me. Even my students took an interest in feeding me. One Mongolian girl brought me the most sumptuous treat, "buuz," (pronounced like booze) a kind of dumpling filled with meat. I gobbled them all up for lunch one day and thanked her for the buuz she brought me, howling under my breath at the double-entendre she didn't get!

My two other children were living their lives with remarkable detachment from their sister. Carlos was thirty-one in 2008 and Caroline was twenty-seven. My obsession with Angie pretty much consumed whatever maternal energy I had left after a day of teaching. I didn't thread their lives together with Angie's very much at all. But I should have.

I'll never forget a friend I had years ago. She was the youngest of three girls in her family. The middle sister had suffered from cancer years before and had died. My friend was ten when her sister died at age fourteen. But it wasn't the death that traumatized Jillian so much. It was the years of care, heartbreak and obsession with saving her dying child that her mother endured — to the exclusion of her other two girls — that turned Jillian into an angry, rebellious teenager. She did not get her share of mother love, she felt, and to this day she has not forgiven her mother. I should have remembered that story while I was obsessing over Angie.

Caroline had been living in San Francisco for eight years and was doing well. She graduated from college there, had lots of friends, and enjoyed the work she did. Since she was three thousand miles away and seemingly happy, it was easy to put her on a back burner. Carlos went to college in Virginia and remained in D.C. to live and work so I saw him regularly. It wasn't Carlos who was getting short shrift; it was Caroline.

At that point I was so vulnerable; I needed her more in my life. So I reached out to her in a number of letters. I wanted my other kids to circle the wagon more, but at the same time I felt like I had to be a paragon of strength for them. Even though they knew about Angie's addiction, they didn't share their concerns with me very much at all. Maybe they felt I had enough to deal with without having to worry about them too. But as their sister continued to deteriorate in her illness, I would feel compelled to bring them into the loop with more details of Angie's life in addiction. I had always avoided this — wanted to protect them from the horrors — and they never pressed me to know what was going on. Was this denial on their part? Self-protection? Didn't they care about Angie at all? They had all grown up together all over the world.

And, of course, our family was far from perfect; it was dysfunctional in many ways. Xavier and I had our faults, but there was never any doubt that we loved our children. So when our family was stricken with Angie's illness, I had the naïve hope that her brother and sister would pull together more on her behalf. But as I wrote in the early pages of this memoir, addiction has acted like a bomb exploding — and my children scattered to the four winds.

Reading over some old letters I wrote to Caroline, it seems as if I was trying to stir up the drama and excitement of my codependency, but thankfully she didn't play along with me and never responded. She detached naturally. What a healthy kid! Of the four of us survivors, I was the one who was the most outwardly affected, because I too am an addict. "With every lash of the whip at her, I felt the pain on my back too." Knowing intimately what she was going through and being powerless to save her tore me apart quite differently from parents without such baggage. At this point in my journey I guess I preferred the relief of insanity, however briefly, to watching Angie die a slow death.

Fortunately, I got better by spring, and my food honeymoon was over. But what a sacrifice I was making by giving up my job. What a toll this miserable disease was taking now, on me. I needed to be strong for Angie, and I felt I was letting us both down. Very few people knew that I had had a breakdown—none of my good friends at work—and I downplayed it to my other two children. I was terribly ashamed.

Doc and his family were selling the farm in Fredericksburg, and would be moving farther south soon.

"For Sale, Hilltop, Greek Revival, 18.88 acres, 6243 sq. ft. Year Built ca. 1859: Asking Price $1,000,000."

This is where Angie and Joe found sanctuary last December. This is where they had a chance to start over, in the care of a man who knew what they were going through, because he'd seen addiction in countless young people for decades. And this is what they walked away from, so firmly were they entrenched in their addictive disease.

Doc invited Gene and me down to collect the things Angie and Joe had hurriedly left behind. It was a bittersweet reunion after all they had been through with the two of them. But I would never meet a kinder or more forgiving group of people. That made her betrayal seem so much worse. We ate hot dogs, talked of other things, and they lifted the boxes of belongings into my car.

"God bless you, Doc, for all you tried to do to help my daughter."

"I'm just sorry I couldn't reach her, Maggie, but I'll keep you both in my prayers."

When we got home, I was anxious to see what Angie had saved from her last home in Richmond. There wasn't much I cared to keep except one thing: a beautiful mug with a Virgo symbol on it that I had given her for her birthday. I had bought it at a crafts fair and given it to her on that last (brief) visit in Richmond. I like to think that she kept that mug so that she would have something from me. And so I have it now, with me on my farm in New Mexico, a tangible reminder of the fragility of life, of love, of our health and well-being.

All spring I had a new routine at school. I made sure to set out a week's worth of work in all my preps, just in case I needed to take a week off. I nurtured a fantasy that Angie would call me, and I would go to Baltimore to get her. But she never called. I needed no time off, and not missing a day of school until I left in June, I think I did the best teaching I'd done in twenty years. I knew I'd probably never have a job like this again, and I threw myself into it, savoring every moment I could. My last months on the job were bittersweet, all the retirement celebrations were bittersweet, and then I looked at my classroom for the last time.

I was on my knees, finally, ready to surrender. This is where I started to sever the umbilical cord. This is where Angie and I began our separate journeys.

I'M ALMOST DONE. (HA HA☺)

5-10-09

Mom,

I love you so much ..
Thank you for not giving
up on me.

♡ always,
Angie

TWO

"Alice: 'Would you tell me, please, which way I ought to go from here?'

The Cheshire Cat: 'That depends a good deal on where you want to get to.'

Alice: 'I don't much care where.'

The Cheshire Cat: 'Then it doesn't matter much which way you go.'

Alice: …'So long as I get somewhere.'

The Cheshire Cat: 'Oh, you're sure to do that, if only you walk long enough.'"

(Carroll 66-67)

Out Of The Valley

Nearly a year had passed since her disappearance from the psych ward in Baltimore. There was no word for a year—nothing. I assumed she was dead; I was sure of it. My daughter, once upon a time, was the most faithful and loyal child any parent could wish for. And even though this memoir has shown numerous instances of the drug-induced change in her personality, I still believed, needed to believe, that my daughter would never torture her family without any word for a year, not unless she couldn't contact us. She would never be that cruel. Therefore, she must be dead. This is when I wrote her eulogy. I was just waiting for the end to come. The only thing missing was the body.

Ah yes, the body, that tool, that means, to fund her habit. How could I forget what had happened not that long ago? I was wrong. I was wrong and still unbelievably naïve about the power and the cruelty of drug addiction. There was a living, breathing body living just outside of Baltimore. Only now she called herself Anna.

Angie's father couldn't stand not knowing what had become of her any longer, so he hired a detective to find her. And right after Christmas of 2008, she was found. This happened without too much difficulty because of the paper trail she had left behind: two things that were on record with the local police. She had been raped one night on her way home from work; she reported this, and it was on record. The second thing—a near-fatal overdose—the EMT report. The paddles broke a couple of ribs, she said later. Pissed her off, it hurt so much. She needed her painkillers.

Xavier, braver than I would have been, drove to the address where she was living outside of Baltimore. There he found her, with her sugar daddy coke addict older boyfriend. Her father offered to drive her back to D.C. right then. She would leave the life she was living in Baltimore, and we would put her in a 30-day rehab in northern Virginia. She said OK, but she needed to detox first, on suboxone.

"Come back in a week," she said. "I promise I'll leave with you then."

So he did, and she did, and before we knew it she was in a rehab facility in northern Virginia.

At any point in this timeline, she could have escaped, but she didn't. At any point, she could have called him and said, "No, Dad, I've changed my mind. I'm not ready to do this. Let it go. **Let me go.**"

But she didn't.

Later, much later, she would throw in our face how unready she had been to leave Baltimore, how coerced she felt to do what we wanted. How thousands and thousands of dollars in rehab was such a waste because she never really wanted it.

There were a number of times on this odyssey when we questioned our dedication to our child. This was one of them. We weren't saints, after all.

This was the first time Angie's father and I sought her out with the help of a professional. And I'm glad we did because it bought her time — time to be safe and in recovery — time to clear her head of drugs and reevaluate her life. But if I had it to do over again, I'm not sure I would intervene in quite the same way. For recovery to work, the addict needs to want it. Angie had not yet reached a point where she was ready to turn her life around. They say an addict needs to hit bottom before he can be motivated to look for a way out. But if being raped and overdosing wasn't her bottom, what was?

Angie's father and I manipulated events by luring her away from the life she had been living there. All that has occurred in the years since we found her in Baltimore might never have happened if we had left her alone, and we'll never know what might have happened if we had stayed away. Maybe she'd be dead. Or maybe she'd have reached for recovery in her own time.

But, for now, safely detoxed and living without drugs for a month, she was (almost) her old self. A good friend she had been close to in high school faithfully journeyed with me out to see her in rehab every weekend. She was in such a hurry to see her she even got a speeding ticket one time. "Oh, fuck," Priscilla moaned, knowing she couldn't afford any more moving violations. "But that's OK — Angie's worth it," she assured me, as if I needed assurance. We took Angie shopping at the nearby mall, spoiled her with love and hope. Then my daughter confided that she had hepatitis C. Her coke addict sugar daddy had taken her to be tested because he was concerned for her. It didn't seem to upset her much, though. You could live a long time with hepatitis C, and she knew it. And it seemed a small price for her to pay, the way she had been living. She was very lucky to even be alive.

I knew that thirty days was not enough rehabilitation for her. So I found a 90-day facility in the desert of California: Palm Springs, land of movie stars and Betty Ford. Good company for her to be in, not the movie stars, but Betty Ford, a recovering addict herself. Betty had four kids, an adoring husband, and a life everybody knew about. Lots to live for. What did Angie have? Her job in the next ninety days was to answer that question for herself.

On February 1, 2009 Xavier and I drove out to rehab to take her to Dulles Airport for her flight to California. We had been racing around like crazy in the weeks prior to this, trying to dig up birth certificates, and/or her passport, long since lost in all her previous domiciles, so that we could have an ID made at the local DMV. She wouldn't get very far in an airport without one.

Saying goodbye to her new friends from rehab, Angie knew she was one of the lucky ones. Most of them would come and go from this facility, trying to stay clean and get a job in the local community. They were kids from there, a rural town at the foot of the Shenandoah. Palm Springs, California might as well have been Paris, France. They said goodbye, good luck. She never looked back at them.

At the airport we had to leave Angie at Security. They don't let anyone but passengers go any farther. But Xavier and I waited on the airport side, watching her go through the lines, watching her every moment that we could, before she blew us a kiss, waved goodbye, and was out of sight.

So this was what it was like: we'd been here before; we'd taken her to rehab, we'd visited her in rehab; we'd silently prayed on our side of the great divide that God would have mercy on our child and intervene—that He, or anyone, I didn't care—would help her see the light and want to get well and return to her family. This rehab was different; it was farther away. Maybe it would be easier for her to get a better perspective on her life. Maybe, maybe, maybe—she had her own higher power, and I had mine. *Oh, God*, I pleaded under my breath, *it had to work this time.* "Let her go, Maggie," I heard Him answer. I lingered, half hoping she'd backtrack and blow us another kiss. She didn't. We turned around and walked to the exit.

Goodbye again.

Sahara Springs in Palm Springs, California was a Shangri-La compared to where Angie had been living: fabulous buffet meals, an indoor gym, pool, shopping expeditions, horse therapy and Librium!

Sunny skies again, both in Palm Springs and in our hearts, all of us who loved her and plugged for her. The beginning of 2009 was a time of joy and tremendous hope. This roller coaster ride had been exhausting, and though it was far from over, we had every reason at this point to believe that Angie was finally going to beat this thing. She, herself, said so, in her letters to us. And that, hearing it from her own mouth, was the most crucial and pertinent truth: this was a cunning and baffling disease; but it could only be fought, wrestled and conquered by the addict. Not by the addict's mom, or dad, or best friend.

Now that Gene and I were both retired from teaching, we decided to make a radical change in our life together. We were veteran hikers and campers, and one of our favorite places was New Mexico, home of the Santa Fe Opera and sunny, sunny days! Coming from the swamp of northern Virginia, this was very appealing. So in February we pooled what was left of our resources and bought a rustic little farmhouse in Sandoval County, about forty-five minutes south of Santa Fe. It was meant to be a second home.

But this man took one look at the view of the red mountain at sunset from our new back yard and said "Adiós Babe, come visit me in the summer!" And that's exactly what we did for a couple of years. I didn't mind. He was busy building a fence on the property and teaching college English. And I was busy in Virginia working on a two-year retirement project for my former school district. Angie was in Palm Springs now, safely in rehab, and I had a lot of time to write her letters.

February 11, 2009

Dear Angie,

I've been so happy to receive your three letters. It feels like Christmas to me!!! We have so much to say to each other. But let's just take one day at a time and write down whatever comes into our heads on that day. Recovery is a long process, and it never stops; it just gets easier as time passes. What will facilitate both of our recoveries is improved communication: honest, sometimes happy, sometimes sad, but always honest, to be effective. That's the purpose of our letter writing. I hope we keep it up!!!

You know, even though I've been a teacher for twenty years, I still think of myself as a lifelong learner. The older I get, the more I realize I don't know. So life is just one lesson after another. And learning how to navigate those lessons, the successes and failures, with a balanced and healthy perspective, is what life for adults is all about.

I'm glad you love Palm Springs. The weather is a lot like Greece. Gene and I just came back from New Mexico where we bought a house together. The weather is a lot like southern California, except it's a high desert and it's cold in the winter. Anyway, I still have another year on my contract here, and Nana is still alive and in need of my TLC, so I don't plan on moving out there permanently. I still have my condo in Arlington, so that I can go back and forth whenever I want to.

Your honesty about the drinking binge at the airport is such an important step. It shows a level of maturity I haven't seen in you in years. But with heroin and heavy drugs, 'half measures availed us nothing.'

Not to provide excuses or blame, but both sides of your family have addiction histories. That knowledge should arm you. I've told your brother and sister to be careful with alcohol, and I hope they're listening. As they say, information is power.

You and I are so alike: we both have addictive personalities. But I never took hard drugs to the level you have, not because I'm any better, but, I don't know, maybe because I had three little reasons at home to motivate me to stay alive and well. I guess I'll never know; but I do know that I thank HP every day for getting to be this old because I've been so blessed along the way. If I had remained in the depression that has consumed me at various points since I was very young, I would have missed out on so much!!! We don't ask to be born, Angie, but if we're very lucky, we learn to value ourselves enough so that we choose to live well (most of the time). It's the best revenge!

I hope you'll continue to write to me and share your thoughts, good or bad. I'm glad you're so happy now, but you're bound to have bad days (and thoughts) as well, so feel free to unload on me. I'm your mother, and I will always love you no matter what!

Love, Mom

Recovery in the Program, time and the perspective it brings us, has given me a lot of new information. My own recovery has also graced me with a healthy amount of humility. I used to confuse humility with humiliation. I used to think that admitting my faults would produce shame in me and threaten my self-worth. But in recent years I have a different understanding of this word.

Having taken the Fourth Step ("Made a searching and fearless moral inventory of ourselves"), and later the Seventh Step ("Humbly asked Him to remove our shortcomings"), I began to see myself in a healthier light. I began to see myself in relation to my higher power. I am just a speck in the universe, no more, no less. I've been playing God for much of my life. It doesn't matter any more why; what matters now is that I remain ever mindful of the amount of power I have over others and stop trying to play God with them.

I was also emailing back and forth with Angie's therapist. I was tirelessly doing everything I could think of, saying everything I could think of, to make a difference with Angie. I knew that this was the last rehab I would be sending her to; I was retired now and running out of any disposable income, so I guess I felt a sense of urgency to reach her—again, as if I had the power to talk her out of her addiction, as if any part of her recovery were up to me.

February 15, 2009

Dear Angie,

I want to tell you a story. When I was twenty, I went to the rain forest of Puerto Rico to be a volunteer English teacher. On my way home I spent a few days in the capital. One day when I was swimming I went out too far and got caught up in the current. Then the waves kept crashing over me and I was powerless to fight them. They were too strong. Every wave was pushing me into a jetty of rocks and I knew I was about to crash into them. For the first time in my life, I prepared myself to die. I said goodbye to my life and I let go. Miraculously, someone on the beach spotted me and swam out to rescue me. He helped me get to shore, and I was very grateful! I've often wondered why I didn't die then and why I was kept alive. I've spent much of my life trying to earn the gift of life I was given that day. I've always tried to make a difference as a parent, teacher, and friend.

You've almost died, yourself, a few times. But you were saved (by people, circumstances, dumb luck). Have you ever asked yourself the same question I did? "Why was I allowed to live when I should have died?" Maybe your HP has better plans for you than to die so young—something to think about anyway.

You have said in all of your letters that you "can do it this time." Well, of course I completely agree with you; you have strengths you didn't even know about. But some good questions to ask yourself are "Why **wouldn't** I be able to do it this time?" Or "Why **wasn't** I able to do it before when I tried?" "What's different about **this** time?" How would you answer those questions? The answers might shed some light on things for you.

I love you, Angie. Be well.

February 22, 2009

Hi Angie,

Words of wisdom from two great minds: "We are what we repeatedly do. Excellence, then, is not an act but a habit" (Durant 61).

That's why Nana introduced me to volunteer work when I was thirteen: she knew I had low self-esteem, and she knew it would make me feel better about myself. If I could get out of the self-centered rut I was in, and think about other people who needed help, I might get some perspective. Later on in my life I got rid of much of my self-defeating behavior—not all at once, to be sure, but I did learn to value myself enough to change my habits and make good choices most of the time as I got older. Volunteer work, maybe in an animal shelter, would be so good for you. Whenever you get around to doing the Eighth Step, don't forget to put yourself at the top of the list. I love you honey, Mom

Of course we wanted her to get well. But until she was willing to dig deep, take up the yoke and do the work herself, the love we all felt for her was irrelevant. Not wasted, love is never wasted. My capacity for love is what had brought me to this point. But, yes, it was irrelevant for Angie. My daughter needed to do whatever was necessary to say yes to life. I knew at long last that I had to let go and let God. And I could only hope that she would too.

Parents' Weekend at Sahara Springs was in March, halfway through Angie's stay there. Palm Springs is a relatively small community nestled at the foot of a mountain range separating it from Orange County and Los Angeles. I had never been to southern California, and I looked forward to my trip. What a gas getting off the plane and coming out of the airport! Palm trees, the San Jacinto Mountains ahead of me in the distance. It was March and the weather was very warm! I raised my head to the sky for a moment and basked in the warm sun. I had a good feeling that this time Angie was going to make it. I grabbed a cab and went to my hotel to shower and unwind before the late afternoon briefing. My hotel, fortunately, was close to the main rehab building where Angie was living so I didn't need to rent a car. It was a five-minute walk to the facility.

When I checked in at the front desk, they called my daughter on the intercom and I saw her coming out of her room in the pool area. I crossed the floor to greet her, hugged her and – *Omigod* – she hugged me back! I felt my heart melt like ice cream on a cone right there. I thought if I died tomorrow I would die happily. Everything I had been through with her all these years was worth it for that one hug.

"Hi Mom! Did you have a good flight? How do you like Palm Springs? Not like Virginia, is it?" she asked excitedly.

"No kidding. Remember I told you Gene and I just bought a farmhouse in New Mexico? Guess I'll finally feel the difference soon enough. You'll have to come visit us as soon as you're out of here."

"Cool. Yeah, that would be great. How is Gene?"

"Oh fine, loving the change of scenery. He doesn't want to go back to Virginia, so I'll finish up his GED classes for him through June. But I want to hear all about you," I pressed.

"Later, Mom. First we're all meeting upstairs in a few minutes. This place is great; and you wouldn't believe the food!"

She looked better than I had seen her in years, rested and anxious to show me around. That would come later after all the parents checked in at the main desk. Then we met in one of the conference rooms upstairs, joined by our children. It was only four o'clock but I noticed the sun seemed to be setting already. The mountains to the west that hijack the sun shadow Palm Springs, so evening comes sooner here.

Sahara Springs was a luxury facility compared to the three rehabs she had already been in. Angie proudly showed me around, later taking me through the buffet line for dinner: crabmeat salad, avocadoes galore, broiled fish, soups, salads, gelatos for dessert—quite a step up from her first rehab. She took me into the exercise lounge and showed me some new yoga moves and poses she had learned. She was still the agile gymnast I remembered from so many years ago. As she bent to do a back flip I noticed the scar she still had on her forehead from years before—and I still missed her wearing bangs. I guess they recalled a time of innocence in her life, before she got so sick.

Every day there were seminars and workshops for families—sometimes with our addicts, and sometimes without them. This was a sad but hopeful group of people, just like me, some of whom were mortgaging their homes, happily, to give their kids a chance at recovery.

Xavier and I had spent a lot of money on rehabs. But it didn't matter. I'd already hurt my health, ended my career. But none of that mattered to her. The only thing that mattered, the only thing, was her willingness to do what was necessary to get well.

If she had had cancer, and the doctor said she needed chemo to get well, she would have needed to go for her chemo treatments. If she'd had diabetes, and needed insulin to stay alive, she would have needed to take insulin. She held all the cards, all the passports, to a healthy life, the life her parents had dreamed for her when she came into the world. But could she do it alone? I didn't believe so. Some addicts recover without having faith in something outside of themselves; they rely on willpower, among other things. Faith in God or any "higher power" is, for many addicts, a difficult idea to embrace. And Angie, ever since she was little, had been a confirmed atheist.

In 1987 when Angie was eight, she was visiting my mother in Massachusetts. She adored her Nana, and confided in her things that I didn't know about. During one of these chats, Angie said,

"Nana, do you believe in God?"

"Well, of course, Angie, don't you?" my mother responded.

"NO I DON'T, NANA, NOT ONE BIT!"

My mother, before she died, used to love telling me that story. She was tremendously amused by Angie's stubbornness and independence. But now, at this point in her life, Angie needed faith more than anything, because whatever she was using up to this point was having no lasting impact on her recovery. In the Program, they define insanity as "doing the same thing over and over again, and hoping for different results." Well, flooding your brain with dangerous drugs clearly does make you crazy, temporarily or otherwise. Angie needed to change course if she was going to get well. She needed to do things differently. But what I realize now is that what she chose to do and how she chose to do it was/is none of my business.

On Saturday night the patients were allowed to leave the rehab facility and stay with their parents in their hotels. It was fun mostly, until, high on hope, I started to think that Angie's recovery this time erased twenty years of my parenting: the good, the bad and the ugly.

We had never talked to each other about intimate things when she was growing up. I really wanted to, but she always brushed me off. She'd always been intensely private, and I think I gave up trying after the divorce. Maybe for a teenager it was normal to behave this way, but I so wanted to be closer to Angie on this level. My own mother had never been someone I could confide in, and I wanted to do things differently. "Doing things differently" — yes, I see a pattern here. I wanted to raise my girls differently from the way my mother had raised me. But my choices weren't necessarily better ones.

Anyway, out of the blue I asked Angie if she'd ever been in love. A look of shock morphed into simple disgust as she turned and looked at me like I was the lamest duck in the pond. That look sobered me up very quickly as I returned to reality. Reality was that Angie had never trusted me with intimate details of her life, just as I had never trusted my own mother. She was thirty years old. She wasn't likely to view me differently now, and certainly not at such a vulnerable time in her life. I changed the subject quickly.

The rest of the weekend was fun. I didn't let our interchange from the night before spoil our time together. While we were in workshops many of the parents bonded, and I gave my number to a couple of people. But I never heard from them. It reminded me of a crack another parent had made to me in a recent Nar-Anon meeting. His daughter and mine were both living in San Francisco in various stages of recovery and relapse. When I said to him, "Wow! What a coincidence to have both our kids in the same town!" He retorted "Yeah, let's hope my daughter never meets yours." *Thanks, pal,* I murmured to myself, *I needed to hear that.*

Those of us who live with addiction are aware of the stigma society places on it. Right or wrong, I'm very discreet about Angie's situation—at least with the general public. But I expected more compassion from Program people. That crack from him hurt and surprised me. But I also think that he was just venting his own judgment on all addicts, something I, too, have had to fight. My letters at times show that I've been every bit as judgmental toward Angie. Parents of addicts need to remember that addiction is not a choice: who in their right mind would choose to stick a needle in their arm day after day and live in the gutter? It's an illness, and has been recognized as such by the American Medical Association. Victims of addiction of all forms deserve compassion, and hopefully they will avail themselves of the recovery opportunities out there.

Maybe the other parents in Palm Springs felt similarly, that the last thing their kid needed was to be friends with another drug addict. Angie told me once that that's why she hated NA meetings: pimps, dealers, and strung-out junkies just itching for their next high often attended them. But in Angie's case I don't think that's true. I think she didn't go to meetings because she needed to deal with her addiction her way, and not be told by anyone else what to do: CSR—compulsively self-reliant—just like her mother.

Or maybe she just wasn't ready to embrace recovery at all, a painful possibility I had not yet considered. I was still determined, at that point, to believe that she was going to beat her addiction and that I, of course, would be the glorious savior she would spend the rest of her life thanking, handing me my redemption on a silver platter.

I would finally, thank God, let go of the oppressive burden I was placing on my daughter by demanding she get well so that I could be OK. My mother unconsciously did the same thing with her children: she was a demanding perfectionist, beating back the pain of self-doubt and unworthiness by raising "successful" children. I'm very glad to have found recovery from my dysfunctional upbringing. It has helped to "relieve me of the bondage of self" (*Anonymous Press* 63). And most importantly, most importantly of all, my recovery has freed my children.

MOUNTAINTOPS

Rehab was mostly clear sailing for Angie. But there was one incident at the end of March that was upsetting: she snuck out beyond curfew with a friend and got drunk. She came back eventually, very repentant, and good-naturedly accepted her loss of privileges. The staff felt obligated to call me about the incident. I wasn't sure what it all meant, but I joked with Gene that she has acted out more since she was twenty-one than she had in her whole life!

I've heard it said that once drug abuse takes hold in someone, they stop growing emotionally and remain stuck. Angie was thirty that year but clearly acted like a rebellious teenager. And up until the present when she found the courage to break away from me, she had been almost completely dependent on her father and me. But we, addicted as we were to her, made that easy for her. From time to time throughout her addiction, she fought to establish her independence from us. Then she would turn around and ask for help. I wanted so much for her to take charge of her own life, but later on it would be crystal clear: Addiction was in control and was happy for any handouts. Drugs cost money.

But for now, Angie was in a blessed period of recovery, and we were feeling very happy and hopeful. The end of her time at Sahara Springs was approaching, and we had already found a sober living house for her to transition to. But her brother was getting married in Texas, and she wanted not only to go, but also to participate in the ceremony because Carlos had asked her to. So we gave permission for her to leave the rehab for the weekend, and for once, we did the right thing. This twelve-year struggle with Angie has shown precious little sunlight through the clouds. But our joyous celebration that spring was made the more joyous because Angie was there and healthy. I will always be grateful for the gift of her return to her family, however briefly, on this occasion.

It was a warm and sunny April weekend in Austin, Texas. Carlos and his bride, Carrie, had planned everything themselves, right down to putting up all the out of town guests. Carlos had just earned his MBA at the University of Texas and he and Carrie were living there before they would relocate; that's why they chose to get married there. Destination weddings were very popular, but the price you pay for getting married in an out of the way place is that fewer guests can attend. My mother, for example, who adored Carlos, wasn't well enough to make the trip. Neither was my sister Lucy. But I really appreciated that she sent all three of her sons in her stead. My brother didn't make the trip and neither did any of his children. There was also a Cuban contingent from Miami, aunts, cousins and second cousins, but Abuelo and Abuela couldn't make it either for health reasons.

On Sunday at the brunch the day after, we found out that Abuelo had fallen out of his bed and died the day before the wedding. I'm grateful that they waited to tell us until after the wedding. He had been ill for a long time, but it was still a terrible blow and loss to us all. Carlos wrote a very touching tribute to his grandfather and posted it on Facebook that weekend.

The wedding itself went without a hitch. It was all outdoors in a garden on an estate used for functions like this. And God was good: it didn't rain, even though we were in the "green" part of Texas. Caroline flew in from San Francisco, as did Angie from Palm Springs. Carlos had specifically asked Angie to be part of the wedding. I was so touched by this, and I knew that he had forgiven his sister for stealing from him years before. He asked her to do a reading during the ceremony. I'll never forget how beautiful she looked, in a long, black Chinese dress with pink flowers stitched along the seams.

In the cabana the wedding party used to shower and change, Angie and Caroline were fooling around and giggling like they used to growing up. Of course I was nervous about everything going smoothly for the wedding, but somehow I had no fear that Angie would spoil things with some ugly scene. No fear at all. It was almost, for one glorious weekend, as though the previous eight years had just been a bad dream.

The reception was really sublime — lots of great food that Carlos and Carrie had planned, capped by a red velvet wedding cake. Gene and Carrie's dad are musicians, along with a number of Carlos's friends from college. They set up a band and had a grand old time showing off their talents. We danced and danced until I thought my feet would fall off. But the best parts, the parts that stay with us forever in our memories, were the toasts. The toasts were wonderful and memorable, but for the father of the groom, Xavier, this was one of his sterling moments. I don't remember exactly what he said, so I let the pictures tell me. Xavier and Carlos embracing, Xavier with tears in his eyes. And the photographer caught a candid of other guests reacting to the toasts. This guy really knew where to put his camera lens. He caught Angie wiping a tear away from her eye.

It had been years since I'd seen my daughter show that level of emotion. I had such a peaceful and happy feeling that day. I felt at long last that this was a time of healing for our family.

In the months ahead, there would still be times when, given the opportunity, I would cleave to her, I would spoil and indulge her. I would bend my rules, readjust my boundaries, and ignore my gut feelings. Severing the umbilical chord, separating from my daughter, would be terribly hard. My illness kept me stuck too; I was very stubborn.

This journey of mine, this parenting journey, would involve going two steps forward sometimes and then three steps backward. It was not vertical progress I was making, but it was progress. And strangely, the more I kept the focus on myself and striving to be happy, the easier it was to let go of my child. I knew I had paid my dues, and I feared no one's judgment, least of all God's.

I've railed at God many, many times during these dozen years of joy and pain, this God they speak of at Twelve-Step meetings. How many times had I sinned in my life? Many, more than I want to remember. And so the child in me had been sure, earlier on, that I was being punished for all of them. It was my karmic payback. "What goes around comes around," etc. Indeed, for all of my life, before my breakdown, I had no faith in any thing or any one other than myself. I grew up very lonely and isolated, and if there was a god, he wasn't paying any attention to me. So I learned to be very independent and self-reliant.

But when I finally found myself on my knees, I felt broken and whole at the same time: broken because my MO for dealing with my problems hadn't been working; and whole because I finally let myself believe in something outside of myself to strengthen me, to fill in the gaps that were missing in me, and to help me cope. I was starting to develop and cling to a faith that assured me that I was not being punished and that I would be OK in the end, no matter what happened to my daughter. And I realized that fighting Angie's battles for her was not only a waste of time; it was also useless and of questionable value.

My energies, spent though they were, would be better directed toward reclaiming my own life, which had been sorely compromised in the fight to save my daughter. And in reclaiming my own life, I was bidding for my redemption, long overdue, but just within my reach. This was my journey now, I knew it; I sadly accepted it. I wanted us to be connected but we weren't. I wanted her struggle to be our struggle, but it wasn't. I wanted to save her life but I couldn't. I could only save my own. And I'd keep working at it, tirelessly, or this relentless disease would claim two more victims instead of one.

And so, graduated from her fourth rehab facility in May, Angie transitioned into a sober living house in Palm Springs. There were lots to choose from. This was a Mecca for rehabs and sober living houses. The fact that she was willing to live in one gave us hope. The fact that she stayed in two rehabs back to back for four months gave us hope. A few of my friends had kids who just walked out of their rehab, as Angie had in her second one. *As long as she's alive,* I thought to myself, *there is reason to have hope.* Hope, I discovered, is a living, breathing organism; but it must be fed in order to survive. I fed it and nurtured it like a flower; when its leaves wilted, I gave it more water. I carefully nourished my hope because beyond that there was so little I could do. She was three thousand miles away from us and so vulnerable. Angie's Mother's Day card to me that spring of 2009 was a tangible reminder of the precious daughter I had known before Addiction claimed her: "Mom, I love you so much. Thank you for not giving up on me. {heart symbol} Always, Angie." Cards like that, quite naturally, filled me with optimism. For days, I felt like I was walking on air.

In her memoir about her daughter, Carrie, Carol Burnett shares a diary entry. Carrie was midway through one of her times in a treatment center:

> "Dare I hope? YES. I'm not going to fear the worst. I'm not going to give fear any more power over me. I'm going to hope for the best" (30).

In retrospect, I wish I'd had the funds to lock her away somewhere for at least two years. As they say in the Program: "It takes time to get time." If I had accomplished anything by putting her into four rehabs between 2002 and 2009, it was buying her some time. I'd hoped and prayed that she would straighten her head out if she could just stay alive long enough to do so. She needed sober time, a lot of it, first of all to reverse the brain damage that had altered her personality and then to try to put the pieces of her shattered life back together.

June 5, 2009

Dear Angie,

I love you so much and I want you to be well and settled, but this may take a while. So I know that I need to just let go of the struggle, which isn't mine anyway, and have more faith that you will find your way to a sane way of life. Between meds and months of therapy, you have the tools inside of you now to do this. All you have to do is use them. This transition to the real world is difficult, I'm sure. But try to concentrate on the positive and be grateful: for being alive and clean, for your sponsor and the discipline you learn by going to meetings, for the humility you gain when you stop thinking you're in charge and turn it over, for the fact that you have a future and will eventually be working so hard that you'll wish you could be on vacation like you are now. Use this time to grow, reflect, read, grow up, and care about other people far worse off than you. As to the volunteer commitment you would have to make, I understand why you can't in case you get a job. But you probably won't work on weekends. Surely in all of Palm Springs, there must be some place that could use a weekend volunteer!

I love you, Angie. Be well; do good things, Mom

Angie eventually found a job as a bartender in an upscale restaurant in Rancho Mirage. We paid the rent, but she was responsible for her other expenses. Her life revolved around Twelve-Step meetings and other recovering addicts. One day I received a welcome phone call:

"Hi Mom. Guess where I am! My sponsor took me on a ride on a tram in the San Jacinto Mountains! It's gorgeous up here. I can see for miles and miles."

"Thanks for calling, Angie, and sharing this with me. I love you!"

I always ended our communications with those three words. Even if we were fighting, and the words got ugly, I made sure she knew that I loved her. I no longer took for granted that this was just another phone call. I never knew if this was going to be the last one. High up on the mountain with her sponsor, could they see what was coming? In the movie *Out of Africa*, Karen Blixen said, referring to her imminent illness, "The world was made round so that we couldn't see what was coming down the road." And that's a good thing. How would our lives be altered if we all had a crystal ball?

That summer I wanted her to come visit and see our farm in the Southwest. In she flew from sunny Palm Springs to sunny New Mexico, and it was a joy to have her with us for a few days. Angie is, among other things, a very talented artist, and I asked her to paint a little sign naming our farmhouse Casita del Mar, so named because of my huge shell collection. It still hangs on the post in my front courtyard, though in the years since her visit it has sustained a lot of weather damage.

We had fun, tooling around Santa Fe, and visiting the Georgia O'Keeffe Museum. I knew she would appreciate seeing this artist's work. Angie had a gift for expression, both in the spoken word and in her renderings. As a child she wrote a lot of poetry. She also could capture on paper a face or expression with great accuracy. In art school I was good at drawing elevations and brick walls, but I couldn't begin to draw someone's face. Angie had a great gift.

We continued north up the slow mountain road to the Taos Pueblo, where we visited a potter we knew and bought some more of her pieces. The next day we took Angie up the tram on Sandia Crest, where you can see for miles in three directions. Looking out for hundreds of miles—and looking within. I knew I was doing a lot of that in my own recovery, but Angie never shared her recovery work with me. On our last day together we celebrated her birthday at dinner in Corrales. Of course, she had to get back to work. We hugged at the airport and said goodbye. Again, there were so many goodbyes—so much uncertainty. I will never allow complacency into my life again. I will never, ever, take a moment of happiness for granted.

Matriarch

My mother, Angie's beloved Nana, died two months later in October 2009. I had retired from my teaching job eighteen months before, so now I had the freedom to visit her every three months or so. While I was in Massachusetts three weeks before she died, I went to see her every day where she was living.

Mother was ninety-nine when she died. The average length of time spent in a nursing home is less than two years. Mother was confined in three different supervised settings for three years. How can anyone live that long? She was a stubborn lady. But her obstinacy couldn't save her from the slow growing cancer in her lung that had taken root two years before. Lucy and Bill had elected not to attempt invasive surgery at that point — just let it run its course.

It did just that, but very slowly. She was bedridden most of the time, so the cancer grew about as quickly as her body moved. But when the tumor started growing, it took off with a vengeance, and I'm so grateful she didn't linger more than a couple of months. It was frightening to watch. I couldn't bear to see my mother suffer.

She wasn't in pain like so many cancer patients. The way she died was worse, I think. She couldn't breathe. You can control pain with medication. But how can you clear your lungs of the cobwebs that made every breath smaller than the last? The struggle alone was terrifying: taking a breath as we normally do a million times a day and having it yield so little. Mom called the nurse in a panic, her eyes pleading, and said she couldn't breathe. By now, we had brought Hospice on board, and they had authorized a little crushed morphine be put under her tongue to calm and relax her. It didn't cure the cancer, but it allayed her fear. Mother opened her mouth like a hungry bird so they could put the medicine under her tongue.

"Here ya go, Mrs. C., this'll make ya feel betta," Julie offered, in her best Southie accent. The nurses there were very kind and I know Mother appreciated it.

"Feeling better, Mom?" I asked as I held her hand.

"Yes, Maggie, thank you for being here," she said, squeezing my hand before she closed her eyes.

I stared out the window. It was painful for me to witness this. Growing old must be the loneliest feeling in the world. I thought of all the times I had needed her to talk to when I was young and she had shut me out of her bedroom, sobbing on the other side of the door. I'm sure at times I did the same thing to my own children. Mother's depression got worse as Daddy's alcoholism intensified. And I was sucked into this sad trio of human interaction, feeling extremely depressed myself and unable to break away. I had felt so helpless in my isolation all those years ago.

But now my mother was the helpless one. I didn't care anymore what my mother had done to hurt me in her life; I was over it. I could only feel great compassion for her. Here in front of me lay the matriarch of our family, nearing the end of her life. I had learned many things from this woman in the schoolhouse by the lake. Both of us had been thrown into the maelstrom of addiction and we had both been wounded by its effects. In the end, though, my mother demonstrated an ability to let go of the control that had been strangling us all in different ways. She surrendered the fight, the anger. We shared forgiveness with one another. And I would become able—a few years down the road—to let go of the stranglehold on my daughter—my addiction to her—and let her continue on her journey in her own way. The compassion I felt for my mother spread through me like a warm tonic. And I would pass it on to my daughter, a final gift from her Nana.

When she was awake, I repeated my assurance to her that she would be crossing over to a better place where all her loved ones would be waiting for her.

"Do you really believe that, Maggie?" she asked me, full of skepticism, but at the same time with hope in her eyes.

"With all my heart, Mom."

I wanted Mother to believe that her aged body was just a prison she would soon be free of. I don't know if telling her about my faith helped her at all. But she did stop clinging to life quite so tightly. The morphine helped; it relaxed her. And she started to let go.

The last day I saw her she was given morphine twice, and was pretty out of it, so we didn't talk. I didn't mind. I had already made my peace with her years before. I had nothing more to say. I just sat on her bed and held her hand as she dozed. It was getting late and I needed to go, so I said,

"Bye, Ma. See ya later. I love you." Then she opened her eyes and answered:

"Bye, baby. I love you too."

She didn't cling this time and beg me to stay like she usually did. She just let me go. It's such a powerful lesson, this letting go thing. When I think of all the years I've gone through in my life, sometimes joyfully, sometimes with sorrow, it is the letting go of the things we most cherish that for us is most difficult.

My mother and I had had a very difficult relationship for a long time. She criticized me harshly for many of the choices I made in my life. Her perfectionism suffocated me, and for years I felt the weight of her on my back. She used me to live out her unfulfilled dreams as much as she could. Her discomfort around my obesity and other embarrassments cloaked her love for me. Yet at that point I, a grown woman now, could distill everything into that one simple thing: her love for me. No matter how she parented, she loved the three of us very much, as best she could, just as I have always loved my children. I could overlook her shortcomings, so laden I have been with my own. In the end, I was able not only to make peace with my mother but also rejoice in the time we had left, however she wished to play it.

In that moment, rejoicing was as simple as holding my mother's hand as she faced death. And most important, most important of all, it was the sublime knowing as I admired the zinnias and marigolds in the garden that I had done the work necessary to forgive my mother and let her go.

Just as she let me go. Just as I must let her granddaughter go. I was grateful that she had stopped asking about Angie. Even though at that moment Angie was in recovery, Mother had never been told about her struggle with drug addiction. She had last seen my daughter several years earlier when Angie flew to Massachusetts to see her. But Angie relapsed right after that visit, and my mother never saw her again. I wondered if she had any intuition about what had been happening to Angie. Would she have preferred her granddaughter dead to the life she had been living while she was on drugs? I'll never know. But I didn't feel that way. It was going to be an uphill battle for Angie, but as long as she was breathing there was still hope for her recovery.

All the years of coming up to Massachusetts to see my aging mother, I always wondered if each visit would be the last time I'd see her alive. She would always insist on walking with her walker to the front door of the nursing home so she could get one last peek of me driving off. She loved the drama of saying goodbye. Maybe she was rehearsing for her final bow.

"Pull around the front as you leave so I can blow you a kiss."

"OK, Mama. I love you. I'll be back again soon," as I gave her a big hug.

I Remember Mama was one of her favorite movies, the one with Irene Dunne and Barbara Bel Geddes. Mother's fantasy was to have a family like that: so functional, so normal, so full of love and forgiveness and, most of all, the mother of the family was worshipped as a tower of strength and perfection by her daughter. Mother wished to be adored by her children; she wished she had been the perfect parent and hadn't felt so guilty about her shortcomings as a wife and mother.

"Have I been a good mother, Maggie?"

"Of course, Mom. You did the best you could."

Just as I have. This was a key component to letting my mother off the hook; I needed to be equally kind to myself and let myself off the hook if I was going to live well in the years I had left. She asked me the same question every time I saw her. There was no quenching her thirst for forgiveness. But I had forgiven her years before, and all I could do was assure her over and over. I know that "being a good mother" is not the same as "doing the best you can." But this is how I chose to leave things with my mother as she neared death.

It was a great weight lifted off my back, and I kept hoping that the angels would carry her off soon. Between the guilt she couldn't seem to free herself of and the growing cancer in her lung, living was becoming more than she could bear. And I wished for her to be set free.

I often feel the same way about Angie. Angie's guilt must be hard to bear. It's unbelievable what my daughter has done to herself and others under the influence of drugs. Her moral fiber has been girdled, like the bark on a tree. She's left now, vulnerable, to the needs of her master, Addiction. This thief has robbed her of her dignity, her very self. She, like my mother, is in the grips of something outside of herself. Mother had lived a long life and was preparing to cross over to the other side. But what about Angie?

Still more questions sprout like seeds in my mind. All my talk about morality and guilt—perhaps I've been projecting my own issues onto my daughter. Maybe, in fact, Angie feels little or no guilt. When she's under the influence of drugs, it's hard to know what thoughts or feelings are driving her. But I do know that this journey has been very much about separating in a healthy way from my daughter. And that would involve keeping my issues to myself to work through, and leaving Angie to hers. It might surprise me one day to discover that they're very different.

That day as I walked out of my mother's room, I turned to look at her one more time. When she was young, she was a striking beauty, with brunette hair. As she aged her hair lost its color prematurely. I'll never forget the dreadful blue rinse she used to put on her hair to cover the gray. Then there was the reddish dye. Finally, I'm not sure exactly when, she stopped messing with the color and one day, like a full moon against a dark sky, her hair was as white as freshly fallen snow. It was gorgeous.

Her eyes had closed and she looked so peaceful. This time, I knew, was the last time I would see her in this body. I just knew. But I didn't feel sad. I didn't run back to her and hug her one more time, the way we do when we want to push back death. Any anxiety, had I done that, would have transferred right to her, undoing all the journeying Hospice was at that moment attempting. But I had no anxiety. I walked away. I knew she was embarking on her own journey now, and there was only room for one passenger.

When Bill's wife called me three weeks later and told me Mother had died at ten o'clock the night before, I let out a small cry but that's all. Lucy and her grandkids had been by to see her in the afternoon, but they went home for dinner. I wonder if my sister knew, as I did, how close our mother was to crossing over. The nurse said that Mother picked at her dinner a little and went to sleep early. Mother was very willful—just like me, just like her granddaughter—a real triumvirate of wanting to do things our way. But in the end, finally, she gave up her will to God and let Him take over. She never woke up.

There was no funeral, and Mother was cremated. Lucy planned a beautiful memorial service for our mother three weeks later. But the thing about living that long is all of your friends are probably dead and can't make it to the service.

Her only sister was ailing in South Carolina and couldn't make the trip. But the three of us attended with our children, along with assorted cousins and her one remaining sister-in-law, my Aunt Mimi, Daddy's sister. Angie was in recovery during this period, so she flew in from Palm Springs. For once, her problems were eclipsed by her Nana's death. How lovely that Angie, who was much beloved by her grandmother, was there when it counted.

It was a gorgeous fall day where we all gathered at the chapel for the service. A few of the brilliant reds were still clinging to the trees, paying homage to Mother and her love of bright colors. Angie sat in the pew behind me with other family members. I don't recall any sense of awkwardness among the guests or any nasty looks sent her way. People had other things on their mind.

Whatever any of us had thought of my mother, she was a force to be reckoned with for many of her ninety-nine years. She had had a number of friends she was devoted to, she spent years of her life in volunteer service, and she did the best she could as wife and mother. My father adored her until the day he died, and the three of us, especially Lucy, doted on her endlessly right up until the end. So I'd say my mother had a very good life.

From the chapel we drove around the winding road on the beautiful cemetery grounds and met at the family crypt where Mother's ashes were placed next to our father's in the family vault. The minister made a few remarks and it was over. The ceremony of our mother's passing.

As I stood under the swaying trees saying goodbye to my mother, Angie saw me staring at her across the grass. When our eyes met, I wondered what all this had meant to her. We held each other's gaze for a long time, clinging perhaps to this interlude of her recovery. I, certainly, clung to the hope that being here with her family would make a positive difference to her.

What was she thinking? What was behind those deep brown eyes, once so full of love for her family? I should have asked her, but I didn't. I had no answers that day as we all turned and walked back to our cars and went our separate ways.

Every year that passes I understand my mother more, as I am learning to understand myself. Whatever it is that enables us to forgive our fellow man—for big hurts or little ones—I have been graced with it. Will my children miss me when I'm gone? I don't know. But I can only live my life as best I can now, using the losses and lessons of my life wisely. I thanked my mother often in later years for all she had done for me, and I'm so grateful that I was able to do that. She loved and accepted me when I needed it later on in my life. I know when we meet again, she'll be happy to see me. And I'll be happy to see her.

Coming Home

I was an orphan now. My father had died twenty-four years before, his body ravaged by too many years of alcohol and cigarettes. Now Bill, Lucy and I needed to go to the front of the line. But death doesn't always work that way. Often it culls the young who haven't lived very long, prematurely separating them from loved ones. It also takes the young — many of them, mercifully — who have lived too long. Now that she had witnessed the passing of her grandmother, and observed the finality of death, would my daughter remain firm in her recovery and stay with us all who love her — among the living?

Angie's six-month agreement to stay in sober living was up, and she had to make a decision. Was she going to stay in Palm Springs or move on? She decided that Palm Springs had been a good place for her, so she found another recovering addict who needed a roommate and moved in with her. This woman was a nurse, and well into her recovery, and the living situation worked out very well. I kept trying to keep the lines of communication open:

November 19, 2009

Dear Angie,

I hope you're doing well. I'd really like to hear from you on a regular basis so that I can know for sure that you're fine. Trust takes a long time to reestablish, and I never know how you're doing if I don't hear from you.

I've been thinking about you kids a lot. You've always had such a big heart. When Carlos and Caroline were out on their bikes or with friends in Greece, you were sitting on the balcony with Nana watching the sunset. Day after day you spent time with her like this. And when we came back to the States, you were the one who left your friends and interests in the summer to go and spend time with Nana. See what I mean? Your heart is very big. We're all so glad you came to Nana's memorial service last month. I'm sorry we didn't have more time together. I know you had to get back to work.

I look at your Mother's Day card often. You know I'll never give up on you. Please let me help you secure a healthy future by getting your interferon treatment done. Don't procrastinate. You need six months to complete it, and you said you wanted to leave Palm Springs by next June.

Last year at this time, I thought you were dead. This year at Thanksgiving, I'm full of gratitude that you're alive. ☺

Much love, Mom

P.S. Not this Christmas, but next Christmas, I'm planning to go to San Francisco to spend time with your sister. It would be cool if you could join us there. Carlos will be with Carrie's family in Buffalo, so it would be a nice reunion for the three of us.

November 27, 2009

Hi Angie,

Thanksgiving I was alone this year, so I went down to serve turkey dinner to the homeless people at the mission in Arlington (remember when I used to take you and Caroline to do the same thing?). Then I went to a Program friend's house for dinner and had a wonderful time. How did you spend the day?

Call me soon, so we can chat.

Love you, Mom

But life keeps happening. Every day that we get out of bed, we make choices, judgment calls. One day in November, just after Thanksgiving, Angie made a bad one at work. She neglected to ID someone who was buying a drink. He turned out to be an undercover cop, and she was fired on the spot.

She was very badly shaken by this, though we tried to convince her that it was a mistake anyone with so little experience as a bartender might have made. Oh, how I tried to control her reaction once again to life as it was happening! How I tried to cushion her from the pain of life's simple ups and downs, as if my telling her it was no big deal would sink in to her mind.

She knew we were on her side, that we weren't judging her. But this was one of those times when I would cleave to her and indulge her, against my better judgment. The holidays were upon us, and she was lonely for her family. She had just been fired from her job, she felt like a failure, and she wanted to come home. So we said yes. We sent her the plane ticket.

Hindsight is 20/20. I should have realized how vulnerable she was at that point, and that bringing her back to the D.C. area, where it all began, might have become a disaster.

But at first, having Angie back in the area was great for her father and me. I was commuting between New Mexico and my condo because I still had a contract job with my old school district to finish up. She wanted to live right in D.C. because commuting to a job would have been hard without a car, and, bless her heart, Priscilla, her old high school friend, said she could sleep on her sofa as long as she needed to. So that's where Angie landed. She got a job walking dogs, no surprise, and came out to Virginia weekends to stay with me in my condo.

That February there was a mammoth snowstorm in the mid-Atlantic region, often referred to as "Snowpocalypse," and we were snowbound together. For the first time in years, we enjoyed each other's company. She even offered to shovel me out. We played scrabble two, sometimes three times a day, and she almost always beat me.

"Angie, let's play another game. I'll make us some tea."

No matter what she was doing she dropped it and joined me. This was a one-on-one activity, being together close up for an hour at a time that was precious to me at this point. And she never refused or had something better to do.

"Sure. Make mine chamomile, OK?"

I tried but I usually couldn't beat her. She had a steel-trap mind. I remember how she used to do all those Sudoku puzzles that I couldn't fathom.

"Well, you beat me again. But by a narrower margin."

"Mom, you're really good. You just need more regular practice with a good player. When you get back to Gene, he'll help you bring the level of your game up."

"Thanks, honey," as I hugged her on the way to the kitchen. "I'm just glad to have you here with me now."

"Me too."

God, I felt so happy with her then. Though she wasn't my little girl anymore, I started to feel a little like she was the person I had raised. Living with her on weekends I saw things I didn't see when she was in Palm Springs. She was considerate and sensitive toward me, for one thing. Yet I knew that not enough time had passed to really test the strength of her recovery. I knew that she needed much more time. And so

I didn't let myself get too comfortable or relaxed around her. My gut was telling me to slow down; don't get your hopes up too quickly. She didn't get this sick overnight, and she wasn't going to get well any quicker.

Angie came out to stay with me at the condo just about every weekend, and on one of these visits I had to take her to the emergency room. She had a bad case of cellulitis in her hand and needed a heavy dose of oral antibiotics to clear it up. As we were leaving the doctor said that if the oral meds didn't work she would need to be hospitalized for IV treatments. I was a little puzzled by this; it looked like a simple infection to me. Why, possibly, would she need such extreme intervention? Angie explained it away as a symptom of her hepatitis.

I should have seen what was right in front of me; I should have questioned her bland explanation. A year later when I got more educated about drug addicts and what they do when they run out of veins would I realize what had really been going on. These last few years I've gotten more involved in support groups around addiction, and I've seen a few movies about what addicts do, where they inject. Strange places I hadn't thought of: their ankles, their necks, and their hands. At the time, I didn't realize what she had started doing—again. At the time, I was too focused on my daughter promising to rebuild her life—again. At the time, I didn't dare face the fact that bringing her back to D.C. might have been a very bad idea. But this suggestion that I played a role in her relapse is what the Program calls "stinkin' thinkin." I accept now that she could have relapsed anywhere, anytime. It wasn't my fault.

Maybe it was good that I had an opportunity to get away. My sister had asked me to come up to Massachusetts so that we could divide up all of Mother's things. Mom had been gone now for six months, and it was time to let go of her material possessions.

Angie was back at Priscilla's, and so I drove up to Massachusetts in late March. I put Angie out of my mind and put an audio tape on to listen to on my trip, *The Shell Seekers* by Rosamunde Pilcher. I loved this romantic story of love and loss, of a dysfunctional family and how they worked through their difficulties to emerge stronger and happier together, at least in the movie version.

Interestingly, it was one of Mother's favorite stories too. This particular story involved dividing up among her three children Penelope Keeling's most valuable possessions: her father's Victorian paintings. Our family, too, struggled over material things as symbols of Mother's love. It often happens in families when wills are read and possessions are dispersed that uncomfortable feelings spring up: feelings of loss, abandonment, and so often, entitlement. But on this visit to see my sister, getting my share of Mother's love took a back seat. She would reveal to me a secret that might explain a mystery that had haunted me all my life—and would sorely test my recovery.

Sistah

It's a long ride up to Massachusetts from Virginia, and I was tired when I pulled up to her house. But I was just in time for dinner. She had one of my favorite meals ready for me: Swiss chard sautéed with goat cheese. I appreciated that, and a relaxing glass of wine, and her insisting I go upstairs to bed afterwards. We'd have plenty of time to catch up the next day.

For the first few days we were enjoying our time together. We tooled around to thrift shops, one of our favorite pastimes. Her grandkids came over so I could see how they had all grown. I took her and her husband out to dinner at a favorite seafood restaurant to thank them for their hospitality.

But we had work to do. We had to divide up Mother's things that were taking up too much room in her basement. One morning, she called upstairs to me as she was putting her laundry in the dryer:

"Maggie, I'm in the basement. After you finish your coffee come on down and let's go through as much as we can this morning."

"Sure, I'll be right there."

We pored over every scarf, every skirt, and jacket. I hated Mother's taste in clothes, nor did anything fit me, and Lucy felt the same way. So most of the clothes went to Goodwill. I took some books and other small items. There was a lamp and a table in Lucy's attic that I wanted, and they fit in my car, so she let me take them. The family albums were hard to divide up, so Lucy's husband spent a couple of hours that morning Xeroxing pages that we both wanted so that we could both have them.

As we were finishing up our work for the morning, my sister approached me where I was standing and looked me right in the eyes.

"Maggie, there's something I've been meaning to tell you. When you were born, actually before you were born, Mother and Daddy sent me to live with Aunt Lila in New York. Apparently, Mom couldn't handle Bill, me, and a new baby. So I lived there for about a year before we all moved up to Massachusetts."

I looked at her, incredulous: "Why didn't you tell me sooner? Why did you **never** tell me?" I felt as though I had been hit with a jackhammer, as though so many truths I had been clueless about were jarred loose inside of me and were tumbling out all at once like so many puzzle pieces, needing to be reconnected.

"I don't know. It was too painful for me to talk about."

It was too painful for you to talk about? I thought to myself. *What about painful for me to live through?* This was the missing piece that made sense to the puzzle now. Looking back, I wonder how Lucy might have felt when I entered the picture and she was sent to live with our aunt. My head was spinning with all the repercussions of our parents' decision. Why had no one told me? They had all watched me growing up, so lonely, depressed, acting out and wildly rebellious, developing eating disorders, in need of intensive therapy. How could they be so blind? Didn't it occur to anyone that my problems might have sprung at least partially from this event that our parents had set in motion before I was born?

I was too stunned to respond to this news. I've never had an ounce of wit, never been able to respond in the moment, or appropriately, to news that leveled me. At least not in that moment, not with my sister in March 2010, after all the work we had done on our relationship and all the inroads we had made together as adults. I didn't want to toss our relationship away because of what I perceived to be an incredible oversight. And anyway, it wasn't an oversight to her. She had been in terrible pain her whole life for having been sent to live somewhere else. She didn't care about my pain; she was consumed with her own. When I asked her over the phone once: "Didn't you feel any anger toward the baby whose arrival prompted Mother and Dad to send you away from your family?"

"No," she answered, "I wasn't aware of any anger."

As a child my six-year-old eyes saw my big brother leave home the year before and I felt abandoned. That child saw her father and older sister spending a lot of time together and she was jealous. And that same child sought solace from a depressed mother who was emotionally unavailable to her. These are reasons enough for many children to act out in their family. The problem in mine is that there was no healthy resolution, no justice — and no forgiveness. I was left to carry the burden and the consequences of my behavior. The difference between guilt and shame is that with guilt, we feel shame. For the latter, we feel down to the core that we are shame.

Whatever motivated me to lash out against my sister, feelings and events that followed set the stage for emotional illness and activated the addiction gene in me: first food and then later, drugs. But I didn't want to argue with Lucy then. I wasn't the same angry child anymore. And I wasn't the same angry young mother in the 1980's struggling with recurring bulimia.

When my children were little we used to spend summers with my parents in Massachusetts, and Lucy and I, both in our thirties, had many opportunities to get together. After I put the kids to bed, I drove over to her house and we had it out, night after night in an effort to work through and improve our relationship. I was so scared of her I used to shake like a leaf. I had always felt intimidated in her presence.

I vividly remember one night in July 1982. I parked the car on the street facing the way home so I wouldn't need to turn around. I might want to leave quickly. This evening I came over earlier. Mom and Dad would feed my children and put them to bed. Mother was anxious for me to see my sister as often as possible, because she knew we had serious issues to work through. Mom spent a lot of energy wringing her hands and wishing that Lucy and I could be closer. But it was out of her hands. We were grown women now and we needed to do the work ourselves.

I neglected to eat at home, hoping Lucy might throw something together so that we could relax over a meal before we started talking. I thought it might disarm her. I was wrong.

When I asked if she had anything I could eat, she was extremely put out. I couldn't believe my eyes, but she heated up some canned Franco-American spaghetti and plopped it down in front of me. Canned spaghetti! I always thought they looked liked wriggling worms as a child, and if I hadn't been so hungry I would have passed on them. She had a house full of veggies, fruit, cheese, and leftovers that she could have offered me. But I swallowed my meal, just as I swallowed my anger. I didn't say a word; I probably even thanked her. This was certainly an ominous start to our evening together.

"It's all about trust, Lucy, and your inability to trust me. I remember after I got married and I was visiting Mom at Terraces. You were there with a friend of yours and you were looking at all the bridal portraits. Your friend looked at yours and mine and remarked, 'Oh, you each wore the same dress when you got married.' You shot back without thinking, 'Yeah, that's something else she stole from me.' Don't you think I would have liked to have my own dress? Mother, of course, wanted to save money, so once again I got a hand-me-down! I was so mortified then, right in front of your friend, that you still, after all those years, thought of me as a little thief."

I had already started shaking. The angrier I got—and the more terrified—the more I shook. This was a physiological reaction I had had to my sister and confrontations with her for years. I was terribly embarrassed, and I never said anything. I think it probably would have baffled her. Years later when I told her of my shaking spells, she didn't say much. And then when I stopped having shaking spells, she said she was glad. To this day I don't believe she has ever understood or accepted the role our dysfunctional relationship had played in my growing illness as a young adult.

"Oh lighten up, Maggie. I was just joking."

"My ass, you were just joking. You've never gotten over my stealing your shoes. You would think, having raised three children yourself, that you would know something about sibling rivalry. But you've never been able to forgive me. I think part of you wants to, but you just can't let yourself trust me. I'm sick to death of feeling guilty for my behavior as a child."

Of course, the great irony was that so much of the resolution I sought might have been buried in the family secret I knew nothing about at the time. If I had known about Lucy being sent away I would have seen her in a completely different light. I would have reached out to her with the compassion she deserved. But since everyone kept it from me, I only saw a sister who didn't like me. I knew nothing of her reasons, which kept growing anyway because I kept behaving so horribly. Lucy waited until our mother was dead to tell me. Why? I guess we'll never know now what would have happened if secrets hadn't been so carefully kept for so many years. For one thing I would have asked her forgiveness for violating her space and possessions over and over again. I like to think that she would have forgiven me years ago when we were much younger.

My sister and I spent three or four summers like this in the boxing ring before I moved with my husband and children to Greece in 1987. But thirty-two years have gone by since we began those early and fruitless confrontations. We're grown women now with more years behind us than ahead of us. There's no question that Lucy was wounded at a very young age. There's no doubt, too, that I was an angry and increasingly depressed child. I look back on events in my life, but I don't dwell there. My recovery has given me much courage to consider other perspectives, to change my attitudes, and to move on in my life with an openness of mind and heart.

I've learned to let go of the past that I can't do anything about and focus on the present that I can change. I can choose to be grateful for all the lovely gestures Lucy has made and continues to make on my behalf. My brother and his family are very welcoming when I visit. Though we can't rewrite our past, it's enough for me to enjoy what we can in the years we have left. Between us there are fourteen great-grandchildren growing up, some of whom knew and loved our mother. Addiction is a sad inheritance, but my parents gave us an appreciation of many valuable things as well: all forms of music, literature, history, and the wealth of education. She and my father left a rich and lasting legacy.

My sister has three sons but no daughters. So I asked her to be Angie's godmother. She agreed, and there was a christening ceremony in Massachusetts at my old church when Angie was a baby. In my mind, this gesture on my part was a gift to my sister, and Lucy accepted it as such. So began a warm and special relationship with my daughter. Angie spent a number of summers in Massachusetts, and she and her aunt had a special place they always went to shop. It was on the wharf in a nearby town, a little place that sold all kinds of things related to shells—jewelry, wind chimes, and many large items like anchors on the back porch awaiting a buyer with a truck. My sister has always had a special fondness for Angie. It has been painful for her to watch Angie 's illness progress over the years and not be able to help her. She sent me an email recently: "I often think of Angie, and of how hard this has been for you and your family all this time. I hold her in my heart."

Another sign of our healing around my guilt issues are a number of birthday cards I've given Lucy over the years. One had an elaborate high heeled shoe glued on the front in 3-D. The message inside was, "When the going gets rough, the tough buy shoes."

I've gotten her a number of cards and objects with the shoe theme. I found a pretty jewelry case in the shape of a long boot that I've been holding onto for years. I know I had her in mind when I found it in a thrift store. I gave it to her recently; she should have it to put all her baubles in.

The fact that Lucy and I can laugh around the topic of shoes is a sign of our health and growing affection. In fact some of the best shoes I have are those she has given me. We exchange clothes, scarves, lots of things, but mostly shoes. She has bursitis in her feet and many shoes she bought in a hurry became too painful for her to wear. And since we wear almost the same size shoe—Mother, Lucy and I were nearly the same height and shoe size—she gave me her castoffs. And my sister, who has flawless taste, knew I'd be grateful. Her castoffs include $150 Dansko clogs which she may have worn once and which I wear every day. I don't remember the last time I had to buy any shoes, thanks to my sister. Isn't that ironic? In these acts of sharing and exchanging our possessions, she continues to show me that she is shedding the burden of carrying an old grudge. I'm grateful for that.

On that visit in March 2010, Lucy also told me that she had a small urn of some of Mother's ashes, and she offered to split them with me. Before the burial last October, Lucy had taken some of Mother's ashes for herself. And now she was offering to share them. I appreciated the gesture. I put some of them in the soil of a burning bush I have at my condo in Arlington. And I brought the rest back to New Mexico to put in my rose garden. But what were these ashes anyway?

"Mother" was not in these crushed bones, not to me. She was nowhere and everywhere. Our mother was what I chose to hold onto that was positive and good. My mother taught me the love of beauty and beautiful things. She showed me an appreciation for literature, the classics, poetry and opera. She taught me how to stretch a dime so I could have more things that mattered. She introduced me to volunteer work for all the right reasons, and those hours of helping others made me feel good about myself, a key component of my healing. My mother was not in these ashes. The best of her walks as I walk through life every day.

We spent the rest of my visit dividing up mother's earthly possessions: her jewelry, furniture and personal items. But it's funny how the circumstances and events of our lives change us. My children have been life's greatest gifts to me. Yet I have watched my daughter struggle with drug addiction since 2001. Jewelry, tables, and oriental rugs? I would sell them all and my soul with them, in a heartbeat, to see Angie healthy again and living well.

My ability to let bygones be bygones, and appreciate the best in my mother and sister, has everything to do with the

Twelve-Step work I've been putting into practice for twelve years, specifically Steps Eight and Nine:

8. Made a list of all persons we had harmed, and became willing to make amends to them all.

9. Made direct amends to such people wherever possible, except when to do so would injure them or others.

I've told Lucy more than once that I was sorry for the hurts I'd inflicted on her as a child. A few years earlier I looked her in the eyes and held her hands as I spoke to her. If I could undo it all I would, I told her. I asked her for her forgiveness, as I have learned to forgive myself. The rest has been, and continues to be, up to her.

The wisdom in the Serenity Prayer shines a light on my life every day:

"God, grant me the serenity to accept the things I cannot change, courage to change the things I can, and the wisdom to know the difference."

Now that our mother was dead I said, "Enough! We can't undo the past; we can't relive a thing. But our mother has died, and we can try to make the most out of what's left of our lives and be sisters. Whadya say?"

She said yes.

Cunning, Baffling, Powerful

Driving back to Virginia I had a lot to think about. But I put it all aside to focus on Angie. She continued to come out to the condo on weekends and she continued to beat me at scrabble, though competing with her made me a better player. We went for long walks together around Roosevelt Island on the Potomac River. Wishing to freeze that pleasant moment in time, I took a picture of her in front of the statue of Teddy Roosevelt. She looked so sad in that photo—almost bewildered—as if to say, "Mom, how did I get here in my life, and how am I gonna get out of here?"

Once again, life was happening, and this time we got a curveball we weren't expecting. Priscilla got a job in New York in May, she sold her condo, and Angie needed to find another place to live. She didn't want to be out at my house without a car, so she found a room in a house in D.C. and moved in with her few belongings. She wasn't walking dogs anymore but she worked in a bar nearby. Then the bar burned down, and she was out of work. Still, I didn't like the crummy neighborhood she was living in; she was riding a bike, and I felt she was a target in that section of the city.

But now my time was running out; my contract job at my old school was finished and I needed to get back to Gene in New Mexico. So I offered to let her live in my condo in Arlington. When she started to reject the offer, I reminded her that she'd have the place to herself; I'd be in New Mexico from now on.

Well, as I had feared months earlier, it did prove to be a disaster, Angie's coming back to D.C. The day I flew off to New Mexico in July, that same day, she entreated me to leave her the keys to my car. *She hasn't had enough recovery time*, I warned myself, *don't give her the keys; don't indulge her like this. You don't know that you can trust her yet. She hasn't proven herself to you."* I didn't listen to my gut, and I left her the keys to my car.

I started to get a little cocky over the summer, telling myself I made the right decision. We were in touch regularly. She was looking for work in restaurants, but she said no one was hiring right then. She saw her dad and stepmother every now and then for dinner. Xavier was a great cook, and she always devoured his meals. So I didn't worry.

Then, in late September, I got a call from a policeman in D.C.:

"Hello, Mrs. Romero? This is Officer Jones. I'm calling to let you know that I picked up your daughter going 70 mph on Beach Drive. I pulled her over and gave her a ticket for reckless driving. She'll need to come in to take care of this."

"Yes, sir. Thank you for calling and letting me know. I'm sorry, Officer, but I have to ask you this: did you check the contents of the car for drugs of any kind?"

"Yes, ma'am. We found a small amount of marijuana, so miniscule that we couldn't charge her with possession. But, believe me, Mrs. Romero, your daughter was on something. She was driving like a maniac."

"Thank you for calling, Officer. Goodbye."

We were enjoying our houseguests from California up to that point. But, as I had so many other times in these years of struggle with Angie, I felt I was back "in the valley of the shadow of death." I tried to hide my shock and grief from our houseguests, but I couldn't entirely. Gene's sister later told me that after the phone call the color had left my face, and she knew I must have had bad news. At the same time I was grateful that Angie hadn't hurt herself or anyone else. She dodged a big bullet there. Early October arrived, and it was almost time for me to go back to D.C. to check on things. But before I went, I received more bad news about Angie: she was near death in the hospital in Arlington.

Things come in pairs, or is it threes? I don't know. All I knew was that I had two daughters, and my younger one, Angie's sister Caroline, was also critically ill in a hospital in San Francisco at the very same time. I was in New Mexico in October, and I chose to fly to California to be with my younger daughter. Angie's father was in D.C., and I left it to him to handle the crisis with her.

Caroline had been living in San Francisco since she was eighteen. She was living an alternative lifestyle: a neo-flower child, new-age hippie — whatever they call themselves these days. She was very happy with her life there, and though they had grown up very close, she was as different from her sister as night was from day.

The choice I was making now was a concrete example of how I was letting go of my obsession with Angie, how I was perfectly able to choose one over the other. No matter what would happen down the road, I don't regret for a moment my decision to run to Caroline's side. And I don't believe, deep in my heart, that at that point in Angie's addiction, it mattered what I chose to do. It was beyond my ability to influence her, whether we were together or apart. This runaway train was refueled once again. And though at the moment derailed, she would take off again in search of, what? Peace? Redemption? Nirvana? To those of us who have loved her so well, that was and remains the great mystery. Why?

But in the Program, we learn to stop asking that question. I watch my friends week after week scratching their heads, desperate to understand why this has happened, and even more desperate to be relieved of the guilt that is consuming them. "Don't take my word for it," I tell them. "The AMA has declared that addiction in all its forms is a disease, and because of that insurance companies had better start stepping up more." I feel some of them don't want to listen to this. They want magic answers, the silver bullet that will end it all. If our kids are stricken with brain cancer, do we ask why? Why, then, do we torture ourselves with that same question that has no answer?

In any case, I was at peace with my decision. It was a warm October day when I flew into San Francisco, settled into Caroline's apartment, and went to see her in the hospital. She was deathly ill with Crohn's disease, tubes snaking in and out of every orifice I could see, including her heart. She was losing so much weight, twenty-five pounds and counting, mostly because they had to starve her to keep her digestive system completely clear. She was so sick, and hungry, it just about broke my heart.

There was nothing I could do for her other than being there by her side to hold her hand. Her friends, ex-boyfriends and all, hovered around, bringing scrabble boards and food when it was allowed. She was in good hands at this teaching hospital, and she was fast getting better. However, on a scale of 1 to 10, her Crohn's was an 8, a very serious case. She would need intravenous medication pumped into her every six weeks for the rest of her life. Knowing this, it was so hard to leave her after three weeks. But, ever the independent one, she encouraged me go without a fuss. She had lots of friends who would happily take care of her. And she knew that on the other side of the country her sister was also fighting for her life, and she needed me as well.

Another drama of sorts was unfolding at my condo in Virginia. I don't know if I'd call it a drama so much as clear irrefutable evidence of Angie's active and ongoing drug addiction. While I was on the West Coast with Caroline, and Angie was in the hospital, Gene's son needed to get clothing of his father's that was still in the condo.

I'd heard my friends recount the tales of their children living in the most squalid surroundings, seemingly oblivious to it all. And, remembering her place with Hope in Takoma Park a few years back, I knew that my daughter was no different. James unlocked the door and immediately had to cover his nose because the smell was so strong. Food left on plates, everywhere, rotting. Un-flushed toilets were on all three floors. But worst of all, the syringes, the crushed up pills on the bathroom sink. Clearly Angie was back full force in her disease. But right now, damage control was in order. I called my loyal cleaning lady Gladys and she came right over to clean up the mess. She had to come twice.

Gladys had known my daughter since she was twelve. She loved her like she loved her own child. Several times she went to see her in the hospital that was right around the corner from her house. It broke her heart, she told me, to see Angie in a fetal position like that. The nurse told her that she had nearly died.

By the time I got back to D.C. in late October, Angie had already been transferred to a rehabilitation facility in Annandale, Virginia. They couldn't justify keeping her in the hospital any longer, and they knew she had no insurance. She had a massive infection in her groin and needed a few more weeks of IV antibiotics. So they moved her to a very nice facility nearby, where she had her own private room.

Xavier and I went right back into our familiar mode: our daughter had nearly died, and we were grateful she was still alive. We spoiled her with special treats, and never once questioned that the infection was from a "bikini wax," an ingrown hair that had gotten infected. A bikini wax? Honestly, sometimes I think our brains had gone soft, her father's and mine, to still be so gullible and trusting this far into her disease. Later, Angie's stepmother went back to the hospital to talk to the nurse who had treated her. "That was no bikini wax, Mrs. Romero."

I visited her every day, and we talked a lot of Twelve-Step recovery. I wasn't pussyfooting around the topic of recovery anymore, and she was open to talking about working the Program. Nearly a decade had passed, nine years of her life lost, and I knew she wanted to get them back. We all did. My attitude and delivery had changed, though, over the years; I had changed.

At first, in the beginning of her illness, I was often too mortified and in shock to confront her. I was in a terrible state of denial and was blind, deaf and dumb much of the time. But in December 2001 I did react appropriately when I removed her from my house.

Gradually, I started to find my voice. I was getting a lot of help: therapy and support groups. I was starting to understand what had up until now been incomprehensible to me.

In time, but only sporadically, I began to assert myself and establish boundaries. I learned to push back, that I had a right to push back. My chest pains lessened in frequency and I very rarely have them now. My cardiologist gave me two separate tests, and concluded it was stress, nothing more.

Eventually I got to a place where I admitted—no, I accepted—my powerlessness over her disease, though it was counterintuitive for me to do so. By accepting her disease it still sometimes felt like I was giving up, like I didn't care. Nothing could be further from the truth. But I had to walk over a lot of hot coals before I would know how much I loved Angie. In time I became detached enough to look at her, feel nothing but compassion and love for her, and discuss things intellectually. It was no longer my personal mission to try to change my daughter into the person I wanted her to be. I was not Angie, and she was not me. We were separate people, and I no longer felt that her illness and/or what she chose to do about it reflected on me. This was tremendously freeing for me.

Or, as one parent writes in *Sharing Experience, Strength and Hope*: "Let go, or be dragged" (214).

Angie joked that she was like a cat with nine lives, and that she was running out of lives. She said she was working on her Fourth Step. That made me happy, as she knew it would. She was working on her moral inventory — this girl who had lost her moral compass years before — was she really going to find it again?

Angie stayed in this rehabilitation facility through Thanksgiving. She had a permanent catheter, called a picc line, in her arm that they pumped antibiotics into two times a day. She had been very, very sick, and this was standard procedure to flush her body clear of the infection in her groin. Xavier and I brought her a turkey dinner with all the trimmings, and we gave thanks that she was still walking among us. Silently we prayed to the Lord God Almighty that this second near-death experience would be the end of all our trials and that she would be ready and able to embrace life now.

But I no longer gave God lists of what I wanted. That's not how faith works. I was not in charge — He was. I had spent too many years hopping on and off this freight train to hell, and I wanted, I deserved, some peace in my life. Only by turning my willful, arrogant self over to Him would I be able to achieve the serenity, now and again, that they talk about in the Program.

And so, several years ago, I started keeping a daily gratitude journal. At its worst, it's a distraction from the pain of losing someone you love. At its best, it's a transformative tool. Every day when I wake up I write down something to be thankful for: from the gift of my grandchildren, to my favorite rosebush, now in full flower. And as the list grows, so, too, does my sense of abundance.

It's all so true: my attitude about my life is everything. And I was seeing on this journey of mine that I had a clear and irrefutable choice about how to live what was left of my life. I didn't want to be miserable anymore. It was my decision when I brought Angie home from that rehab facility to be happy. And I still feel that way. It all depends on how I choose to see things. And I choose to raise my spirits with a daily remembrance of all the good things in my life.

My best friend Jeanne and I had taught side by side at the same school in northern Virginia for many years. She was one of the few people who had borne witness to Angie's illness and decline since 2001. Jeanne had retired from teaching the previous June, and she built her dream house on the Outer Banks of North Carolina. She built this home on land that her father had bought years before. Fortunately, he was farsighted enough to know that land on the Sound side was a safer investment than oceanfront property.

Hurricanes have ravaged this fragile coastline for centuries. More recently Dennis, followed by Floyd a month later in 1999, soaked the state, causing record flooding. In

2003 Hurricane Isabel caused widespread power outages and downed countless trees. In 2011 Irene destroyed more than 1100 homes in the area. And Sandy in 2012, though she didn't make landfall, still caused a lot of water damage.

These storms have turned many beachfront homes into a crumpled deck of cards. Jeanne and I drove down the beach road to see the old devastation and felt very lucky that there was less damage on the other side of the milepost highway where she had built her retirement home.

Now that I live in New Mexico most of the year, I have missed the smell of salt in the air that I remember from spending summers at Cape Cod where my parents sent me away to camp. So whenever I come back East, I happily make the five-hour drive from D.C. to see Jeanne. Angie was home with me now, graduated from the rehabilitation center. It was early December, when we might still catch some of the migratory birds on the way south at the bird sanctuary down there.

And so that fall Jeanne invited Angie and me down for a few days of rest and relaxation. My friend thought it would be a good opportunity for my daughter and me to spend some quality time together. I would have made the trip anyway without her, but was so gratified that Angie chose to come. Another opportunity, I thought, yet another opportunity to show my daughter how much I still valued her, no matter what had gone before. Despite all my work in Al-Anon, a small part of me I wasn't even aware of anymore still believed that my love could propel her forward into her own recovery. I would be cured of that delusion soon enough.

The three of us first decided to take a long walk on the beach across the road from the bird sanctuary. I liked it that the beach was empty, so we had the pick of all the shells the tide had brought in. I have a huge collection of shells from several foreign countries as well as my own, so many that they overflow in both of my homes, some ending up in my rose garden as fertilizer.

The best ones I ever found were when I ripped Carlos off my nursing breast — milk spurting out all over the sand — and plopped him onto higher ground so I could race down to scoop up the contents of an incoming wave. He was seven months old, and Xavier and I were on our way back to the States from Guatemala, visiting the Yucatan in Mexico for the first time.

Before we went down the peninsula to see the temples on the east side, we stayed in Merida for a couple of days. We visited a few of the Mayan villages and went up to the northern beaches one day. I couldn't believe all the beautiful and colorful shells just sitting there for the taking. They were so small and seemingly hand-painted, unlike the big sun-bleached clams in New England. I brought home with me as many as I could fit into my carry-on luggage. The Gulf of Mexico, I decided, had the prettiest shells.

Three years later, again on the Yucatan with our toddler Carlos and his baby sister Angie, we stayed in a cabana near Tulum. Right on the porch front was a conch someone had left with a beautiful peach interior. It must have weighed five pounds with the animal dried out inside it. And it was bulky. I had two youngsters to carry and all our necessities — diapers, bottles, toys and books — for the trip from South America back to the States. But I somehow found the energy to drag that conch with me too. I'm not sure why shells are so important to me — maybe to show me that something always remains long after the occupants have left — a small dose of immortality.

Angie has lived with my shell collection collecting dust on the shelves in ten temporary and permanent homes we had been living in over the years. She knew how much I loved collecting them, how they brought me back to my roots in New England. Jeanne and I each had a bucket, and Angie had a plastic bag. There wasn't much brought in by the tide that day, but my daughter decided to walk in the opposite direction. She thought maybe she'd be luckier.

She was. As the wind was picking up, Jeanne and I were getting cold and decided to turn around and go catch up with her. I saw her running toward us in the distance and wondered what had lit a fire under her. Getting closer to us, I heard her exclaim excitedly, like when she was a child coming home from school year after year with a perfect report card:

"Mom! I found a whelk! A perfect whelk!"

With furrowed brow I said, "Let me see that. My God, you're right! Not a crack or split anywhere. How did you manage to find this among all the seaweed and garbage?"

"Good eyes, Mom. I have good eyes."

She still had good eyes then. She could still walk without a limp then. We could still enjoy being with each other then, on that day, in that blessed moment. She spoke with such confidence right then, as if she had completely forgotten what it had been like to lose herself. As if she were the person she once was before Addiction had claimed her.

Why don't we cherish and cling more fervently to good moments when they occur? Because we assume there will be more of them? This is why in the Program we learn to live "one day at a time." We learn to cherish the good when we have it because, as this disease has taught me, it could be gone tomorrow. Carrying the onus of our loved one's addiction for more than twenty-four hours is a terrible burden. Dwelling on yesterdays that we can't do anything to change, and focusing on a future that hasn't happened yet is an appalling waste of time. My ninety-nine-year old mother, so uncertain about death, and so grateful for every day she had left, used to repeat this saying to me over and over again: "Yesterday is history;

tomorrow is a mystery; today is a gift. That's why they call it the present."

This afternoon with Angie was a gift.

But just as the sunshine of Angie's discovery brightened my mood, the clouds descended once again, and she started turning mean. I suppose I should have been used to the mood swings by now. But they had been infrequent in our recent time together. And it's always hard to weather them. Especially with her near-death experience two months before, I had a very ominous feeling in my bones. I once again started to feel that Angie survived this time only to fall harder and deeper into the addiction that had been trying to take over her life.

It was getting very cold and we decided to visit the bird sanctuary the next day. We all piled into Jeanne's SUV and went home to fix dinner. My friend dropped Angie and me off at the house and went to the store to pick up some things we needed. Angie went upstairs to read in the living room while I changed my sandy sneakers into some warm slippers. Even though I was tired from our walk on the beach and would have liked to lie down, I didn't want to miss a moment of my time with Angie. And today had been such a happy day. So I walked back upstairs to join her.

As I approached the couch where she was sitting, she looked up from her book and the look in her eyes hit me head on like a brick wall. Oh, how I know this feeling, this dread. But it wasn't fear for myself anymore, as it used to be. Just fear for my daughter, fear that she was losing herself again. I knew Angie, and I knew that goat-eyed, soul-less look. I'd seen it many times in the past eight years. And I knew what it usually preceded — even before she opened her mouth.

Out of the blue, she started pounding away at me about the divorce back in 1991, how it was entirely my fault and how it destroyed Dad. "You never think about Dad anymore and how he suffered when you got divorced," she accused, turning to face me on the couch, her eyes two slits and her hands nervously fidgeting.

"Angie, where is this coming from?" I asked, anxiously reaching for some way to fend her off. "Your father has been married to Roxanne for fifteen years. I would hardly say I destroyed him." I sounded defensive. She knew how to wound me and access an old guilt I thought I'd been rid of. I moved nearer to her but stopped suddenly. An invisible wall erected itself. I didn't want to get closer.

This was the wall of pain that separates all addicts from their loved ones. It is not a smooth or pretty wall. It is repellant and odorous. It is rugged and high. Those who try to scale it are often at risk themselves.

"Please, honey, we're having such a nice time here with Jeanne," pleading with my addict to play nice during our visit, as if she had any power over her moods. "I don't know why you're thinking about the divorce right now, but it happened a long time ago and both your father and I have moved on with other people. Daddy's not destroyed and neither am I," I reasoned, again, trying to fend off the unpredictable Monster that took control of Angie's mind when I least expected it. "Can't you just let this go?" my plaintive tone again giving her (Addiction) power over me. Even as I begged, though, anger welled up in me. I was tired of getting pummeled; I didn't deserve it.

It was a senseless attack. It's like she was in a time warp and was still the hurt twelve-year-old that saw her parents separate and turn her world upside down. And maybe, in many ways, she still was, despite all the interventions she'd had over the years. In so many ways she was still that hurt child.

And short of returning into that time capsule with her where I relived every hurt I'd ever inflicted on her, begging her forgiveness, I didn't know how to help her. But there was also a voice inside of me screaming to get out, a voice that said "Enough! You've done enough! Have you learned nothing in recovery? Just let it go; let Angie and the illness that is mummifying her go. Whatever the course of events from now on, you know you don't have the power to alter them." Throughout my own recovery, this voice had been growing louder, and now I was listening, but it felt like walking on broken glass to do so.

Fortunately, we heard Jeanne's footsteps, and that put an end to this nasty exchange. I wondered if Jeanne had heard Angie yelling at me as she walked upstairs. I felt mortified, but Jeanne knew all about my daughter's addiction. I was sorry though that she might be getting a front row seat to the unfolding drama. Angie and I brushed it under the rug, for Jeanne's sake, the rest of the evening.

"Can I help you fix dinner, Jeanne?" she asked, as if being helpful and pleasant would produce amnesia in my friend.

"Oh, sure, honey, why don't you peel the potatoes and wash them while I make the meat loaf?" Bless her heart, Jeanne was going along with the charade.

It was amazing how Angie could pour on the charm when she wanted to. Gone was the brittle, cold addict hurling accusations at me. She was relaxed and even funny all evening. You would never know how she had just raged against me. A real Jekyll and Hyde—like my father was sometimes.

Relentless, mother-fucking disease, I screamed under my breath. *You are a demon, a life force all your own. How can any human being think that they have the power to fight you and win?* And those, like Angie, who want to think that they do have that power, are just being seduced, as Luke Skywalker would say, by the dark side.

The next day we kept busy and I was grateful for that. We could pretend the nasty specter of Angie's addiction wasn't once again knocking on the door. Jeanne knew, even if she didn't hear Angie's exact words, she heard her tone of voice. Later that evening she and I went for a walk outside, and she raced to my defense: "How dare she talk to you like that?"

Too frightened by the prospect of what might be coming, I simply put her off. "Oh, honey, you have no idea. This was nothing."

We left the Outer Banks early the next day, not looking forward to a five-hour drive back to northern Virginia. The SUV was crowded enough with all our suitcases, food, and other paraphernalia. But now we had another passenger. I felt the presence of her illness in all its demonic glory, and I know Jeanne did too, from having overheard Angie's outburst a couple days before. Jeanne told me months later that she thought Angie's tone of voice sounded really frightening. Welcome to the world of drug addiction, my friend. But fasten your seat belt. It'll be a bumpy ride.

By the time we got back to the condo, it was no longer a feeling; it was a certainty. Angie was falling fast again into the madness that wanted to reclaim her.

Made A Decision

The stressful climate of these past three months, from September through December, all the drama, were soon to wear me out even more. Things with Angie were going south fast. Our trip to North Carolina was just the beginning. In fact it all happened so quickly that I was too caught off guard to react appropriately. And the truth is, I knew too well what she was capable of, and I was starting to fear being around her—again.

The next three weeks were extremely tense and unpleasant at the condo. She was prickly, became annoyed at just about anything and was quick to pick a fight. Was this the same daughter who ten months before had loved hanging out with me, playing scrabble with me sometimes two or three times a day? It was the same body. But then I was remembering that back in March, before I went to my sister's, there had been signs of drug abuse, though I hadn't recognized it as such at the time. There was the speeding ticket and the certainty of the policeman that "she was on something." And finally there was the drama at my condo in October, the squalor, the needles, and nearly dying from a groin infection.

It was all so clear to me then as I was putting the pieces together. Angie was deep in relapse and had been ever since she came back to D.C. from Palm Springs last winter. And it was her father and I who had enabled her to come back here. But I wasn't responsible for what was happening. Yes, we brought her home, and the wheels of fate kept turning. Our daughter was an addict, and whether she was living in D.C.

or Uganda, Angie had a disease that she alone must wrestle with. At this point we could only stand by and watch. Angie knew what she needed to do if she wanted to fight her illness and get well.

She no longer wanted to be in the Washington area; in fact, she wanted to get as far away from it as she could. Clearly, she knew what she had been getting back into, and she thought she could run away from it in another place. She said she missed her sister and wanted to get reacquainted with her after so many years of estrangement. She knew I would warm to that, and perhaps over look that she had been treating me very badly as she slid backwards into the insanity of her disease.

There are many different kinds of pain: physical pain, say, from arthritis; emotional pain, from losing someone you love; and psychic pain, the kind that crosses the line to insanity. I'd known all three. And I felt myself, temporarily or otherwise, crossing over to a primitive place I'd never been before.

I've lost count of the dips and climbs on this journey and I saw that I was in for some more. But my breakdown a few years earlier was an excellent lesson for me. As a teacher I'm always looking for lessons and giving them away. Pain is one of the best teachers I know, and my pain was continually instructing me to let go. I wasn't always, though, a very good student.

I didn't know what to do with my building rage and frustration. So I took it into nature where I always had growing up, near the schoolhouse by the lake. "Where am I happiest?" the secret question to get into my bank account asked. "In the woods," I always answer.

It was a cold and very windy day in December, but I didn't feel it when I left the condo to get into my car. My internal engine had been heating up since North Carolina, and I felt something break loose inside of me. I knew where I wanted to go. It was as if the car were steering itself back to my kids' childhood home just ten miles away. And maybe to my own childhood home as well. We used to take our dog Oscar up to the woods next to the Potomac River to run free. I used to run free in my woods too.

I felt as though I had stepped outside of myself and been taken over by this raging, howling, maniac. Arriving at the park along the river, I parked my car in the lot and locked it, zipping my keys into my coat pocket. It was 2:00 p.m. on a Tuesday. Dog walkers and runners use this park and there's no time of the day when no one is here; it's a very popular place. But I thought there might be fewer people at this time, a lull before they came here after work. The days were shorter and colder now, and it was dark by 5:00 p.m.

I saw the brook on the left, much wider than my childhood brook. I walked along the wide footpath but soon left it and climbed the hill to the right. I was glad I was wearing my hiking boots to give me traction because I left the well-worn trail to go deeper into the woods. And I was glad to be wearing my heavy gardening gloves. There was no one around.

I felt as though parts of my life were raining down on me in these woods. This reckoning was long overdue. I was once again the little girl who longed to be close to her big sister and missed her big brother, the little girl who needed attention from her father, and the young woman who needed to be free of her domineering mother. Losing Angie again felt like a death to me even though it wasn't. There was no real closure, like the day I put Oscar down, Mahler's Ninth Symphony pounding in my head. I was back in the woods of my childhood where I could scream my frustration and no one would hear me. This was not my whole life—just the parts I needed to purge, the parts that held me back, and the ones that told me I deserved to lose my child.

"You had this coming to you!" the voice of Guilt shouted.

"NO I DIDN'T!" I screamed back, "No, I don't."

The leaves had already fallen to the ground and I could feel them kicking up from the wind around my ankles. I saw the branches moving so I knew it was windy but I couldn't hear the wind. The noise in my head was crowding out the sounds of nature around me. I felt my body once again inhabited by something bigger than me, taking over. But this wasn't the troll of my bulimia egging me on to numb my pain with donuts and ice cream. This wasn't my depression reaching for an easy pick-me-up. I wasn't depressed. I felt energized—far from the paralyzing sadness that had limited me when I was young.

I felt that day in December, with my temples pounding and hearing nothing but the train racing in my head, that I was powerful. I was reclaiming what was left of my life. I'd been in recovery for years and was happier because of it—no question. But often when Angie relapsed I'd felt myself start to crumble like a week-old cookie. I'd want to scramble to help her fight off the Monster. I'd start to cling, listen for her footsteps, and anticipate her movements, her moods, utterly lose myself in my codependency, allow myself to be controlled by the uncontrollable, and panic at the ensuing chaos.

"Can I drive you to a meeting? There's one in the same church as mine. Same time," I implored, as if going to a meeting would bring some order to the chaos.

"Mom, stop. You know I hate meetings."

When she said that I used to feel enraged, and impotent in my rage, with nowhere to go with it. Addiction had a life of its own. I had spent so much energy fighting a useless battle and worse, not allowing my daughter the dignity of fighting it herself.

But not this time—not this day—nearly a decade into her illness. For the moment, anyway, I was done. This struggle with Angie had worn me out, over and over again, and I wanted to put an end to it. All the hurt and pain from my childhood, all the agony of watching my daughter commit slow suicide, were racing through my head at breakneck speed.

I made my way to a clearing in the woods. I was, for a while anyway, transported back to Massachusetts. But I didn't go back there that day to revisit the judgments of my childhood. I went back to the same place where I had grown up to try to end the battle inside me—and the battle to save Angie—for so long seemingly one in the same—and now, forever separate.

Using my gloved hands I fashioned four small spaces—four bedrooms—my brother's at the end of the hall on the left, then my little room on the right, Lucy's big room next to mine, and our parents' room across the hall. These rooms bordered the center of the house, the family gathering place. But there was no big granite rock there, as there had been in my "courthouse," where I used to bang my "gavel" and pronounce judgment on myself. Here there was a huge uprooted ancient oak on the forest floor. So I straddled it. Looking up at the sky I watched the wind howl through the swaying branches. Then I studied my little house, remembering my life there all those years ago. And once again my anger and sadness found my voice. I yelled out loud, and I started sobbing.

I was raging against my daughter.

I was raging against the demon Addiction that had claimed her.

I was raging against that same demon that had claimed my father, and pushed him to an early grave.

I was raging against that same Monster that might have claimed me.

And I was raging against a God who took my childhood away and now was taking my daughter.

Then I remembered: God had nothing to do with it. All these years in the Program had brought me this far. I knew there was no one to blame, least of all God. Addiction is a terrible disease, made more terrible because it so often kills slowly, claiming not only the victim but also often anyone else who loves him or her.

And as I felt all the rage and frustration drain out of my arms, I let go of my childhood and left it there. Let the woods house my pain. They'd seen plenty of it.

Taking the first three steps of the Program again, I was restored to sanity. I, once and for all, made a decision to entrust my life to God. And I felt my faith return to me like a floodtide. I knew and had no doubt that whatever was going to happen from now on would be the embodiment of God's will. I would be OK, if I held onto my faith.

So, right after Christmas, I put Angie on a plane to San Francisco, and we said goodbye. I had no idea if this would be the right change for her, but I was heartened to know she would be back with her sister. And at the same time I was relieved to get her out of my house. I had been "saving up chips," as a former therapist used to say, lots of chips. I was furious with her for treating me so badly while she was living with me, and I was about to release the Kraken on my daughter.

I may have felt my faith restored, but that didn't mean I was abandoning my rights and ceasing to uphold them. I had a few choice words for my daughter, and they were long overdue—not the content so much as my attitude. I'd been treating her with kid gloves on and off since the beginning of this nightmare, and I was tired of it. Did it help, anyway, to ignore her and/or duck every time she came out punching? So I took the gloves off and sent her a letter soon after she got to San Francisco.

January 5, 2011

Dear Angie,

During much of your stay here, not all of it, but much of it, you behaved like a spoiled, self-centered, arrogant, ungrateful brat, and I will never tolerate you treating me so abusively again. It's good you got away from me; you are absolutely toxic for me to be around.

Your sense of entitlement is overwhelming, the way you prance around my home demanding this and that, all the while trashing your room so badly that Gladys could barely clean it. And speaking of Gladys, I was stunned that you didn't thank her for visiting you in the hospital when you were at death's door. I guess you're above thanking people who've been kind to you.

Not cutting me an inch of slack, too many petty complaints to mention, making an issue out of every goddamn imperfection in my thoughts or deeds, twisting simple, well-intentioned praise into an insult, expecting, and thinking you have a right to, much more than you got, the only thing you're entitled to is a giant kick in the butt.

I imagine in your mind you feel justified in treating me so badly. But I'm here to tell you: no, you're not, not now, not ever again. If you can't muster the consideration and respect that I deserve, then we need more space. And that's my recovery at work.

I hope the time away from me will give you a clearer perspective. I would love to have a healthier relationship with you. I love you very much. But I'd be a very poor parent if I let you get away with such unacceptable behavior. Right now, I seem to bring out the worst in you. So it's good that you are where you are, and I'm glad your sister is close.

I really hope you can one day learn how to be happy. Maybe things can be better between us. But that's up to you now. And in the meantime, good luck with the room search, job search, and all the other challenges that await you.

I love you, Angie. I say all this because I love you, Mom

She was in San Francisco now and crashed on her sister's sofa. Caroline, still recovering from her initial bout with Crohn's disease back in October, was very welcoming and didn't put too much pressure on her to find her own place. But Angie needed to find some space of her own and was fortunate within a couple of weeks to find a group home right around the corner from her sister, on Harrison Street. She bought a bike and enjoyed tooling around the Mission.

Then, while I was still reeling from December, she ended up in another hospital at the end of January, on IV antibiotics for the second time.

Whereto, Persephone?

Something snapped in me back in the woods of Virginia. Not because I saw with such clarity what Angie was falling back into. In fact, my wailing in the woods had very little to do with my daughter. Losing her to the madness of addiction was just the final loss in a string of losses I had never properly grieved or shouted out or laid to rest. Loss of self more than anything—that was my greatest loss. I'd been carrying the empty weight of that around since I was a child and I wanted to be free of it.

The way I'd been managing the challenge of Angie's illness, certainly in the beginning, reflected an unhealthy lack of self-regard much of the time. It wasn't my load to carry anymore and doing so only slowed my progress in my own recovery. Slowly through a decade of Twelve-Step work I'd become a better person, though being only human, I've had plenty of slips. But somehow Angie's latest relapse pushed me to the front of another perfect storm: of old useless attitudes confronting renewal, growth—and love. Love in all its forms: from detachment with love to a joyful embrace of myself. I was finally letting go of my painful past and moving forward lighter and freer.

Angie ran away from Virginia only to find out that she couldn't leave the addict behind. I'll never know exactly how she ended up in the hospital for the second time, and it doesn't matter. Angie was a grown woman learning to live in a new city. Her sister was close but unlikely to be drawn into her drama. Caroline knew a few addicts and knew plenty about addiction. But she was carefully and lovingly detached. Angie was really on her own again with no parents around. She was at yet another crossroads where she was faced with the same choices that had confronted her many times before. Would Addiction continue to squeeze the life and humanity out of my daughter as it had in the past? Or would she be able to fight her demons on her own?

I was back in Virginia in January, after a three-week visit to New Mexico, for a testing gig at my old school. I chose to stay there and not run to San Francisco. I chose to handle this crisis long distance. All my past rescuing hadn't accomplished anything and it was too late for that anyway. Angie had already put herself back in the hospital. I felt it was best to let the medical establishment take care of her. My daughter knew better than anyone how much I loved her. I didn't have to keep proving it.

Angie's version of how she ended up in the hospital is that she fell off her bike and injured her femoral artery, that groin injury that put her in the hospital five months earlier in Virginia. Well, I never thought to grill her about the truth of that. What was the point? It was what it was, and now she was in the hospital for another two-to-four weeks on IV antibiotics, just like the last time. Only at this teaching hospital, the same one her sister had been in, they let her stay to conclude her treatments. I also pressured her to start the interferon treatments while she was flat on her back.

The Medicaid people came around to sign her up, and I wish she'd had the good sense to go on it. She refused to sign up with them because she had every intention of working. If you're on Medicaid, there's a very low limit to how much you can earn, and Angie had bigger plans for herself. She still planned, or at least convinced me that she was planning, to get her life back better than ever. So she didn't sign up, and instead of getting on the government dole, she remained on her father's and mine.

We agreed to keep supporting her until she got a job. But she kept saying how bad the job situation was in San Francisco, how no one could get a job. In retrospect, I see how laughable that is. I know people who just got out of jail who have gotten jobs. She was behaving the way drug addicts behave, and using us. But we kept making that easy for her.

Her new roommates came to visit her, along with Caroline, while she was in the hospital. Everyone spoiled her; I sent her a new phone so that we could communicate better. She got through her treatments and eventually went back into her group home on Harrison Street.

It was March 2011, and she said she was job hunting. For a while things were quiet. We continued to support her. We were being patient—sure that any day now she would find work. But she was over spending and after a couple of months of this and not working we chastised her on the subject. She responded that we were right and promised to be more frugal. Promised to look harder for a job. Assured me that she was getting better, slowly, but surely. "Be patient, Mom. I'm getting better every day. xoxo"

I was so heartened to get emails like that. *Throw me a crumb, Angie!* I pleaded. *That's all it takes for me to feel hopeful.* And so I was. It was hard enough to see her in active addiction and hope for the best. But when she told me herself that she was getting better, I bought it hook, line and sinker. I believed her—so great was my need to. But towards the end of the summer, a new crisis presented itself in her life, and as always, she sought my help to rescue her.

Angie's story is that she was sick of living in a house full of people. She said it was like a commune. She had made friends with someone, and this friend said that her boyfriend was moving out and Angie could move in with her. So my daughter gave up her room on Harrison Street, trusting this new friend to come through and let Angie move in with her. Well, of course, this plan fell through and Angie found herself on the street with nowhere to go.

Over Labor Day she moved into a hostel in the Tenderloin, not a terrific place to live in San Francisco, but it was where she landed. At the end of September I journeyed there to see both of my daughters. I rented a car as usual and stayed at the Day's Inn north of Market Street. That way I would be close to Angie's hostel. I determined to see both my girls—Caroline just to hang out and have fun—Angie to help transition to a more affordable living situation because the hostel was more than I could afford. I gave her a deadline: I was getting good now at setting boundaries, and said I wouldn't support her at the hostel beyond November 1. That was still quite a hefty expense on my Discover card. Christmas came and went that year, for me, without much gift giving.

My week with her and Caroline was OK, but I got tired running around so much with Angie, dragging suitcases and garbage bags full of stuff she had brought with her from Harrison Street. She said that her bike and other things were still in the storage room there. So since I had a car I offered to go get it so she could consolidate her stuff.

Turning on me like a rabid dog, she barked, "Don't you dare ever go over there, Mom. Things were very tense between my roommates and me when I left. I will be very angry if you go over there. Promise me you won't, OK?"

Well, I didn't need to be hit over the head to see she was hiding something. I could only speculate, and what did it matter anyway? Right now she needed to find an affordable place to live. That was in the forefront of my mind. And by now she was such a pro at manipulating me; she knew how to take advantage of the conflict in my mind.

She loved to push the envelope with me, but on November 1 she moved in with a man that she found on Craigslist. His name was Wayne Chin, and he worked for the transportation department. Angie liked that because he was rarely home and/or had weird hours. So she had the place to herself. What was she doing with all her free time? I don't know. We had stopped supporting her, so I guess she found some kind of employment. But she never told us what it was. She left it to our fertile imagination.

As if by now we didn't know what female heroin addicts do to support their habit. As if we had blocked out the memory of Baltimore. Her father and I were so inured to everything over the past ten years—so resigned, I guess, to what was and our inability to influence our daughter. *Our daughter*, we moaned to ourselves, *where was she?*

I was starting to feel desperate and wanting to bring my other daughter into the loop again. The holidays were looming and they've always been an emotional time for me. I'm flooded with memories, both happy and sad. But more than anything, I remember the anxiety, the frantic covering up, the alcohol-enabled keeping up the appearance of being happy that I felt in my childhood.

As I felt Angie slipping away again, I wrote to Caroline and said I'd hoped she was OK and not getting sucked into Angie's drama too much. But I needn't have worried. She and her brother have been able to detach pretty well all these years. Or have they? They haven't talked to me about what they were feeling, and I haven't asked. But sometimes I think the bomb that exploded back in 2001 is still exploding, here and there. We're all still licking our wounds, carrying on.

I went back to Virginia again in late January for that same job at my old school. My neighbor who had been collecting my mail brought me bags of junk mail to go through. But one of the envelopes wasn't junk mail. It was a letter from Wayne Chin. He had to do some research to get my address in Virginia. It must have been important.

As my heart sank reading it, I felt sick to my stomach all over again. Like when the Moneygram people back in 2004 told me I should have had Angie prosecuted, I didn't do anything then and it was a big mistake. What had I learned in the Program about enabling and protecting our children from the consequences of their behavior? Now I was faced with yet another life Angie had touched. Wayne's letter further confirmed that Angie was still a loose cannon. She was such a stranger to me.

Wayne informed me that Angie had stolen $2500 in cash that he had kept in his house. He had a limited income, he said, and that was a lot of money. Then—strange little man— he complained that Angie had ruined his hardwood floors, and did I know how to repair them? Ending his letter, he said he hoped "I could rectify this and provide a solution."

I still went to see my former therapist occasionally while I was in the D.C. area. At first all he could do was laugh at Wayne's emphasis on the destruction of his hardwood floors. But both Dr. D and I knew only too well that the greater concern was the fact that Angie was running ragged over anyone in her life she came into contact with if it suited her. She was no longer the daughter I raised, Carlos and Caroline's sister, Aunt Lucy's niece. She hadn't been for years. Angie was a using drug addict transformed by her addiction into an immoral human being, serving only her addiction. All of us who had known and loved her for over thirty years were irrelevant to her, unless we pandered to her addiction in some way—usually by funding it.

This was what I realized reading Wayne's letter. Now, how was I going to manage the damage control? Was I going to step in as I always had in the past? Or was I going to bow out of this latest drama?

I was no longer wondering what she was up to while she was living with him. His letter says it all. But still I was stunned. With all her history, all the antics and clear disintegration over the past dozen years, I was still shocked. What does that say about me? I'm not sure. That I still had faith that my daughter carried something within her — some sense of right and wrong — that I had taught her when she was a child? I still needed to believe that my moral guidance counted for something.

It didn't. And it doesn't.

Angie and I had not been communicating at all, not since before the holidays. I was holding my breath, something I would often do between clear sailing and stormy skies: that in between state of grace when things looked good, she seemed functional and more important, communicative. She even remembered my birthday in January with a loving text and that, of course, threw me off.

Wayne had called the police and she conned her way out of this one too. Pointing to the security camera in the building, she fabricated a story pointing the finger at someone else who might have taken all that money. There was reasonable doubt, so no charges were filed.

But there were, thankfully, consequences. Angie came home one day after all this and found the locks had been changed. When she called her roommate, he said all her belongings had been placed in a dumpster and hauled away. Angie, for the first time in a long time, just had the clothes on her back.

I sent Wayne a very nice, sympathetic letter in response, but no money. I chose to stay uninvolved. I felt very sorry for him, another one of Angie's victims. And I was really fuming at my daughter. She moved into a city motel, texting me every now and then about how she's happier than she's been in a long time, primarily because she's not dependent on her father or me. But after I got that letter from Wayne, I was sick of the hypocrisy. I confronted her the same day about his letter to me:

"Angie, I want to tell u why I've been so silent and keeping my distance. Wayne Chin wrote me a letter last month saying u took more than $2000 from his house. I was very shocked. I only tell u this to explain y I've been out of touch. I have no interest in shaming u or calling u out. I wish he'd never written me that letter because it's none of my business. Here's my bottom line, and it's important that u believe this if we're going to move forward: If u did steal from him, u should return as much as u can to him. Guilt has always been ur waterloo, and this just adds to it. If u didn't take anything, then he's just a scam artist and we shouldn't be having this conversation. Either way, whatever u do or don't do, it's between u and him to work out. I want no part of it. I want us to start talking again and reestablish a relationship. What do u think? Xoxo"

Well, what would my friends in the Program say about that? Pretty good, no? I did a great job of sitting on the fence, detaching pretty well. I like the part about it being none of my business; that's really fine, "none of my business." My daughter's choices: none of my business. If she were an ax murderer, would it be none of my business? *Let it go, Maggie; you are separate people, remember?* I told myself. My Twelve-Step recovery, so far, has brought me a great deal of gratitude and serenity, mostly when I remember that voice from God telling me to let go of control and resistance. Yet there's another part of me that hurts terribly when I witness the destruction of my daughter at the hands of Addiction. How can I be well while

Angie is so sick? I've spent all these years searching for an answer.

Meghan O'Rourke, author of *The Long Goodbye*, in an interview discussing her own grief about losing her mother, says this: "I'm changed by it, the way a tree is changed by having to grow around an obstacle."

It's the subliminal mother force in me. Grief and loss — they change us. I keep getting beamed onto Planet X, then back again, my molecules getting rearranged every time. Just as Angie has changed, so have I. I've loved my daughter as best I could for half of my life. How can losing her to this living death **not** change me?

Cool as a cucumber, her response by text the next day:

"I'm in the process of suing Wayne Chin. I have a lawyer and everything, although now I guess I'm adding slander to my lawsuit. Yes, his supposed money disappeared the same time my purse and some of my clothes disappeared (from inside the apartment). The apartment building is extremely secure and there are cameras everywhere. Camera footage showed an Asian female entering the apartment at about noon one day (half an hour after he always left for work). I know about the footage b/c Wayne called the police, after frantically insisting to me that I give him back his money. We weren't getting along anyway for a number of reasons, but it's going to take me a year to write this all out so if u have time u can call me."

Part of me believed this story, but a bigger part knew that I was being manipulated. So I didn't respond. We retreated to our corners and I left her alone. Then a few weeks later she came calling again:

"Hi Mom, sorry I've been out of touch. I actually came down with food poisoning sometime late last week and spent half the day in the hospital on Mon getting IV fluids b/c I had become dangerously dehydrated from all the vomiting and diarrhea. Actually I wanted to give u a heads up. I got charged $500 (at Walgreen's) for my food poisoning medications (fenergen) b/c I have been temporarily kicked off Healthy SF…so I have to pay full price for everything."

It's easy to go into my Walgreen's account and see what has been bought. She's never purchased any of the medicines she said she had. These lies about the cost of meds have been going on for a year since I set up the Walgreen's account. It was originally set up to pay for her hepatitis medicine, interferon, which was costly. But she gave up on the treatments six months earlier anyway because they made her too tired.

I responded to her email about food poisoning and told her I needed to close the Walgreen's account. No drama or big confrontation. I just said that I couldn't afford it anymore and she would need to take care of her own health expenses. And she came back at me punching. She bombarded me with a series of angry emails, screaming at me for being so uncaring and cheap. This wasn't my daughter's voice. It was the voice of Addiction.

Toward the end of May, I made my annual pilgrimage to San Francisco to see both of my girls. Always looking forward to seeing Caroline, I was very apprehensive about seeing her sister. If I escaped without too many scratches a week later, it was because I chose not to confront her with what was right in front of me.

The day after I got to San Francisco, I called Caroline and we made plans for dinner that night. I had emailed and called Angie about my upcoming visit but got no response from her. So Caroline said she would call her about where we were meeting for dinner that night.

I picked up Caroline and her friend Seth at her place in the Mission and we drove to Blowfish over on Bryant. It's a very nice sushi/fusion place but a little pricey. I figured what the hell—how often do I come to San Francisco? I wanted to spoil my girls a little. I hadn't heard from Angie since that nasty email exchange about closing the Walgreen's account and I didn't know what to expect.

She pulled up in a cab with Loki, her terrier she took everywhere with her. Breezing in she sat down next to me. Caroline and Seth were sitting across from me at the table so Angie didn't have a choice.

No "Hi Mom," hug, "How ya doin?" Nothing—just a chip on her shoulder the size of Alaska and just as chilly. Caroline and Seth were already on their second margarita by the time she got there, and so I decided in the chill air that I needed a drink too. This was going to be a long meal. So I ordered one. I tried to engage her with affectionate chitchat, but she wasn't buying. She was still mad at me. This is an angry text she sent me in April:

"You really seem to think that just because you go and whine to a bunch of people once a week while sitting in a circle that you are in ANY way qualified to advise, that you are somehow an authority? As far as I'm concerned, they've made you even more of a pain in the ass."

Sitting in the restaurant, it's like I wasn't there. She chatted back and forth with Seth and her sister. But the strain was obvious and I sat through it feeling more and more uncomfortable.

Well, at least she came. She didn't blow me off completely. She still cares a little, I thought to myself. I still needed to believe that Angie cared about me as I so clearly cared about her. What mother wouldn't have these needs?

Then, out of the blue, she announced that she had to go back to work, threw a hundred dollar bill on the table, picked up Loki, and left.

Hmm, I guessed, *she's getting good tips.*

Angie texted me the next day and suggested we meet at my motel. As sick as she was, she was still into propriety and avoiding public scenes. But now, I knew, she could say what she needed to say in private. And at 5:00 p.m. that day, she did.

Angie knocked on my door and I went to open it. She came in and didn't sit down but she put her terrier down. She stood rigid against the door as if she might want to leave quickly. Her body language was very clear. She kept her boxing gloves on.

She looked like hell—bruises all over her neck—a dead giveaway that she was out of veins and injecting there now. Another dead giveaway that she was indulging in behavior I wouldn't want to know about: the hundred dollar bill she threw on the table to help pay for dinner the night before. Later in the visit she would help me pay for bags full of clothes at Goodwill. And then on the last day of my visit, more hundred dollar bills to help me pay for the two nights of a hotel stay I put on my credit card. These were hundred dollar bills in her purse—not tens or twenties. Where did I imagine she got them?

I didn't indulge that question and quite frankly was glad that for once I was on the receiving end where money was concerned. My daughter was injecting drugs into her neck and refused to tell me how she was supporting herself, but I was momentarily glad because **she** was giving **me** money for a change. She was burdened, I think, with guilt from years of taking advantage of me, so I kept the hundred dollar bills, grateful for the payback.

I spoke first. "Well, Angie, it's very clear that you're still angry with me."

Relaxing her posture, she loosened up a little. "I'm just so sick of you telling me what to do, how to recover. You don't have any idea what I go through and quite frankly I don't want to discuss any of it with you."

"Fine," I said, holding my hands up to show my boxing gloves were off. "Angie, I'm done trying to manage you and your life. I've done too much of that for years and it's gotten both of us nowhere. Please accept my apology for all that. You know I was well intentioned, but I just wouldn't let go and stop trying to tell you what to do. I will now, OK?"

Visibly appeased, but still a little skeptical, she concluded, "Well, I hope you mean it this time. OK." Moving to sit down on the bed to stroke Loki, she asked, "Do you want to go have some dinner before I have to get back to work?"

"Sure. There's a good place right up the street. You've pointed it out to me before."

"Ok. Let me rinse off in your shower first and then we can go."

While she was showering, I stroked Loki and got to know him a little. He was a very needy little terrier, constantly pressing for attention. Angie told me that she had rescued him from an animal shelter, so he may have been abused earlier on. This relationship between Angie and all her animals was an eloquent reminder to me of her kind and compassionate nature. I was so heartened by it. And then I thought suddenly: *Who will care for Loki if Angie dies?*

We walked up to this Italian place just beyond the intersection on Market. They served fabulous take-out in big bins, like a salad bar but hot food. Angie and I got what we wanted and sat down. We talked a little about her massage therapist, the apartment she had found and was planning to move into, the pending suit against Wayne Chin. These were safe topics—topics of her choosing. Conversation was awkward. There was no real engagement, no honest connection between my daughter and me. Blissful dishonesty; play it safe. Don't push her away. I can't begin to describe the loneliness I felt carrying on this meaningless conversation—and being with this stranger I barely knew anymore. All I could think of was how much I missed her bangs.

As I got ready to pay at the cash register, she said, looking at the sumptuous desserts in front of us, "C'mon, Mom. I know you want one. Treat yourself. C'mon!"

So I did get one. I think it was a piece of cake. But I was keenly aware of what she was doing: she had her addiction, which she felt I kept reminding her of; and I had mine, which she was now reminding me of. I was in recovery from my food addiction, but she didn't know that. She knew that desserts used to be trigger foods for me. So why was she pressing me to eat one? If this was a game, I didn't want to play anymore.

A couple of days later, I agreed to take her thrift store shopping. Parking the car at Goodwill, "the best one in San Francisco," she'd said, she told me to go on to the store and she would meet me there as soon as she walked Loki around the block. I said "Sure," and went into the store.

I waited and waited inside the store, and after forty-five minutes I was getting angry, so I went outside to look for her on the sidewalks. I got in the car and drove around the block, several different ones, hoping to spot her with the dog. I didn't seem too worried about losing the parking space we had found earlier. I was livid, so I pulled over to collect myself. I was remembering more than five years before in Miami when she disappeared around the corner to take her suboxone while we were shoe shopping. At the time in Miami

I had no idea that she had become a heroin addict, so I was pretty clueless then. But now I knew only too well what Angie was capable of. When I luckily found the same parking spot I had given up to look for her, I went back to the store and there they were. She was stroking Loki on the floor as I approached her. Looking up at me, all wide-eyed and innocent, she asked,

"Where you been, Mom?"

It's amazing the levels of deception addicts are capable of. They are so utterly cocooned in their little world that they lose touch with the people around them. They also lose any sense of time. She was off getting high for an hour and acted like I was late for our shopping spree.

I didn't make a scene in the store. I said nothing. We went up and down every aisle filling her cart with clothes and shoes that would fill three large garbage bags. I even found some stuff for myself.

I chose to spend these five days in San Francisco in blissful dishonesty, knowing full well that Angie was using drugs right under my nose, but saying nothing about it. Maybe that's a sign of my ongoing recovery, my letting go. Is it possible that I could have halted in its tracks more than a decade of methamphetamine, cocaine and heroin abuse with a reprimand?

"You little, fill in the blank. What are you doing now? How could you ruin my visit this way?"

No, I don't believe so. I've known it for years, knew it then and put it into play this last time I saw her on her turf: whether or not my daughter chose recovery and gave up drugs was not up to me; it was up to her. She herself had to embrace recovery from addiction—using whatever method worked for her. I know many addicts who have recovered. I've prayed that she would join them.

From *Courage to Change*, one of my favorite daily readers:

> It's not easy to watch someone I love continue
> to drink, but I can do nothing to stop them. If I
> see how unmanageable my life has become, I
> can admit that I am powerless over the disease.
> Then I can really begin to make my life better.
> (74)

This is the hardest thing about letting go of those we love strangling in the clutches of addiction: watching them do the dance by themselves — and staying on the sidelines. If I live to be as old as my mother when she died, I'll never experience anything harder.

Angie was surly much of the time in my company, though, and not pleasant to be around. But still I was determined to see her as much as possible before I flew back to D.C. When I wasn't with Angie, I was with Caroline. Other than that first dinner at Blowfish they couldn't coordinate their work schedules, so I saw them separately. I was determined not to use Caroline as an intermediary or as a sounding board to whine about her sister. She was already very sick with Crohn's disease, and I didn't want to add to her stress by spending our precious time together talking about Angie. We had a lot of fun thrift shopping, and I marveled at her ability to detach and live independently with her sister falling apart right across town.

Angie was flitting back and forth between hotels in expensive cabs, with garbage bags of stuff and her terrier, Loki. Sometimes I think she got that dog to stay alive — to be accountable to something or someone other than herself. She and Loki stayed with me a couple of nights in my motel. By the time I checked out I was covered with fleabites. When I told her that she should have the dog defleaed, she flew into a rage.

"It's not Loki, Mom, you're just too cheap to stay in decent motels. You always pick fleabags to crash in." Whatever.

When Angie was in her first psych ward back in October 2007, they used art therapy on the patients. She made me a bead bracelet. "These are your favorite colors, Mom," she said, carefully placing it on my wrist. I finger those beads now and again, like Greek worry beads, a reminder of the hope I nurtured then. On one of the nights she stayed at my motel, she was out all night while I tossed and turned, wondering where she was. When I awoke, there was the most fragrant smelling flower in a glass of water at my bedside. She had picked it outside of her hotel in Japan Town and left it for me to enjoy in the morning. I still have what's left of that flower, all dried and brown, another reminder that "Joy & Woe are woven fine" (Blake 491).

It takes two to fight and she tried very hard to engage me in battle while I was there. She brought up examples of what she perceived to be parental neglect from years earlier.

"Carlos had <u>green teeth</u> when you took him to the orthodontist in Greece (in 1988). You never supervised our dental hygiene! How could you let him get <u>green teeth</u>?!"

Beverly Conyers began writing about addiction when her youngest daughter became addicted to heroin. She shares some of her insights in this passage:

> Most parents, when looking back on how they raised their children, have at least some regrets. They may wish that they had been more or less strict, that they had expected more or less of their children, that they had spent more time with them, or that they had not been so overprotective. They may reflect on difficult

events, such as a divorce or death in the family, and see these as turning points in their child's mental health. Some may bear heavy burdens of shame over past difficulties, such as an infidelity that damaged the family and caused mistrust. Whatever the parental failings may be, it is almost inevitable that the addicts will recognize these vulnerable spots and take advantage of the parents…

Addicts may have many complaints, including major and minor grievances from years past. Some of their accusations may, in fact, have truth in them. Families may well have caused pain for the addicts. They may well have failed the addicts in some significant way. (After all, what human relationship is perfect?) But addicts bring up these problems not to clear the air or with the hope of healing old wounds. They bring them up solely to induce guilt, a tool with which they manipulate others in pursuit of their continued addiction. (qtd. in Sheff)

Angie was just pulling things out of the air. I think I was so stunned by this that I kind of laughed it off — big mistake — and that only enraged her further. But after she got it out of her system she calmed down and suggested we have brunch the next day before I left. Still throwing me crumbs, she knew I'd flown three thousand miles to see her. She still had some humanity left.

But, a surprise to me more than anything, I bailed out on brunch the next morning because I was very sick all night and exhausted from lack of sleep. The last thing I wanted was to go out to eat. So I called her and Caroline and cancelled, sorry not to see both my girls one more time, but sure that the best self-care I could do now was to stay in bed until I had to drive to the airport and catch my plane back to the East Coast.

So we left each other on a good note the next day — her bruises still on her neck — mine confined to my aching heart. She took a cab over to my motel to reimburse me for the hotel expenses I'd put on my card.

"Bye, Mom," as she crossed the floor to hug me, "I'm glad you came. I love you."

"Bye, honey," hugging her back, "Love you too."

Blissful dishonesty — that's what I indulged in for five days in San Francisco. We were walking in parallel universes. Well, we had been for years, but it's a strange feeling when you're together up close. I chose to overlook the obvious. One word from me, one reprimand, one emotional "Give up drugs, Angie, or you will die!" would have sent her back across the cable car tracks and I wouldn't see her again. This was the truce we had made together at the beginning of my visit. It ensured that she would see me at all. And I wanted to see her. At this point in our long goodbye, I never knew if I would see her again. It was such a desolate, helpless feeling. *Let go, Maggie,* I thought to myself, *she has her own Higher Power and you, dear girl, had better cling to yours. You're gonna need Him more than ever now.*

This was where I was in my recovery as I left San Francisco, at that hard won place I'd fought through years of resistance to find: the end of the battle — acceptance. I had tried to help her over the years and admittedly made so many mistakes: I begged, I pleaded, I covered up, I manipulated, I enabled, I moved boundaries so often I couldn't even find them anymore. I confronted her behavior; then I did the opposite, lapsing into momentary denial.

Obviously, my relationship with my daughter has often been very unhealthy and codependent. And another truth I cringe at is that keeping her dependent on me by supporting her and endlessly bailing her out of her messes made me feel important and needed—not erased as I had so often felt. If I was her bank, then at least I heard from her regularly. But Angie hasn't been in recovery for a long time and the only connection she has recently sought with me was monetary. As long as she was in her disease that wasn't likely to change. So I decided to close the bank for good, knowing I probably wouldn't hear from her again.

I went back to Gene and the farm in New Mexico, trying to lose myself in our growing orchard, the price of white peaches, and my ongoing recovery in the Program. I continued to attend several weekly meetings, enjoy my service work, and continue my daily meditations. This discipline kept me focused on my own personal growth. I immersed myself in the daily rhythms of life, kept busy, and hoped that Angie really was a survivor. I was in New Mexico—she was in San Francisco—probably a blessing for me that she wasn't any closer and she would have to fight this battle on her own. But soon her birthday month, August, arrived, and I had an excuse to contact her. Once again, I would waffle on the money issue.

Angie emailed me that she needed help to pay for three nights in a motel. "This could be my birthday present," she suggested, "and I promise I'll pay you back as soon as I get my paycheck." Ask any shopaholic if she really needed to buy all that stuff. Ask any enabler if she doesn't get a high from giving money to a needy child. Did I question the veracity of her story? No, I relapsed— briefly. I got sucked right back into my disease.

Well, the money I had agreed to give her wasn't enough. Three nights in a hotel wasn't enough. Loving her the only way I knew how and/or could afford just wasn't enough. I was in Austin in early August, celebrating my granddaughter Madison's birthday, when she asked for more.

"Mom, I'm so stressed out. They're really taking their time to de-flea my room at the hotel. I can't move back there yet. Can you float me a loan for another night? I promise I'll pay you back."

These are the moments many of us parents face when trying to set and enforce boundaries with our children. I've been here before with my daughter, and I've usually caved in under the pressure she exerted. But this time was different. This was where the rubber hit the road for me, and this time I said no, I've given you enough; my son and family were waiting for me with the car running. Amazingly, I hung up on her to go out to dinner on Madison's birthday.

So, I drew a line in the sand, telling her over the phone that I was not willing to pay for any more nights in a hotel. The following text is the price I paid for setting boundaries, taking care of myself, and forcing my daughter to face the consequences of her own irresponsible behavior:

"Do not contact me. Ever. I want absolutely nothing from you and I feel nothing but unadulterated hatred for u. Enjoy ur grandkids while u can because when they're older they'll come to loathe u just like all three of ur children do."

Cut with a knife through my heart, I went out to have dinner with my grandchildren. Oh, she knew where to wound me. Go right for the jugular. Angie knew that my children have always been my greatest joy — and my deepest sorrow.

After I stumbled back to New Mexico from Austin, I discovered that my bank account had been hacked into. Someone had set up "Bill Pay" for $500. The name of this poor sap, his address and phone number were right there in black and white. Whoever set it up, used him. Fortunately for me, the bank emailed me to verify the transaction. I denied it and it was cancelled. But my first thought was Angie. When

I confronted this man by phone, I actually had the chutzpah to ask him if he knew Angie Romero. He said the name was familiar. After I called the police to report the attempted theft, naming my own daughter as a suspect, I spent hours changing all my ID's and passwords to all my bank and brokerage accounts. *I've been here before*, I thought. How many times have my hopes soared and collapsed since then?

In *Cherishing Our Daughters,* licensed clinical psychologist, Dr. Evelyn Bassoff, writes:

> For Veronica, letting go means accepting that her adult daughter, Anne-Marie, is less than Veronica had hoped she would be. Her task is especially difficult, first because it is natural to personalize your child's unhappiness, seeing it as an indication of your failure; second, because it is excruciatingly painful to see someone you love falter. Bright, talented and pretty, little Anne-Marie skipped through childhood with barely a stumble. But...for reasons hard to discern, she began to make bad choices: falling in with a fast crowd...and experimenting with street drugs. Now... having flitted from one disastrous relationship to another...Anne-Marie also struggles with a substance abuse problem; she tells Veronica that she goes to AA meetings, but Veronica doubts that her daughter's attendance is consistent and her commitment to rehabilitate sincere. Veronica is in therapy herself, learning to live with her real disappointment and to be supportive but not overly invested in her daughter's life. 'Every mother wants her daughter to be the happy ending to her own life, but unless Anne-Marie

makes dramatic changes, it may not turn out this way for me,' she confides. 'I am learning important lessons in therapy. One is that the only life you can direct is your own; my 'good advice' to Anne-Marie only falls on deaf ears. Unless my daughter musters the courage to make changes, I cannot do anything more for her. And so, over and over again, I say to myself, I am not responsible for the way Anne-Marie chooses to live. Another is that you love your child forever not because she is happy or successful or makes you proud but because she is your child. (218-219)

THREE

"When it is dark enough, you can see the stars."

Charles A. Beard

Progress, Not Perfection

Life continues to unfold as it is meant to. We are often too close to events to have any clear perspective. But I continue to live my life as best I can, with deliberateness and purpose. From *Courage To Change*:

> Progress can be hard to recognize, especially if our expectations are unrealistically high. If we expect our negative attitudes or unhealthy behavior to change quickly and completely, we are likely to be disappointed — progress is hard to see when we measure ourselves against idealized standards. Perhaps it would be better to compare our present circumstances only to where we had been in the past...
>
> Today I am no longer seeking perfection; the only thing that matters is the direction in which I'm moving. (76)

I have faltered many times in my recovery. But learning to focus less on my desired outcomes and more on the journey has enabled me to learn more things along the way. I'm learning to slow down and enjoy the ride. And most importantly, it has kept me out of the driver's seat and open to receiving life's valuable lessons.

For a confirmed perfectionist, prone to black or white thinking, this has been a big change for me. Looking back, I see where my perfectionism came from. My mother's mother was demanding and critical, and my mother passed that on to me.

A number of my defects grew out of my upbringing in an alcoholic family. My mother was powerless to control my father's drinking, so she dominated her children instead and was a powerful influence on their life choices. My eating disorders as a young adult were, among other things, an attempt to establish a sense of control in my life. Purging masked my food addiction and kept my weight down. To others, I appeared normal; no one knew how sick I really was. It was paramount to my mother, and therefore to me that I keep up appearances; so I hid my true self from the world. How could I admit how utterly imperfect and flawed I was? I was so sure that I would be shunned and disregarded. So I locked myself into a lonely and isolated prison for more years than I like to remember.

Ever since I was a very young child I'd been fragile, like thin ice on a lake—don't walk on it; you might fall through and drown. My sense of being OK was always shaky when I was younger. Many of us who grow up with low self-worth become chameleons. Chameleons change their color out of fear to protect themselves from predators. We don't have clear personal boundaries, often not recognizing where we end and others begin. We don't really know who we are, so we attach ourselves to whomever we're around, often seeking their approval by pretending to be like them. But like the chameleon who turns green in the jungle, we are afraid to distinguish ourselves. I remember telling Angie back in 2010, "I know who I am now." Well, that's an ongoing process.

Now I accept who I am, warts and all. I know that absolute perfection doesn't exist anyway. My years of growth in the Twelve-Step Programs have brought me out of isolation while I've celebrated my humanity. As I dare to take new risks I continue to learn new things about myself. I respect my imperfections because they keep me humble and swimming in the stream of life with other fellow travelers also struggling like me. I am never alone.

Xavier and I have been shouldering the grim reality of Angie's addiction all of these years, rarely unloading on family or friends. It's just been too painful. And there was still the stigma. Our society is very judgmental about something that is so commonplace. But this attitude nevertheless has increased my sense of isolation at times in my own family, with certain friends, and propelled my recovery into a deeper and more spiritual place.

The holidays have been hard since Angie got sick. I've been trying to honor the gift of life, the celebrations, the blessings of my friends and family. But it's not so easy to compartmentalize, keep the Angie problem off in a drawer somewhere. My child has been fading away right in front of me, and all those close to me knew it. That made my situation even harder, because I was always negotiating what and how much to tell people, not out of shame, but out of consideration for their feelings. They were suffering, too, for me.

They say misery loves company but not in my case. I've had no need or desire to disrupt the lives of my friends and family with the intimate details of my heartache. Many of my friends, in and out of the Program, have blanketed me in my sorrow over the years. They are always high on my gratitude list I keep up every day. I am very blessed to have so many good people in my life. And Gene's on the top of the list— because he makes me laugh.

I've cried a river since this all began, and now I can usually talk about Angie calmly. But my dearest friend, Jeanne, sometimes tears up when I give her an update. And when this happens I wonder, as I have many times over the past decade, if updates are really desirable with my friends and family. They are concrete reminders that I am not alone in my suffering, that this disease has cut a wide swath in our lives.

Melody Beattie's wisdom has been instrumental to my ongoing recovery from codependency:

> "We need to know how far we'll go, and how far we'll allow others to go with us. Once we understand this, we can go anywhere" (166).

For the first years of Angie's illness, as I felt I had less and less control, I was becoming obsessed with her — utterly addicted to her and her problem. Melody Beattie, a recovering addict herself, had written a number of books on codependency, and I've read most of them. I recognized myself as the classic codependent she had described: people-pleaser, and losing myself in the process; poor self-esteem; caretaking, to the exclusion of self; obsessive; perfectionist; reactive; controlling; poor boundary setting.

Setting boundaries keeps us focused on protecting ourselves. But they're supposed to function as bridges, not walls. They're not intended to shut us off from those we love. Nevertheless many of us when dealing with addicts maintain this defensive posture because a using addict has the power to hurt us. We learn to be careful.

But in all areas of life, it's healthy to establish clear boundaries. Over the years I've learned to be discreet about Angie with friends and family members — not dishonest, just careful. Growing up I had never learned the importance of establishing boundaries, and I've had to learn that skill as an adult. Melody Beattie addresses the need for boundaries often. I've had to recognize what a powerful stigma addiction still carries in our society, so I no longer just blurt out the painful truth to anyone who wants to listen. That's because I've lost a friend or two since Angie got sick. These people don't know how to deal with me anymore; they don't know what to say to me, as if I were defined by Angie's addiction, and the horror of my ordeal is just too much of a distraction.

That's another effect of addiction, how the stigma can burden a relationship just as surely as families of suicides are often shunned (Bialosky 145, 175). I had a friend I'd known for years. We used to love chatting about our lives and our kids. But then Addiction appeared and crashed our comfortable camaraderie. Like an invisible wall between us, there was a discomfort and unease that was palpable. Over the years she's resisted my overtures for dinner, always too busy with this or that. After a while I got the message and stopped trying. But finally I accepted our forfeited friendship as just another casualty in the wake of addiction.

I used to go back and forth: anger — regret — grief — joy — gratitude. Back and forth, back and forth, tossed like a ship on a wave in a stormy ocean. But —

> "I am not afraid of storms," Louisa May Alcott has asserted, "for I am learning how to sail my ship" (*Courage* 150).

Now I have the tools of recovery to pick up and keep me grounded in gratitude and love for all the good fortune in my life. I have had such a good life in so many ways. The ability to remember that is a testament not only to the power of the Program but also to my determination to survive one of life's hardest lessons.

I find myself less and less in thoughts around Angie though, of course, when I think of her it is with sadness and a heavy heart. But doing that would be to remain in the problem, and I don't have the power to change that. Now I try to stay focused on the solution. For me, that is practicing the principles found in Twelve-Step Programs on a daily basis. Just as healthy food and sufficient exercise ensure my physical well-being, so too does my recovery Program lead me to spiritual health.

This road to recovery has followed a fairly steady progression over the years, though at a tortoise's pace, slow and stubborn. But early in Angie's illness, like a blip on a radar screen, I did something for myself that, temporarily anyway, elevated me out of the despair I was feeling. Back in 2003, I found a life raft. I jealously guarded it because, hell, she was packing a chainsaw. I got smart; I took care of myself. I enrolled in graduate school to earn my Master of Arts in Teaching.

Up until then, though most of my teaching colleagues had gone to graduate school, I ran from the idea, full of self-doubt and scared of taking on more of a challenge than I could handle. But for some reason when I saw the flyer in my mailbox at school advertising this new class I jumped at the opportunity. I felt no fear — on the contrary — I was energized and excited about taking on something new. Looking back, I see this healthy move as one of the regrettably few choices I made on my own behalf as I began swimming through the waters of addiction with my daughter. I would have years of recovery work ahead of me. But right then I decided to put myself first.

Angie had been living with me in the basement of my condo at the time. She moved in with me at the end of the summer in 2001 and was finishing up a few courses toward her B.A. at George Mason University. Computers had just been introduced to my school two years before, and I had only one at home. It was with Angie in the basement. Somehow I felt clear that day about asserting myself in a relationship that was crippled with very blurry boundaries:

"I'm moving the computer upstairs to my bedroom, Angie," I told her. "I'm in grad school now and my needs come first where the computer is concerned. I'm gonna be writing all the time."

"Sure, fine, take it," she snapped. "What am I supposed to use now? I'm in school too, you know."

"Yes, I know," I retorted, delighted to be stepping up for myself for a change. "You'll have to use the computers at school or come up to my room to type. The computer stays with me."

I was on a roll for a couple of years. I loved my school assignments, and I threw myself into work. This was a Master's in reflective practice and I was doing a lot of reflecting about my teaching and how my life had impacted it. I spent hours writing "teacher stories" in my reflective journal. I'm so grateful that I accepted the challenge and did all that work because I know it made me a better teacher. But as much as it served as a distraction from seeing Angie start to slip away before my eyes, when I earned my degree two years later I fell right back into my own disease, drowning in codependency.

Melody Beattie shares with us,

> I've made many mistakes. But I've learned that mistakes are OK too. I learned how to communicate, to laugh, to cry, to ask for help. I'm learning to react less, and act more, quietly confident that who I am is OK.

> I've learned to own my power. I've also learned I must constantly return to the act of surrendering to do that. (38)

Melody originally published that book twenty-five years ago. Her insights are as illuminating today as they were then:

Instead of obsessively trying to control others, we learn to detach. Instead of allowing others to hurt and use us, we set boundaries. Instead of reacting, we learn to relax and let things settle into place. We replace tunnel vision with perspective. We forgo worrying and denial, and learn constructive problem-solving skills... we stop expecting ourselves to be perfect, and we stop expecting perfection of others. (13)

Detachment has always been a difficult concept for me to grasp. But, all these years into her disease, having been immersed in the highs and lows that all parents of addicts recognize, I was at last accepting the fact that I could do very little to help my daughter.

Speaking at an Al-Anon meeting a few years ago: "I chose these two readings because they address the idea of "letting go," as opposed to clinging to, much of the negativity in our lives and much of what weighs on us and drags us down into depression.

"The skill of detachment enables us to create a safe distance between our addict and ourselves, because I have learned from experience that if we don't, we might be swallowed up by their black hole before we know it.

"As parents, we often feel we don't deserve this gift of detachment. But we do; I did the best I could with what I had. I have learned how to forgive myself for any mistakes I made with my daughter. It took a long time, but this was an important step, because until we do that, we risk being forever enmeshed in their pain and the mess of their lives if they don't choose recovery.

"Once we are able to reach some level of detachment, we are freer to work the steps. In hindsight, I see now why I couldn't really do the first three steps at first as I might have. Guilt was holding me hostage. I simply had not let go of my responsibility in her life, my importance in her life, and therefore my need to "fix" her life. I needed to be humbled, in the best sense of the word.

"So all the steps leading up to the tenth involve many processes, letting go for starters, and then turning our gaze inward rather than outward. They call this 'cleaning house,' and it never stops. The tenth step reminds us that taking daily inventory and making amends is an ongoing process that helps us live more freely, because nothing is more crippling than guilt.

"I'd like to open up the discussion about ways you've struggled with detachment, both successes and failures, and how you may or may not agree with me that clinging to our guilt puts us at risk in parenting effectively our addict."

It's gotten increasingly easier to detach from this person we call Angie. We can, a lot of the time, be tough with her, set boundaries, and cut her off financially. We can do this because she has become such a total stranger to us. She is, in fact, someone else. Her personality is radically different from the girl I raised. Drug addiction, at its worst, is a living death. We have our weak moments, to be sure, when, fueled more by fantasy than reality, we see what we want to see, hear what we want to hear, and believe what we want to believe. We've kept trying to connect with her, and money is the only language she speaks. But now that has become a dead language to us.

I have dinner with friends, Patti and John, frequently in New Mexico. Patti's son is married to an alcoholic, a source of intense pain to my friend. She wrings her hands incessantly, wondering what to do, how to help. Many, many people I know, parents in particular because it's natural to be protective of a child, feel that it's a demonstration of love to worry about and suffer along with their addicts. And to do the opposite, they feel, is uncaring. I used to feel that way but have learned — to paraphrase A.J. Cronin — that worrying doesn't do anything to change the future, but it sure has the power to ruin the present (*Courage* 15). Or, as John tells Patti, "Let it go, honey. It's not your canoe."

Still, I falter from time to time, tempted to search for my daughter and jump into her orbit again. But I don't. Melody Beattie quotes another woman, Anne Morrow Lindbergh, who found the freedom to live independently — years before the Women's Movement arrived:

> ...I believe most people are aware of periods in their lives when they seem to be 'in grace' and other periods when they feel 'out of grace,' even though they may use different words to describe these states. In the first happy condition, one seems to carry all one's tasks before one lightly, as if borne along on a great tide; and in the opposite state one can hardly tie a shoestring. It is true that a large part of life consists in learning a technique of tying the shoestring...But there are techniques of living too; there are even techniques in the search for grace. And techniques can be cultivated. (qtd. in Beattie)

Much of recovery, Melody says, is all about learning to tie our shoestrings. The techniques I am cultivating are found in the Twelve-Step recovery Programs; they are my daily disciplines. But some days work better for me than others. Some days I'm "all thumbs."

Mother's Days have come and gone the last few years without any word from Angie. But her friend, Priscilla, whom she had lived with back in D.C., always sends me Facebook messages that I treasure. I'm sure she knows — maybe even saw it coming — that her friend has tumbled back into that dark, inaccessible place, and has meant to offer me some comfort:

"Happy Mother's Day. Love and miss you very much."

"Prissy, you'll never know how much your message means to me at this time."

"Of course! I love you very much and I always will."

Love and miss you from a dear girl whom I love like a daughter, but no more words from my own daughter. I have a favorite student from Bolivia whom I also love like a daughter. I was thrilled to attend her college graduation and more recently her wedding. Such a gaping hole in my heart — in my life — Angie's loss has left me with. So I fill the hole with other young women, just a few. I listen for other voices calling me, and am blessed to hear them and respond. But I ache to see Angie again, whole and full of promise, before she got so sick.

One daughter can never replace another. It's been hard watching my older daughter so sick with addiction that she's (unconsciously) throwing her valuable life away. But there are other people out there who are suffering too. Well into her sister's illness, I stepped up my attempts to get closer to Caroline, who had left home when she was only eighteen and chose to live three thousand miles away. I have often felt that the Crohn's disease she is plagued with now was brought on by many stresses in her life — including losing her sister to drug addiction.

These are a couple of the letters I wrote her the year before my breakdown in 2008:

Hi Lammie,

I always used to call you 'little lamb,' remember? Angie was 'Princess' and you were 'my lamb.' And you had that picture on your wall. You probably hate to hear it now, and Angie sure does.

Al-Anon is a program for people with friends or family members with addiction problems. Bopi was an unrecovered alcoholic, Gene is a recovering alcoholic, and Angie is an addict, so that's how I qualify. I've grown so much these years in the Program. I wish I had had it when I was your age. My life might have been very different, and yours too.

The Program teaches us many things, one of which is to apologize to people we've hurt. I know that there were many times when I neglected you while you were growing up. Have I ever told you that I was sorry? I think so, but maybe it bears repeating. You must have felt terribly abandoned, helpless and angry. I wish I could have those years back to be a better mother to you. But another thing that they teach us is to accept the things we cannot change. I can't relive the past. But I do have the present which, when lived well, lays a good foundation for the future.

You are a lovely, talented young woman. I wonder if you really know that. Does your life reflect a solid sense of self-regard and worth? I hope so, because I love you very, very, very much, and I want you to be happy and live a good life.

I just wanted to communicate these thoughts to you.

Hi Caroline,

Hope you're well and moving in the direction you want to go. The past year or so has been a challenge, hasn't it?

I'm learning many things about myself as I grow older, and one of them is that I wasn't a very effective communicator when you kids were little: I often kept things bottled up that I should have said. Daddy's the same way. You know, he and I are good friends. We talk about you kids and other things. One thing we always talk about is how much we miss you.

I've relived in my mind a thousand times that cold January day seven years ago when you and Cathy drove out West. At the time I remember how you hated it in Virginia and needed a change. So I thought that a good parent would let you go without a lot of fuss, as I did. But sometimes I wish I'd made it harder for you, protested more, or made you feel guilty (like many parents would). You've made a life for yourself out there, and I'm so proud that you finished college with a B.F.A. In the end, though, you're there and we're here, and there's such a gulf between us. I don't want to lose you altogether.

Do you think there's any chance that you'll come back East to live someday? So many of us back here wish we could see you more and just plain know you better. Uncle Bill said, 'I guess I don't even know her anymore, do I?' I suppose it's easy to forget that the first eighteen years of your life you were around extended family a lot. And now they're just wishing they knew you better—because you're worth knowing!

So I guess that's my point in writing this: to let you know that I regret not protesting more about your leaving because you might have misinterpreted that passivity as my not caring whether you stayed around your family or not. Nothing could be further from the truth.

I've learned, of course, to accept what I cannot change, and you will live wherever you want. But whatever you decide to do in the future do it with your eyes open, and know that many of us in the East wish you were here too, because you're a valuable part of our family.

Keep smiling, baby! Love you!

Hindsight often provides us with clearer vision. I was making progress in the Program, but I still needed to work harder on letting Caroline go. Reading these letters now, much of my tone seems cloying, even manipulative. If I could write those letters again, I would express my thoughts differently. I wouldn't wring my hands about watching her move to San Francisco; and I wouldn't try to make her feel guilty about leaving her family behind. When I wrote to her, I was still immersed in a tremendous sense of loss around my children. My grief around Angie was an open wound, and I was grabbing on to her sister for comfort. I would learn, in time, to let most of my attachments go, and, anchored more firmly into my own space, live life more independently.

I quit smoking in 2002 after having been a smoker since I was fourteen. I have been making a lot of progress in dealing with my own substance abuse issues. Early in Angie's disease and though deeply mired in my codependency around her, I remember the day I screamed to myself: *Enough! Enough addictions in this family!* And I remember why. I had recently removed my daughter from my house and she was living with her pusher in D.C. That period was one of the dips in the roller coaster ride that would push me toward a nervous breakdown several years later. But at the time, feeling powerless to end her self-destructive behavior, I took back the power I had to end mine. I wore a patch and weaned myself off my menthol cigarettes over a period of six months. And I've never missed them — not for a second.

I know addiction is a brain disease, and I'm certainly no expert on how or why some people are afflicted with it. Why do certain people abuse substances? Why did I depend on amphetamines for ten years? And how could I stop and never start again? Why did I smoke all those years and why was it easy for me to stop? Why have I been a food addict all my life and why am I just one bulimic episode away from relapsing? I have no answers to these questions. But I do know that learning to love and value myself through my work in all the Twelve-Step Programs I attend has made it easier for me live well and put an end to my self-abuse.

Expectations, when dealing with loving an addict, can be killers. We want our loved one to seek recovery and remain there, of course—for the rest of his life. We want the nightmare to end and to stop waiting for the other shoe to drop. As my friend Michael said at an Al-Anon meeting: "We all live in this forest. We can remodel our house, add to it, and greatly improve its value. But we're always going to live in the forest." Philip Seymour Hoffman's recent death reminds us that "once an addict, always an addict." We may stop abusing substances at last—and forever if we're truly blessed. But we always carry within us the addictive gene/tendency to pull us back into that dark world of relapse and—in the case of this brilliant actor—destroy us.

The more Angie has declined and showed signs of brain damage, the more I've needed the discipline and comfort of my recovery program. I no longer regret Angie's illness any more than I would regret a cancer diagnosis. It's a horrific, deadly illness and is particularly cruel because it often destroys our children's minds before it actually kills them.

What was unfortunate for most of the years of Angie's addiction was my reaction to it. All the mistakes I made are the product of my disease, not Angie's. And I have found great relief, joy, serenity and contentment through Twelve-Step study. I have learned many important lessons in this Program, most importantly learning to let go of anything that is out of my control. As long as Angie is still alive, there's always hope that she will recover on her own. It's—and this is the hardest lesson for any parent—out of my hands.

Recovery has been a slow uphill battle for me. I've had to examine and then let go of beliefs about myself that no longer served me. And if they didn't serve me well, they harmed those I loved as well; for example, my tendency to judge myself and assume inappropriate amounts of guilt. Guilt crippled me with Angie and kept me from being a firm parent. That was what she needed, not an enabler.

Many Twelve-Step meetings end with the shout-out: "Keep coming back. It works if you work it—because you're worth it!" If you are blessed enough to grow up feeling loved, valued, respected and cherished then you are fortunate indeed. I grew up on very shaky ground, but there is no one to blame. Alcoholism is a disease, not a human failing, and it has infected my family for several generations. I am an adult child, and many adult children suffer from low self-esteem. So for me now to proclaim, "I'm worth it!" and mean it has been crucial to my well-being. I feel so grateful for the healthy principles I've learned in this fellowship.

> From *Opening Our Hearts, Transforming Our Losses:*
>
> After the acute pain of grief, the one feeling at the forefront now is gratitude—tremendous, overwhelming gratitude…
>
> I'll probably never know why some people are able to find recovery while others are not. Still, I'm astonished to discover that not only in spite of, but because of my losses, I am more keenly aware of the tenuousness, the delicacy, and the beauty of every moment. (170, 172)

I particularly like this book because it's straightforward and puts the stress on positive solutions. It takes the disease of addiction out of the closet and shows it at its worst, which is why people affected by it have earned the right to grieve. I know many people who can't even admit to the disease in their family, much less grieve about it. The book puts our losses out on the table, but doesn't leave us mourning. The shared stories show us how to move on with our lives.

All of the Twelve-Step programs are indebted to the founders of Alcoholics Anonymous who wrote the steps back in the 1930's. Much of the early literature would serve as a guide in subsequent programs. From *Anonymous Press Mini Edition of Alcoholics Anonymous*:

> An illness of this sort—and we have come to believe it an illness—involves those about us in a way no other human sickness can. If a person has cancer, all are sorry for him and no one is angry or hurt. But not so with the alcoholic illness, for with it there goes annihilation of all the things worthwhile in life. It engulfs all whose lives touch the sufferer's. It brings misunderstanding, fierce resentment, financial insecurity, disgusted friends and employers, warped lives of blameless children, sad wives and parents—anyone can increase the list. (18)

I am sometimes at odds with my recovery groups about the nature of addiction: is it a disease or a choice? I don't want to force my views on them. There's a wonderful Cherokee tale told by a grandfather to his grandchildren:

"There's a battle inside all of us between two wolves. One wolf is jealousy, greed, dishonesty, hatred, anger and bitterness. The other wolf is love, generosity, truthfulness, selflessness, and gratitude."

"Who wins the battle, grandfather?"

"The wolf you feed."

Insist that our loved ones are choosing to be addicts, that they want to stick a needle in their arm and live in a gutter, and we feel justified in our anger and our bitterness. Keep feeding those feelings, and they will consume you. I choose to believe that my daughter is wired differently and is prone to addictive disease. That's no surprise, since four generations in my family have all had addictive disease in varying degrees. For whatever reason we still are unsure of, whatever life stresses beckoned her into that dark place, she became a victim of addiction.

Dr. Nora Volkow, director of the National Institute on Drug Abuse, has said:

> I've studied alcohol, cocaine, methamphet-amine, heroin, marijuana and more recently obesity. There's a pattern in compulsion. I've never come across a single person that was ad-dicted that wanted to be addicted. Something has happened in their brains that has led to that process. (qtd. in Sheff)

I interviewed another mother recently, Maria, from my Nar-Anon group in New Mexico.

Maria is beside herself. Her son has been living with her, on and off, and stealing from her. She knows he is on drugs; he doesn't even try to hide it. I have been exactly where she is with my daughter. At what point do parents say enough is enough and start to take care of themselves better? At what point do parents let go of this anchor that will pull them down too if they don't cut themselves loose? All of us are different. Back in 2002 I kicked Angie out of my house because of her outrageous drug-induced behavior. But since then I've waffled back and forth through my own recovery, never able until recently to be steadfast on the recovery path that I have chosen.

"I don't know what to do," Maria laments. "My son is in two parts. I don't see him anymore. He's hidden deep inside."

"Can you explain that a little more and tell me how it makes you feel?" I prod her on.

"I simply don't recognize him anymore. He's a stranger to me. He behaves like somebody else. I feel a lot of things: furious and terrified at the same time."

One of the hardest things for parents to do is to behave appropriately when the addict is in charge. More times than I want to remember, I turned a blind eye to Angie the addict and pandered to her needs. This is enabling at its worst because it hurts both the parent and the child: the parent probably feels his wallet getting lighter as he fumes that "my kid never even thanked me;" the kid feels less and less respect for his parent or whoever the enabler was, in a hurry to get his next fix. The cycle goes on and on like this until it is broken. I remember the definition of insanity: doing the same thing over and over and expecting different results. For years I behaved insanely.

I was always the enabler, but Maria was ready to do things differently. She gave her son a choice: he could get on the next plane to a rehab in California she had arranged for him, or he could get out of the house. They went through this dance a couple of times. The first time he got out. But he came back and the cycle of stealing and abuse continued. She called the police during an altercation, threatening jail time, and in front of the police he agreed to go into rehab rather than be arrested. My friend took her son to the airport, full of relief and hope, but once inside the building he froze in his tracks, sat down, and refused to go any further. What followed was the slow motion agony of detachment and letting go.

Maria went on, "I just stood there like a statue, looking down at him in the chair. Everyone around us was a blur. There were only two people in the world: Michael and me. Nothing else mattered. I begged him to cooperate. I told him this was his last chance with me. He just looked down at his shoes that were cemented to the floor. I told him I'd had it. I just couldn't do this anymore. I didn't even try to kiss him or hug him goodbye. I felt like a piece of wood. I walked out of the airport and left him there. I haven't heard from him since; this was two weeks ago."

The break was over and we had to get back to the second half of the meeting. I hugged Maria, "Thanks for sharing this with me, Maria. Take care."

"Thanks for listening to me. It really helps to talk about Michael and know that I'm not alone."

"You're not alone, Maria. Look around you," as I looked at the sixty people sitting in the room.

Maria has other children, but a few of my friends are grieving the loss of their only child. That must be very hard, to see all of our parenting efforts focused on this one troubled child. But there are endless things in life to be grateful for, and new joys ready to be embraced, if we but open our hearts.

Frequently exasperated over the years when Angie has relapsed, I would even talk to God a little:

"God, I've been at this place before with my daughter. This very same place! I feel like I'm a rat chasing my tail! It's not fair, buddy."

"Maggie, first of all I'm not your buddy. Secondly, you're not a rat chasing your tail. It seems that way to you because you're too close to the situation. Step outside of everything for a while and get some perspective."

"OK, you're right. But what about the last thing?"

"Maggie, who ever told you life was fair?"

From *One Day At A Time*:

My life is a series of unfoldings — incidents and occasions, agreeable or distressing. Each day is full of them, hour by hour, and this makes it difficult for me to take a detached view of all that is happening. I'm too close.

If these occurrences were like so many pieces of merchandise — groceries or dry goods — I would see them clearly, good and bad. Looking at the incidents of my life in this way, I might be astonished to discover that the good far outweigh the bad. And yet I concentrate so heavily on the trials and burdens that I hardly give a thought to relishing the pleasant and satisfying things that happen each day.

This noticing is an acute awareness of our surroundings and what takes place in them. It can be cultivated, like watching a play or film.

Today's Reminder:

If I learn to see everything with a fresh eye, I will find I have many reasons for contentment and gratitude. When I find myself being bogged down with negative thoughts, I will deliberately turn away from them.

Let me observe, with new interest, even the commonplace things that happen in each new day. (345)

In All Our Affairs

I don't see my family very often. Gene and I live far away from our families of origin. We enjoy a quiet life in a farmhouse with a fruit orchard in New Mexico.

Christmas in July, that's what it felt like.

When Gene and I bought this property back in 2009, we were newly retired. He had a part-time job teaching college English, but he was still bored. He sat in his rocker that spring watching the sun transform the mountain into a palette of vermillion hues day after day. He wondered what to do with his life. Included in the property was a half-acre extending east from the backyard. Then one day the idea hit him: "I want to grow fruit trees. I'm gonna plant an orchard."

Like a bolt of lightening he felt energized. Gene bought his first trees from local nurseries, usually two-year-olds. Over the course of the next two years he ordered more trees, some of them whips, or babies, from mail order nurseries. Finally he had fifty trees in the ground, lovingly planted, each one, with his own hands. He used most of his savings to do this. He nurtured every one of those trees as if they were his own children: fertilizer, coffee grounds, water, homemade and store bought compost—whatever would give them the best chance to flourish in the difficult, sandy soil of New Mexico.

You should see them now, how they've grown up since then. Our half-acre is thick with peach trees, cherries, apples, and plums. The cherries didn't do well at first. That year, he saved the one Rainier we got in a bottle until it dried up like a big raisin. But now the trees are thick with them, three different kinds. In previous years we'd lost our battle with the birds. But we recently put up netting, like the top of a circus tent, over the orchard. This year I think we're doing it right. Shamelessly smirking as I watch them perched and ready to attack, I shout, "I'm sorry birds, but you'll have to go elsewhere when the red catches your eyes. We're smarter now." We've also got blackberries that keep sprouting new shoots all over, melons, peppers, squash, cucumbers, and eggplants. We have so many tomatoes we have to give them away, whatever we can't sell at the market. Last year we had tomatoes till Christmas. And basil? I can't believe I used to buy it at the store. We have three or four kinds and so much of it growing wild all over the place that I just grab handfuls of it, wash it, and throw it into my sandwiches, my salads, everything. It's my ambrosia.

So on that morning in July I went down to inspect the orchard and grew wild-eyed at the sight in front of me. I was drunk with the sight of all this ripe fruit on our trees.

"Gene, come down here," I shouted, "Look at the trees!" He was drinking his coffee on the patio and took his time joining me. He had seen the blossoms from months before so he wasn't as surprised as I was. I didn't go down to the orchard much; I was consumed with my rose garden next to the house. So it was a revelation to me how a small white flower could transform itself into a piece of succulent fruit.

"Oh ye of little faith," he intoned smiling, delighted at the proliferation of white and yellow peaches on at least twenty-five of our trees — big ones, big as large apples. We had the trees netted pretty sloppily that year and the greedy birds took pecks out of many of them so they couldn't all be sold.

Reaching out to pick one, Gene let out a cry of dismay when his fingers sank into the open flesh of the peach. "Ach!" he hollered, "Damn birds!"

"They have to eat, too," I reminded him.

But I cooked and froze the mangled peaches that we couldn't sell. Gene said they tasted better than any he had ever bought in the store, and he's very discriminating. We were giddy with delight, went out and bought baskets to harvest them and get them to market that weekend. Gene happily held out samples for our customers on Saturday and Sunday — literally the fruit of all his labor. He has grown very content with our life in the Southwest.

"Giddy with delight" — recovery does wear many faces.

"Recovery is when fun becomes fun; love becomes love; and life becomes worth living" (Beattie Section 1).

Now I tune into the life that is going on all around me. My sadness around Angie doesn't weigh me down anymore. It's there, of course, but I elevate myself when I remember to count my blessings and be grateful. Like a snake that has shed its skin, I feel fresher and more ready for life and its daily renewable force. My son now has a wife whom I adore and two beautiful little girls whom I visit often. They, along with Caroline, Gene, and my wonderful friends and extended family, are the flowers in my garden. They are, along with work and my other passions, my happiness. Every day that I let myself embrace life, I find contentment. I just have to keep my heart open. "Agape" is one of the Greek words for love. Agape — open — ready to receive.

Quite a few of my friends in the Program, still struggling so hard to meet this challenge in their lives, simply don't understand how I can feel one moment of happiness even as I watch Angie further slipping away deeper and deeper into the black hole of drug addiction. But, as I've said so often when I've spoken at meetings, in Al-Anon we learn that we have choices. We do not have to bury ourselves with our loved ones, though we often may want to. Several years ago I paid a heavy price for my involvement in my daughter's illness, and I didn't want to keep losing, one by one, the parts of my own life tapestry I had worked so hard to create. I have had a wonderful and interesting life, and I can say that now, and feel it in my bones, without embarrassment or guilt. My work in this transformative Program has reacquainted me with my own worth and humanity, both of which came seriously into question when this tragedy struck my daughter.

Well, welcome to your second life, Maggie! I guess it's never too late to learn how to be happy. Jennie Jerome Churchill has shared with us her definition of happiness: "Life is not always what one wants it to be, but to make the best of it as it is, is the only way of being happy" (*Each Day* August 17). That sounds like her take on acceptance to me. So how do I make the best of living with a cloud over my head, a cloud that will always be there, even if Angie at last finds recovery? By focusing on gratitude — my recovery is grounded in it.

One of the promises of Al-Anon is that we shall learn to be "happy, joyous and free." I like the free part best. For too many years I've been chained to my own human failings. I never understood with such clarity my own defects and limitations until I started to work this Program. I was so lonely and isolated. But when I came to believe after much trial and error that I was in fact powerless over addiction — mine, Angie's and anyone else's — I fell to my knees and turned this struggle over. And I felt so much lighter. Now, at last, I was off the hook. I've turned over all the lost years with Angie and turned my attention to things I can control now. And that has given me the freedom to focus on other things.

My spirituality is based on three factors: far less EGO (Easing God Out), humble acceptance of whatever my lot is in life, and the vision to appreciate every day for all the good that I can see and experience. In this way, the principles of this

Program have changed my life. It's really great to be alive, and for so many years my life was utterly joyless. That's the power of the spirit coming alive in me through my spiritual Program.

Recovery from the effects of a loved one's addiction—what else is it? It's many things to many people. It's being able to relish the kaleidoscope of colors in life—not just see them but also appreciate them. Life need no longer be black and white, even gray. My friend, Debby, coming out of a meeting recently, exclaimed:

"Oh, what a gorgeous sunset!"

That's what recovery is: being able, in spite of everything, to swim with the currents of life—and be grateful one can still swim. Thirteen years seem like a long time to watch one's child slowly succumb to the disease of addiction, though I know other parents who have traveled this road longer. Angie has bounced in and out of recovery and so have I. I have no wish to outlive my child, but many parents do just that, whether the enemy is cancer or any other disease.

Growing up in the Fifties, we weren't a wealthy family, and my mother taught me to squeeze the life out of every penny. Later on, I was more comfortable financially, but I remained tight just the same. Especially during Angie's illness, I continued to shop at Goodwill and cut as many corners as I could. This enabled me to have more disposable income to enable my daughter! Xavier and I sent her to four rehabs, paid off her college and car loan from years ago, continued to pay her rent and support her much of the time these last few years, and I had set up that Walgreen's account in San Francisco.

Well, poof! Cinderella has turned into a pumpkin, or maybe the other way around, but another face of my recovery looks like a lot of overdue self-care. I've grown so much in self-esteem through my work in the Program. Now I'm starting to spend my money on myself, and what an adventure! I have a regular massage therapist now, a friend in the Program, so she knows me well. She told me she thinks I've been storing a lifetime of pain in my body. I told her she's full of crap — wouldn't I feel it? During our second session, she found a spot in my back that sent me through the roof.

"Jesus Christ, Vivian, that hurts. Stop it!" I screamed, involuntary tears streaming down my cheeks. I started sobbing about I don't know what. She just looked at me, nodding her head. She knows all about my resistance. Week after week she's heard my whole story. She was right. And now she was showing me that the pain in my body was nothing compared to my resistance to it, which is what tension is. I've cried plenty in my life, but I've never had much physical pain or cried as a result of it. This was huge. Every week she has been unlocking points of pain all over my body. She also suggested I start to do yoga. From my work in the Program, I've learned about mental and emotional surrender. Vivian felt that I needed to find an outlet for physical surrender as well.

I really enjoyed my first yoga class. The Yogi had us going for an extended aerobic workout. (I think this summer crowd wanted to sweat more.) With Katy Perry blaring and Michael Jackson belting out "Billie Jean," I started fantasizing. Right in front of me I imagined a huge punching bag, and I was giving it left jabs and right hooks, all the while yelling under my breath:

"I hate you, Addiction! You are the curse of this century and I despise you. You've stolen my daughter and this is what I think of you: Kapow! Boom! Left jab to the right eye. Bleed, you bastard! Angie may not have the strength to fight you, but I do. Here's a right hook to your left eye. Keep bleeding, you son of a bitch. This one's for my dad. Ever since I can remember, you snatched him from my life. This one's for Angie, you piece of shit. Is this how you get off? Turning a beautiful, bright young woman into a vegetable? And this one's for me, you giant succubus. Me, I won't let you destroy. Me, I'm gonna save. So that my children and grandchildren will see that there is hope when struggling with Addiction. It doesn't always have to win."

"God, please, **pleas**e help me break the chain of addiction in my family. Right here—right now!"

Tears streaming down my face, I started slowing down with the rest of the class, deep breathing in and out, as we cooled down separate sections of our bodies. It was a good workout for me, a nice release. At the end of the class, getting up from our lotus position, we all bowed to each other and said something I don't remember. But I do remember how good it felt to hit that imaginary punching bag, even if it didn't parry with me. It couldn't; it's not human. Addiction is a nasty, nasty illness. When it kills its victims slowly for all to helplessly witness, it can be very frustrating. Physical activity helped me and I felt better afterwards.

Well, this wasn't strictly yoga, not at all—more like karate. My instructor kept airily saying, "FREE your MIND of all your thoughts. Just FEEL your body. R-E-L-A-X. Get in touch with your body," etc. So after a couple of classes, I got the message and got rid of the imaginary punching bag. After class that week when we all sat around drinking tea and sharing, I said that I had learned something.

"Oh, yes? Tell us what you learned today," he inquired, with an expectant look on his face.

"I learned to leave the punching bag and all my negative thoughts at the door," I offered.

Everyone was pleased; smiles and light applause all around. *Geez,* I thought to myself, *I didn't realize what a strutz I was being!* And then, all judgment aside, I congratulated myself for being a good student — not so much the stubborn, resistant, willful adult child I was when I entered Twelve-Step recovery.

Another lesson learned.

Recovery from addiction, one's own or from the effects of someone else's, is not an easy accomplishment. My program of recovery has enabled me to grow in self-awareness, self-esteem, and self-forgiveness. I've committed many sins in my life, against my sister and others. There were very few consequences, and so I internalized my guilt. I would be forever crippled until I found a way to let go of that baggage.

This healing Program has shown me how to face myself in the mirror honestly, with gentleness, kindness and praise for the good things I have done. I've learned how to hold myself accountable for my actions and cease blaming others. I've learned the importance of making a simple apology, something I didn't learn as a child.

In fact, I've often said in meetings that I grew up in my recovery groups. And it's true. I am an adult child: chronologically an adult but emotionally immature, though less so as I continue in my recovery. Many of us who grow up with alcoholism have addictive personalities ourselves and find ourselves ill prepared to meet life's challenges effectively. We often marry our addicted parent, or we look outside of ourselves for sources of comfort. There is an absence of differentiation, as Dr. Gabor Maté explains (237). Many of us overeat, pop too many pills, shop too much, drink too much, work too much, etc. Addiction is everywhere in our society. It temporarily fills in our hollow spaces until we feel better. A soundly moral character, among many other things, has gone a long way toward keeping my addictions at bay — one day at a time.

Being able to live one day at a time, one of the basic tenets of the Twelve-Step Programs, used to be a challenge for me. How could I live my whole life in just the next twenty-four hours — without fear or projection? That was a tall order. But particularly for addicts it's necessary to live one day at a time. Life happens — every day — and too many stresses can occur in a mere twenty-four hours to throw us a curve and beckon us back into our addictive behavior. If we limit our vision to the day at hand, it's easier to stay focused on our sobriety.

Early in my Twelve-Step study, I often tormented myself looking at my past mistakes because I'd felt I had it coming. "What goes around comes around," and all that wrathful noise about divine retribution. But I don't believe God has anything to do with my self-punishment because I believe that He is benevolent. And now I can "look back without staring" if I keep my focus on the present and remind myself that done is done, but today is the first day of the rest of my life.

Not dwelling on what happened yesterday, not worrying about what hasn't happened yet, and having the gratitude to appreciate the colors of the sunrise today, or a kind gesture from someone, or a good meal, or a good night's sleep — I'm always sending God thank you notes — I don't know who else to thank! The ability to do this is one of the many rewards this Program offers us.

After that scathing communication from Angie while I was in Austin, I retreated into a furious, uncommunicative shell. Then, out of the blue — apparently she didn't remember what she had said to me in that brutal text — she sent me this one a couple of months later — with all the entitlement that only an addict can muster:

"Why haven't you reopened my Walgreen's account yet? I have a gash in my leg now and need to fill this script. It's getting infected so I need these antibiotics. I just spent $4500 to move, so I'm broke. I NEED TO FILL THIS SCRIPT. I COULD LOSE MY LEG."

My response:

"Ur life is a mess because of the drugs u take. U r cruel and abusive. Were u unconscious when u kicked me out of ur life? U know what u need to do. When u get clean, when it occurs to u to give me the love and respect I deserve, then u can start building a bridge, which u urself burned, back to me. Until then, just know that I will always love you, no matter what u do. I'm always here to support u in recovery. But I will give u no $. Those are my boundaries."

Angie's retort:

"I have no desire to have a conversation with u. I don't even want u in my life, but I will say that my addiction is the best thing that ever happened to u because all of a sudden u think ur some kind of fucking martyr whose fit to judge everyone around u and who fucking knows everything. Maybe any mistreatment u got from me was just ur OVERDUE comeuppances for YEARS of the most miserable, ABUSIVE, pathetic excuse for parenting we suffered under u? Did u ever think about that?"

And again:

"And u couldn't bother to tell me that yesterday before I fucking hobbled to Walgreen's for NOTHING with an infection in my leg that looks like an ax wound, you stupid cunt."

From me in response:

"If you go to Walgreen's on Geary St. I will call the pharmacist and pay for this one antibiotics prescription. Tell me if u want me to do that. I won't do anything unless u text me back."

No response.

I texted:

"I'm going to bed and silencing my phone so I can get a good night's sleep. I haven't heard back from you, so I assume u don't need anything from me."

I read her response in the morning:

"Get fucked u dumb bitch. Thanks for fucking NOTHING. I've gone without antibiotics for so long at this point I have a 102-degree fever and I don't even have the energy to make it. To. The pharmacy. Just typing. This. Text took over an hour"

My response:

"I'm sorry, Angie."

Last text from her:

"I didn't bother reading your last text and I don't plan on reading it. I don't see any point in any further communication."

In her memoir, Carol Burnett shares some of her hard-won wisdom during Carrie's early drug addiction:

"You have to love them enough to let them hate you" (34).

On Facebook, I read a passage by Passion, the anonymous screen name of a recovering addict. It's a compelling essay that offers tremendous insight into the mind of many addicts. These are some excerpted passages:

> You can't make me clean, though I know it is what you want for me to be. But until I want it, I won't be. You can't love me clean, because until I learn to love myself, I won't be. I know you must wonder how I can learn to love myself when I am caught up in a lifestyle of self-hatred and self-destruction... I can learn from the things that happen to me along the path of my own mistakes. I can learn by being allowed to suffer the consequences of my choices. Life has

a funny way of teaching us the lessons we need to learn.

I know it devastates you to watch me hurting myself. I know you want to jump in and save me. This helps ease your pain, but I don't think you understand just how damaging it is to me.

You see, although I look like and sound like your loved one, I am not. That person is in a self-imposed prison way deep down inside of my being and what you see before you is an addict ruled and reigned by my addiction. The main focus of an addict is to feed the addiction...

How can or will I ever be able to get clean, you wonder...

The same way I gave myself over to my addiction is the same way I can give myself over to my recovery. BY MYSELF

It's been very difficult for me to separate Angie, the daughter I raised, from the addict she has become. But this is work that many of us must do in order to gain some objectivity when dealing with our loved ones. A parent writes in *Sharing Experience, Strength and Hope*:

> I could not bear to look at pictures of him, as they were only a sad reminder of what he had been and what was taken from him. I missed his sweetness, his innocence, his loving nature, and his honesty. That was my son, not the shadow of the person he was now. I was losing him and myself while my family was being torn apart. The only thing I was sure of was the fact that I was powerless. (361)

I talk a lot to other parents struggling with this kind of loss about the need to separate the addict from their child. This is so important because it governs how we respond to abuse while our loved one is in active addiction. But for many it's a surreal exercise. Before I had educated myself about addiction I felt angry and betrayed every time Angie hurt me. I was so enmeshed with her, and felt so responsible for what was happening, that I allowed much of my own life to spiral out of control. But when I could finally make the separation necessary for my own well-being, when I could lovingly detach from my daughter, my life got better. I told her that I would no longer support her disease, but I would gladly walk beside her in recovery.

Angie called us several months ago and demanded several thousand dollars. We said no. Since then, she has cut herself off from her family. We've been in this purgatory before, when she was missing in Baltimore for almost a year. We know only too well what it feels like to wonder if our daughter is dead or alive. It's almost as if we're talking to cold air when we have reached her, as if she had vaporized into a ghost. And in so many fundamental ways she is a ghost of her former self. Maybe right now she is in that place between life and death, that living agony of drug abuse where she has all but forgotten the family and friends who have loved her for three decades. I read about those lost souls in Gabor Maté's book, his patients whom he treats in Vancouver, British Columbia. Perhaps Angie is like one of them now, an ethereal creature already with one foot in the grave in the bowels of San Francisco's drug world (184, 220, 260, 346, 430).

Xavier and I still try to contact her by email. I just tell her I love her. It's important to me that she knows this. She never responds, so I can't be sure she gets my message. We've lost countless phone numbers because she keeps throwing away her phones and buying new ones. I believe in my heart that part of Angie feels great love for her family and that estranging herself from us is the only means she has left to spare us the pain of her addiction. Angie knows how to reach us; I pray she does, and soon—unless her mind has forgotten us. All it would take is one phone call telling us she wants to go back into recovery—and all of us who love her would join her in support.

I've called the police department in San Francisco to leave my name as next of kin in case my daughter shows up there. "I'm sorry, Mrs. Romero. We're just not set up to keep a database like that. There are too many addicts out there." "Not set up to keep a database like that?" In my frustration, I call the morgues and get them to take down my name. I visit Angie's old dentist in Virginia to retrieve her dental records. He looks puzzled; I don't explain and leave in a hurry.

My newest concern was not if she was still on drugs. That was patently clear to us all. Now I feared that she would lose that leg, the one with the femoral artery she injected God knows what into when I left her alone in my condo in Virginia—the same artery that got infected again right after she moved to San Francisco. And now that same artery was infected again, threatening to break like a worn out rubber band. She really could lose her leg. And then what will become of her? Whereto, Persephone? A state hospital somewhere in California for the rest of what's left of her life? Would this be the bottom we all pray for and fear at the same time—the one that convinces her that she must embrace recovery or die?

I live with this reality every day. Sometimes I look up and ask God for a sign, some way of knowing something. But this is why I'm learning to replace fear with faith. I've spent much of my life controlled and manipulated by fear, rarely feeling good enough, secure enough, valued enough to just be me. Fear so often clouds our good judgment, and faith releases us from too much responsibility, too much self-importance, and from our need to control. Over and over again in times of crisis in recent years I've accepted what is — without resistance anymore — and I've discovered for myself that faith and acceptance go hand in hand.

My behavior when I was in San Francisco is a good example of this. Expressing any anger to Angie — feeding the angry wolf — would have been an appalling waste of energy. I've known since she was in her first rehab in 2002 that she's not a rebellious child in need of a spanking; she's sick. She may or may not get well someday. But wherever her journey leads her it will be her journey to make. I can only love her and wish her God's speed. I have absolute faith that life is unfolding as it is meant to. Having faith in anything — a rock, a friend, the God of our understanding — is a shared experience, ending our isolation.

Faith, like recovery, wears many faces. I'm not a born-again Christian. When I was a child and young adult in Massachusetts, I went to church because I was told to. My mother had found solace in the religious rituals during her own childhood, and I believe she wanted to pass them on to all of us. But I found no such solace or relief. I felt entirely abandoned by God as a child. Later, when my children were little, Xavier and I returned to church for a number of years in an effort to give our children a spiritual foundation. We went through the motions, but having little or no genuine faith in a benevolent higher power, I can see why my children never bought into it. They, like their mother, went to church because they were told to, and we all stopped going when we moved overseas. Angie, in her conversation back in 1987 with my mother, implied that she, too, felt abandoned by God, just as I had at the same age.

It wasn't until I was tested as her mother that I found my ability to harness any faith at all. My sadness as a child paled before my growing despair as an adult child. The journey I'm on now has given me fresh new insights as I've confronted myself and understood where I have come from. My journey has in turn helped me understand where I have taken my own family. What was given to me has been passed down to my children. Yet I understand now that I could not have turned out differently, nor could I have been a different parent. My behavior as an adult was scripted from my childhood. What I need now is faith in something outside of myself to help me carry the burden—and gratitude that I'm finally able to ask for help. My faith has everything to do with turning over my self-will and accepting the will of another. I have found peace and serenity in acceptance of life as it is happening every day. Letting go and handing over the reins has given me the freedom to live my own life now without feeling shackled to the past or frightened of the future.

From *Sharing Experience Strength and Hope:*

> Thought For Today: When I feel overwhelmed and unable to cope with my problems, I can surrender and let the God of my understanding take control. This is not the act of a quitter; it is an act of faith. (275)

I shared emails with my friend in Virginia a while back—more like swapping war stories. She asks me in one I receive today my advice on how to get through the holidays. I respond to her, grateful that I might be able to make a small difference, but well aware that we each must find our own way to navigate through these waters:

Susan,

Thanks for your informative and heartfelt email. Re the Friday a.m. meeting, no guilt or apology needed for not attending, though I completely understand why you feel those feelings. Anyway, the older I get the more selfish I become. I'm learning to be picky about how I spend my time, because I have less of it than young people. You keep your Friday mornings for yourself; do whatever you want. Your time is valuable; don't waste it.

How will I get through the holidays? My younger daughter is flying in for a visit. And the following week I fly to Austin to be with my grandchildren. That's how I get through the holidays, by focusing on all the good in my life and being grateful. You must do the same thing.

I want to be happy. I've done what I can to help Angie. But all I can do is make the tools of recovery accessible to her (four times in rehab). She has to pick them up with her own hands and use them if she wants to recover. That's it. No more hand wringing for me. I've turned it over to God and will accept whatever is His will.

So how to get through the holidays? It's all in how we see things, our attitude, how we choose to view our world. I make myself look on the bright side of things, not because I'm a goody-goody (Ha!), but because it makes me feel better. At what point in the road did I decide I deserved to be happy? I don't know. But when you reach it, you'll know. And you'll feel like the weight of the world has been lifted off your shoulders. That's what recovery feels like.

All the best to you, my friend, and hope the holidays will be less of a chore for you this year. Keep in touch and take good care of yourself. Maggie

One of the things that we attempt to do in Nar-Anon, not out of anger, bitterness or spite, is to make both parties accept responsibility for their choices, and bear the consequences as well. The principles of this Program are intended to promote dignity and growth in both the parent and the addict.

For a long time I was lost and consumed with my grief. But now I am determined to live my life to the fullest, keep the focus on myself, what I can control, and what I can take joy in. Mustering the self-esteem to do that is the direct result of my growing up not in my family of origin, which was fraught with alcoholism, but in the wise and compassionate Twelve-Step fellowships I belong to.

Now I feel worthy enough to move on with my life and to feel grateful on a daily basis for the gifts I've been given. I focus on all that I have, not all that I've lost, and recognizing my glass as half full is empowering. And if we're lucky we figure out that it's better for everyone—the addict and the loved ones touched by his disease—to try to save ourselves.

If the Program is working, and for some of us it takes years to surrender, we learn to let go, to place responsibility where it belongs, and to focus on ourselves. The Program teaches us to be selfish. We bore these children who didn't ask to be born and we did the best we could to raise them to adulthood. At some point we learn to release them to the wind, cross our fingers and hope for the best.

How I've been able to even think about my own recovery, much less reach for it, on the bones of my daughter is a testimony to the power of transformation through spiritual recovery. And only as my recovery deepens have I been able to withstand this struggle with any serenity or grace.

Speaking at an Al-Anon meeting for parents recently, I said:

"My topic tonight is the second half of the Serenity Prayer: the courage to change the things we can. All of us as parents are united by a plethora of feelings: anger, disappointment, frustration, and often relief and joy in our children's new or continued recovery. There are many lessons for us all to learn, in both the negative and the positive outcomes of our struggle. I have learned and am still learning much about myself. You all have watched me the past few years as my daughter has bounced up and down with depression and drug addiction. And prior to that, hard to believe, she was far more functional, finishing college, working at a good job, driving, and still in touch with her family. So, it's been hard for me to connect the dots, very hard. But as I have, out of sheer necessity, I've found myself more and more in touch with my own purpose for being on this earth. And as I've done that, I've needed to make changes.

"How has this program enabled me to make changes in my life? Well, for me, I can't breathe a sigh of relief and say my child is in recovery right now. So, as I often say to myself and to friends here, 'What am I supposed to do? Do I lie down and give up? Or do I try to keep going?' I do have a choice every day. I've spoken a few other times here and I've always said the same thing: I keep going because there are other voices out there to listen to. There are other people in the world, in my world, which I can touch and make a difference to. I don't want to forget them. I just have to keep my heart open.

"The program has helped me determine what I want to do with my life. I've learned to do more for myself. I've grown a lot. I know myself better, from my Fourth Step work, and I'm trying to improve my relationships with people. I've learned to like myself more, and because of that I want to live better. I value my time more and I don't want to waste it.

"Our mettle has been tested, all of us as parents. We've paid our dues, and in my case, sometimes in service to my daughter's addiction. Now can we go beyond mere acceptance of our lot and transform our lives into one that we deserve? Sometimes, being human, I feel, 'how can I?' But I've reached a point in my own journey where I want not only to survive the effects of this disease, but also to live well. I don't want Addiction to win twice. This is the promise of Al-Anon. This is my hope for my future.

"So, the topic tonight is transformation, and changing the things in our lives that we can. The floor is now open for sharing."

Recently I asked my friend Jeanne if she remembers Angie from when she was younger. While she was in college, she was going door-to-door selling Cutco cutlery. Angie could sell a freezer to an Eskimo—a skill we would all sadly fall victim to years later. Of course I bought a set of knives, which are gathering dust in my basement in Virginia. I can't bear to part with them—such concrete reminders they are of her normalcy, her functionality, of Angie before she got sick.

"Oh yes," she enthused. "Angie called up to make an appointment to show me the cutlery she was selling. I told her to come over at three that afternoon. 'But don't be so formal, Angie! I'm three blocks away from you. Just come on over!'

"When she got to my house, she shook hands with me. So professional! Angie sat down at my dining room table and went through the whole blurb. It must have taken her hours to memorize all that! Well, I was so impressed that I bought the whole set—$750 worth of cutlery—which I use all the time now. It was a great investment, and it will probably last forever."

Then my friend, her eyes tearing up, returned to the present moment in our lives—light years away from those carefree days.

"Honey, I don't think she's gonna make it."

It must have been very hard for my friend to say this to me. I have struggled and ruminated for a dozen years; but rarely have I burdened my friends with my fears and projections. Hearing these words from her struck me hard. Time and again over the years I told myself this was just a nightmare that would be over. It was a storm, and like all storms, it would pass.

But for now, all of us who love Angie are steeling themselves for a final onslaught, a final reckoning, hers with her life, or ours with her death. We still have hope that she will reach for recovery. Her father insists she is a survivor. And as I've said many times at meetings, as long as she's above ground, there's hope.

Now we need to go on with our lives as best we can in spite of the cloud hanging over us. If my beautiful girl can't find the courage to say yes to a healthy life, then I will. I'll do it for her. What could be a better testament to Angie, to all her gifts and possibilities, than to go forward with my life savoring every moment? Wherever she is right now, I know that the best part of her loves me and would want me to be well. I really believe that, in spite of everything her drug-induced mind has spit forth. I have more confidence now. I know without a doubt that I've been a good (enough) mother to Angie. I love her. And loving is enough. Loving is always enough. This has been my lesson.

Though nothing can restore the years we've lost with Angie, I feel more and more able to embrace the life around me and revel in the gifts I've been given. On my gratitude list this morning, I added something else: "I thought the rose bush was dead, but a little more water and it's come back." Simple things—

How is it possible for me to be grateful, even, to Angie, whose illness brought me into the rooms of Twelve-Step recovery? How is this possible?

My unsent letter to my child:

Dear Angie,

Ironic, isn't it, that you have become my teacher and not the other way around—teacher of life, teacher of love, and beacon of surrender.

I'm so grateful that you were born, even though at times I've felt otherwise. God works in mysterious ways, doesn't he? Though you haven't been in my life long, and not always happily, it's been your very existence that has propelled me into a serenely spiritual life, even happiness. I never would have done the work necessary to reach this place without your inspiration.

You are my child, my teacher. As I've stumbled on this rocky path, my thoughts of you have guided me; they guide me still.

All that I've become are gifts from you, my daughter: life lessons, trial by fire. How do I thank you?

By living well—By loving well—Mom

"God grant me the serenity to accept the things I cannot change." I cannot change the fact that Angie is an addict, and I cannot "wish" her into recovery. I can only love her. And— this catch-22 has taken me most of my life to learn—I can only love her or anyone else in my life with any integrity, if I love and value and respect and cherish myself first.

Through my recovery work in the Program, I am no longer prone to feelings of guilt. I've made amends to Angie many times. And though my behavior toward her would continue to be oppressive at times, I've learned to change that as well. Now I see that there is nothing between Angie and her Addiction but Angie. I'm not in the way anymore. I've learned to remove myself from her life and her disease. Freed of my own addictions, particularly my addiction to her, I can distance myself and be more objective, if that's something any parent can ever be. It has taken me over a decade of recovery to do the one thing that would enable me to love Angie best: learning how to love myself.

A few years back before I retired from teaching, I spoke at an Al-Anon meeting. These are some of the things that I said then:

"I'd like to talk a little about the Ninth Step (making amends) because it helps us deal with one of the vulnerabilities that unite us as parents: the danger of feeling guilty and staying stuck in that hole. Many of us when we walk through the door for the first time are flooded with feelings of guilt. I know I was. But not until I started to look at this realistically was I able to live with a healthier perspective about what my responsibility is now and to whom I am responsible.

"This is a blurb in a newsletter that I picked up at the Employee Assistance Program where I used to teach school:

> Regardless of cause, history or contributing factors, feeling guilty about your past role in the development of your child's problem behavior will risk sabotaging your parenting roles. For a more focused relationship with your child: 1) Recognize guilt as negative, self-talk that is normal, but that can be managed or stopped, 2) Acknowledge that a desire for relief from guilt places you at risk for changing the rules, boundaries, and standards that you want followed. 3) Try to act more consistently and proactively, feel better about tough choices, so that you can be less encumbered by what happened in the past. (3)

"What is negative self-talk? It's when your son gets arrested for burglary and you say you just didn't raise him right. You blame yourself, so you bail him out. It's when your daughter gets pregnant and you say it's your fault because you didn't talk to her about birth control. So you take responsibility for her problem, whether it's paying for the abortion or raising her child for her.

"My guilt around Angie is very great, and in seeking to relieve myself of it I have too often spoiled her, not followed through on threats of punishment, and cushioned the falls that might have taught her valuable life lessons.

"Slowly I'm learning to consider tough choices instead of easy ones. And I'm trying to let go of my guilt around my past behavior. But it's a well-worn groove in my character, and I'll need to work very hard to let go of it. It might take a long time.

"Steps Eight and Nine—the apology steps—provide an opportunity to learn the difference between what is and is not our responsibility and to take a more realistic look at the effects of our actions. In my case, my sense of responsibility is inflated. So when I cross the line and try to fix her, out of a sense of guilt, I always mess up. In my desperation to be free of guilt, I became the consummate enabler, a doormat, and a worrywart; basically I felt I had to punish myself because my daughter's addiction must have been my fault. But I don't feel that way so much any more. I'm learning to let go.

"A while back, Angie stole my identity, and then got into my bank account when, thankfully, the bank called me.

"She came to see me where I work, looking very sorry. 'Mom," she said with tears in her eyes, 'I'm so sorry to let you down like this. I know you didn't raise me to steal. It's not your fault. Please give me another chance. I promise I'll never steal from you again. Can you forgive me?'

"Words to melt a mother's heart, right?

"'Oh, honey, I'm so glad we're talking like this! Of course I forgive you. Let's start over, OK? We'll put this behind us.'

"A friend of mine who knew Angie said she was looking mighty happy, like the cat that had swallowed the canary, as she was leaving the building. A year later, Angie stole from me again—a $300 Moneygram. My lesson? See things as they are and not as I want them to be. Or, toughen up, show her some serious consequences, and don't be such a sap.

"I made amends to my daughter a long time ago for oversights I had committed in her childhood. But that didn't stop her from relapsing back into drugs. So why make amends then? To free **me**, that's all. Al-Anon is a selfish program. We find out quickly that we can't save our children, but we can save ourselves. And why should we save ourselves? Because in time, if we've been doing our homework, we learn that we're worth saving. So for me, Step Nine is a liberating exercise. I say 'I'm sorry' very easily now, and it's been so good for my relationships, students especially. But mostly Step Nine has reacquainted me with my own humanity. Now most of the time I just feel like a regular person, with my joys and my sorrows, like everybody else. The Twelve Steps of Al-Anon are great levelers."

Remorse, I think, is a terribly crippling emotion. To be free of it is freedom from a prison of our own design. A few years ago, I wrote a letter to my other two children, asking their forgiveness for obsessing about their sister for so many years. This is my letter to my son:

February 2, 2012

Dear Carlos,

Caroline gave me a wonderful birthday present this year. I asked her forgiveness for being so consumed with Angie that I had little emotional or financial resources left over for anyone else for a very long time—and she gave it to me. It's understandable that I'd be wrapped up in Angie's illness. But my involvement hasn't served any purpose, and it's time to let it go and return the bulk of my energies to my friends and other family members. I'm especially looking forward to being a part of Catherine and Madison's lives. Though losing Angie will always be an unremitting sadness for me, they are constant reminders that life goes on, and I have so much to be happy about and to be grateful for.

Carlos, I'm asking you for forgiveness as well, not just for my obsession with saving Angie for so many years, but also for any other failings I committed as a parent when you all were growing up. One thing I can promise you is that I did the best I could, though being so flawed sometimes my best just wasn't good enough. But now that you're a parent yourself, I'm hoping that you'll find the compassion to forgive me for ways I may have failed you and your sisters, and open the door for my increased involvement in the lives of your children who, as you saw in my treasure trove in New Mexico, are pretty much at the center of my heart these days.

Much love to you always, my dear son, Mom

Families all over the country deal with addiction in different ways. We are no longer living in the Fifties when skeletons gathered dust in closets. It's a brave new world; it's a scary new world. But just as our life expectancy has increased by more than twenty years, so has our capacity to live and deal with the addictions of all kinds that surround us.

Carlos appreciates that his sister is very sick. But he's felt the need to distance himself from her. His wedding and her involvement in it was the one bright moment they shared together in this long ordeal.

I asked my granddaughter last year about her new preschool:

"So Cate, I hear you go to school some days. Have you made any friends there?"

"Noooo…not yet…"

"You go, girl! Let 'em wait!"

I'm delighted by her pickiness, her total ease with just hanging out and letting the world come to her. At her age I was desperate to get my sister's attention, anybody's attention, so afraid I was to be alone. I looked outside of myself for validation instead of the opposite, and so I was always at the mercy of people's whims, circumstance or fate. I get such a kick out of seeing my grandchildren so much stronger than I ever was, encouraging their strength and independence. Seeing this new generation spring up before my eyes, I feel such pride and joy. Life truly does go on.

While talking to my son recently, he inadvertently reminded me that I still have some unfinished business to take care of. He didn't recognize how difficult that would be. So last month I went back to my condo in Virginia, where it all began.

Carlos had been chiding me, "Mom, when are you gonna get tired of burning hundred dollar bills?" I felt jolted by that question and have spent some time reflecting on it. I moved to New Mexico five years ago. Why have I been sitting on the fence all this time? It's a luxury I don't need. Why has it been hard to let go of my condo?

I have an easy answer. It's a beautiful townhouse. I've loved it for fourteen years. My own need for independence had driven me much of my life and it has been a symbol for that, something that is mine alone that I worked hard to keep with no one's help.

It is true that it's an extravagance I don't need. But letting go of it had been unthinkable—until now. Letting go—the learning of it, the doing of it—is a curious exercise. We cling for dear life to things we cherish, afraid that we'll never have something so fine again. But I've learned these past few years that we can also cling to memories of pain and loss. For me, the condo had been the stage for my most recent connection with my daughter—a sad, bittersweet place of remembrance.

Within a year after I bought it, Angie was a methamphetamine addict spiraling out of control. For the next five years she would live with me, crash with me, and torment me on and off. She always slept on a sofa in the basement even though there was a bedroom and her own bath upstairs on my floor. But that was too close to me. She needed her separate space. And still she needed me—for her own reasons.

Digging deep, I see the real reason why I've been clinging to that property. Crossing the threshold on my visit last month, I started facing the ghosts that were holding me hostage. Why have I been holding onto a place that has outlived its usefulness?

This is why: Angie was there with me. I loved Angie there, I lost Angie there, and I began my own reckoning with a lifetime of struggle that ended in the woods a few miles from there. Angie's illness catapulted me into a cave of my own discoveries. And though I began this journey to save my child, it was myself I saved in the end.

The condo will soon be on the market. There is so much those four walls hold inside the beams and drywall. I went from room to room looking for memories, the sad evidence of Angie's presence. There it is, the cigarette hole in my sheets, the burn marks on the porcelain sink where she carelessly left her butts. The black dye she spilled on my new wood floors that I tried to sand away. The bottle of muriatic acid in the laundry room I had no clue about at the time. Why didn't I throw it away years ago? I remembered the night she had free-based and lost her eyelashes, noticed the knife mark on the door she had locked and couldn't open. I walked around and felt the walls she had brushed against, sat in her favorite chair, ate from her Asian bowls, smelled her perfume on the jacket she'd left hanging in the closet. They were everywhere, the reminders of Angie's presence, of the cruel illness that had claimed her, of her loss of self. Why haven't I walked away from all that sooner? Many would have. What does that say about me?

But Angie, my daughter, was there too. I left them around, remnants of her lost innocence: the hand-painted ceramic heart for "The Greatest Mom in the World" on Mother's Day in 1988; the picture of wild geese she bought me at the flea market in Greece; the dried coral roses she gave me for my birthday one year; the Scrabble game we played together on her weekend visits in 2010; pictures of her on holidays there with family while she was in recovery. How could I have known then how fleeting it would be?

I have felt that by truly letting go of the place that witnessed our time together I would be, yet again, abandoning Angie, something I didn't have the heart to do. But I find myself now at a point where I can let go of the memories that chill and sadden me. And it's not an abandonment of my daughter. Just as I have done with my mother, I can carry the best of Angie with me wherever I go. I can let go of the condo now, that proving ground for the redemption I've been seeking all my life. I no longer need to feel the lash on my back.

The last time I saw Carlos he was, as always, very upbeat. This is a man who knows how to make lemonade out of lemons. He had his own struggles growing up. But my son is a survivor—and a joy to know. Sitting across the table from him I brought up the subject of Angie, and it's always hard for me:

"Carlos, the girls are too young now. But what will you tell them when they ask about Aunt Angie?"

"I see it as a cautionary tale, Mom," he answered. "I'm not gonna hide anything from them. They'll know everything when it's an appropriate time. And I hope it will make them think twice before wading into such dangerous waters."

Part of me wanted to see him show more emotion—even shed a tear with me—and part of me was glad that he was so detached. My son had worked very hard to get where he was. He had a wonderful life now and was very happy. But I needed him to know that it was not as easy for me.

"A parent never gets over losing a child, Carlos. I've learned how to be happy and make the most of my life. My recovery Program is strong. But I'll never stop missing Angie and all her possibilities. Never."

When addiction claims our loved ones, we often feel resentful. It feels to us like we had been tagged, even though we had run as hard as we could. It's taken me a few years to get to a place where I don't feel angry or gypped anymore. My lot is no better or worse than any other mother's whose child was struck down by illness. Whether or not she outlives me—as is the law of nature—remains to be seen.

In the meantime, I must remember to watch the mountain turn into a big red watermelon, and enjoy the colors of New Mexico.

"The Mad Hatter: 'Have I gone Mad?'

Alice: 'I'm afraid so. You're entirely bonkers. But I'll tell you a secret. All the best people are.'"

(Alice in Wonderland Film)

Works Cited

Al-Anon Family Groups. *Al-Anon Alateen Groups at Work*. Virginia Beach: Al-Anon Family Group Headquarters, Inc., 2013. Print.

---. *Courage to Change*. New York: Al-Anon Family Group Headquarters, Inc., 1992. Print.

---. *Hope for Today*. Virginia Beach: Al-Anon Family Group Headquarters, Inc., 2002. Print.

---. *How Al-Anon Works for Families and Friends of Alcoholics*. Virginia Beach: Al-Anon Family Group Headquarters, Inc., 2008. Print.

---. *One Day at a Time in Al-Anon*. Virginia Beach: Al-Anon Family Group Headquarters, Inc., 1996. Print.

---. *Opening Our Hearts, Transforming Our Losses*. Virginia Beach: Al-Anon Family Group Headquarters, Inc., 2007. Print.

Alcott, Louisa May, "I Slept, and Dreamed That Life Was Beauty." *AllPoetry*. N.p. n.d. Web. 31 May 2014.

Alice in Wonderland. Dir, Tim Burton. Perf. Johnny Depp, Mia Wasikowska, and Helena Bonham Carter. Walt Disney, 2010. Film.

Anonymous Press. *Anonymous Press Mini Edition of Alcoholics Anonymous*. Malo: The Anonymous Press. 2008. Print.

Arlington County Government Employee Assistance Program Newsletter, October, 2001. Print.

Bassoff, Evelyn, Ph.D. *Cherishing Our Daughters*. New York: Dutton-Penguin, 1998. Print.

Beard, Charles A. *Wikiquote*, N.p. , 2014. Web. 11 June 2014.

Beattie, Melody. *Beyond Codependency*. San Francisco: Harper. 1989. Print.

Bialosky, Jill. *History of a Suicide*. New York: Atria Books, 2011. Print.

Blake, William. *The Complete Poetry and Prose of William Blake*. Ed. David V. Erdman. New York: Anchor-Doubleday, 1988. Print.

Burnett, Carol. *Carrie and Me: A Mother/Daughter Love Story*. New York: Simon and Schuster, 2013. Print.

Carroll, Lewis. *Alice in Wonderland*. London: Puffin Classics (Penguin), 2008. Print.

Collins, Judy. *Sanity and Grace*. New York: Tarcher-Penguin, 2006. Print.

Durant, Will. *The Story of Philosophy*. New York: Simon and Schuster, 1961. Print.

Each Day a New Beginning. Center City: Hazelden Foundation, 1982. Print.

Maté, Gabor, Dr. *In the Realm of Hungry Ghosts*. Berkeley: North Atlantic Books, 2010. Print.

Nar-Anon Family Groups. *Guide for the Family of the Addict and Drug Abuser*. Torrance: Nar-Anon Family Group Headquarters, Inc., 1971. Print.

---. *Nar-Anon*. Torrance: Nar-Anon Family Group Headquarters, Inc., 1971. Print.

---. *Sharing Experience, Strength and Hope*. Torrance: Nar-Anon Family Group Headquarters, Inc., 1971. Print.

O'Rourke, Meghan. "Why We Write About Grief." *New York Times Week in Review* February 26, 2011, 3. Print.

Passion. "You Can't Make Me Clean." OurAnon. Facebook, 29 Aug. 2011. Web. 17 Jan. 2014.

Sheff, David. *Beautiful Boy*. New York: Houghton Mifflin Company, 2008. Print.

Author's Note

I have changed the names of most but not all of the individuals in this book in order to preserve anonymity. Also, some identifying details were modified in order to respect the privacy of those involved. Relying heavily on my own personal journals, letters, and emails, I've needed to mine the depths of my own memory at various stages in order to give life to my story.

And, as often happens in memoir, to see it through a different lens. The Twelve Steps, The Serenity Prayer, and readings from Program literature have served to be the backbone of much of my recovery and are frequently cited. In addition, other historical references as well as relevant contemporary works have brought my recovery into focus. I'm indebted to these others who have gone before me and have lightened my journey.